W9-AXJ-024

THE ESCHATOLOGY OF PAUL

THE ESCHATOLOGY OF PAUL

IN THE LIGHT OF MODERN SCHOLARSHIP

by

Henry M. Shires

THE WESTMINSTER PRESS
Philadelphia

LIBRARY OF CONGRESS CATALOG CARD NO. 66–10339

PUBLISHED BY THE WESTMINSTER PRESS®
PHILADELPHIA, PENNSYLVANIA

PRINTED IN THE UNITED STATES OF AMERICA

To My Family
who have helped me know the love of God

◈ ◈ ◈ CONTENTS

Introduction THE RECOVERY OF ESCHATOLOGY

ESCHATOLOGY, that branch of theology which deals with the "last things" of heaven and hell, judgment, resurrection, and eternal life, is today largely ignored or seriously misunderstood.[1] The categories of eschatological thought have not been completely abandoned, but they have little effect upon our daily life. Thus John A. T. Robinson concludes: "The interest of the modern man in Christian eschatology, if he has any interest at all, centers in the fact and moment of death." [2] This almost complete separation between the practice of twentieth-century man and a traditionally central area of Christian belief has been brought about in the last several centuries by a number of factors that are clearly present in the contemporary world.

We are told that eschatology is simply irrelevant for the very practical concerns of our sophisticated age.[3] Our ways of thought seem far removed from the highly imaginative patterns of Biblical eschatology. The beliefs of the early Christians regarding the end of the world are so different from our assumptions that we are tempted to find a great and impassable gulf between us and them. Scientifically-oriented thinking rejects the projections of eschatology, which apparently have so little to do with real life as we know it.[4]

To many, eschatology means only promises of future

happiness when this life is finished, so that serious concern for the conditions of the present is eliminated or restricted.[5] It has often been noted that there is a basic inconsistency between eschatology and ethics. In general, eschatology regards this present world as hopelessly evil. Matter has somehow become corrupt and helpless. Salvation is therefore to come in the future, in another world, in a " spiritual " medium. Between matter and spirit there is an irreconcilable conflict. The natural realm is, after all, unimportant alongside of that which will succeed it and then endure without change. It is understandable that there should be a strong reaction to such a dualism, which has been rightly or wrongly associated with the very essence of eschatology. J. E. Fison has protested vigorously that " we may not abandon the materialism of the Christian faith in favor of an escape into a more spiritual, but utterly unreal, dehistoricizing of the biblical revelation." [6] If eschatology is necessarily dualistic, it has to be rejected as contrary to the true meaning of Christianity.

Eschatology deals with the belief that the course of world history, religiously considered, moves toward a definable goal that involves the coming into being of a new order of existence. Reinhold Niebuhr has written: " A comprehension of the meaning of life and history from the standpoint of the Christian revelation includes an understanding of the contradictions to that meaning in which history is perennially involved." [7] But what if there is no ultimate meaning in history at all? The succession of time, be it long or short, tells us nothing about significance. Dr. Robinson considers the critical nature of the time in which we are living, and he notes: " Men now may have a more lively expectation of an end. But the decisive factor is whether they think of that end as purposive, not whether they believe it to be near." [8] Those who hold that history manifests no purpose or sense or goal point consistently to eschatology as having no foundation and no reason for being.

In spite of the many influences working to eliminate all references to eschatology in our common thought and life, there is evident a renewed interest in the subject in the present time. In the first place, there is always in times of crisis a concern for the last things which seem to lie close at hand; and we are living in one of the most critical periods of all history.[9] The questions of M. E. Dahl are timely: "The real difficulty . . . is not—Is not Jewish eschatology fantastic nonsense? but rather—Can the scientific method and outlook really answer the questions all human beings really must ask, namely, What are we? Where are we going? How are we to arrive there?"[10] When this world and this age appear to be on the verge of destruction, it is inevitable to wonder if there is another world and another age and to inquire about the meaning of an order that may so quickly disappear.

In a period of uncertainty and despair men search for authority as a sure rock of refuge. The Bible taken at its face value, without the upsetting disciplines of literary and historical criticism, is such a refuge; and the Bible contains a great deal of eschatological material which, when accepted literally, provides a vivid picture of the nature of the coming age that will follow our present. J. A. T. Robinson declares: "The popularity of various forms of Adventism outside the orthodox Christian bodies is a clear reflection of the failure of the Church to formulate a theology of the Last Things which is intellectually respectable."[11]

Whereas a literal acceptance of the eschatological teachings of the Bible will satisfy some, most will look for a form of defensible reinterpretation. According to A. M. Hunter: "Time was when our eschatologically-minded forefathers dogmatized on such themes, and sometimes spoke as if all the secrets of God had been revealed to them. . . . Men now confess their ignorance, and often their doubt."[12] What we do with eschatology will have a large share in determining the place we give to the Bible as a whole. What we must seek, however, is not a way of accommodating our thought to eschatology or vice versa, but the truth of eschatology, if any, that transcends the approach of any single age.[13]

Reinterpretations

Within recent decades there have been two notable attempts to reexamine the doctrines of eschatology with a view to discovering their permanent message. The first of these is the approach of Rudolf Bultmann known as demythologizing. Amos Wilder declares: "Modern study of Biblical eschatology is constantly confronted with problems as to the proper interpretation of the cosmic and transcendental language."[14] For Bultmann the New Testament presuppositions and pictures of eschatology, apocalyptic demonology, a three-decker universe, sacramentalism, resurrection, and ideas of preexistence all constitute a pattern that is unacceptable to the modern mind. In his view, whatever in the New Testament attempts to describe the otherworldly and the divine in terms that are human and this-worldly is a mythology that must be sharply differentiated from the core of the gospel.[15] Bultmann accordingly dismisses the eschatological statements of the New Testament as belonging only to the first century. In their place he turns to an emphasis upon the religious experience of the individual while continuing to use the term "eschatological." He writes: "The early Christian community understands itself not as a historical but as an eschatological phenomenon."[16] And he adds: "Jesus Christ is the eschatological event not as an established fact of past time but as repeatedly present."[17] For him the meaning of all history is to be found in present experience that can then be called eschatological because it is history's goal and purpose. He finds that eschatology determines Paul's understanding of history: "The end of history cannot be the natural result of historical development, but only its breaking off, accomplished by God. . . . To this extent Paul recognizes a meaning in history, but not a meaning which is immanent in history itself." [18] Thus in Bultmann's view Christianity means the termination and the transformation of time. Yet his approach to eschatology is open to serious objections. According to Wilder, "The existentialist view does not sufficiently recognize the time-category in which we are saved." [19] Moreover, it may well be that in arbitrarily altering and subtracting from the form of the New Testament message we may lose the substance. The relationship between revelation and its medium is so close that neither can stand without the other.

The second major reinterpretation of eschatology in our day is that of C. H. Dodd and is known as "realized eschatology." He has reacted against a concentration of attention upon some future time that devalues the present with its obligations and opportunities and obscures the higher aspects of morality.[20] Although he admits that New Testament eschatology allows for finality at the end of all earthly existence,[21] he asserts that "an absolute end to history, whether it be conceived as coming soon or late, is no more than a fiction designed to express the reality of teleology within history." [22] In his view the term "Kingdom of God" primarily asserts the sovereignty of God over all opposition, and as used by Jesus it indicates that in him "the powers of the world to come" have begun to work among us in a series of events that are unique and that cannot be repeated.[23] While, for Dodd, Jesus' undoubted apocalyptic symbolism points to the otherworldly nature of God's Kingdom, his parables teach that the Kingdom has already arrived.[24] In Dodd's view, therefore the gospel is revealed, not in evolution or progress, but in an existential crisis that confirms the universal reality of history as successive generations are confronted with the fact of Christ.[25] The position of "realized eschatology" seems to be open to at least two objections. In the first instance, in such an analysis the extent and the strength of this world's evil are not sufficiently recognized. And secondly, the future becomes almost meaningless because it has nothing essential to contribute that is not already present. Once again the time process is reduced to insignificance.[26]

Yet the search for a satisfying interpretation continues. C. K. Barrett affirms that "Biblical eschatology . . . reveals God as He is, not as man thinks He is, or would like him to be — though perhaps there are few forms of theological thought where there is more scope for human dogmatism (of various kinds) to obscure the revealed truth."[27] It is impossible to eliminate eschatology from the gospel, since it points to its very center. It is the eschatological principle that is involved and not any aberration or perversion of it. Jesus and the early church were clearly eschatological in their thinking.[28] For this reason it is difficult to conceive of the Christian community except as an eschatological reality. Eschatology is not the only element in Christianity, but it is clearly one of the foundation stones. W. Grundmann declares: "The distinguishing feature of the message of the New Testament, that which gives it its decisive quality, is its eschatological sense of history, its conviction that the final stage of the fulfillment of God's purpose for this world has been inaugurated."[29] The gospel message is rooted in the belief that in Christ, God has acted so that his righteousness will be victorious over all the forces of evil.

Myth and History

Many of the words, pictures, and forms found in New Testament eschatology are admittedly incompatible with modern thought. J. A. T. Robinson reminds us: "While theological assertions about the beginning and end of things are, in their essential content, derived from present awareness of the living God, the *form* in which they are expressed . . . is the myth."[30] Since the term "myth" is subject to many misunderstandings, it is most important to know what is meant by it. The form of the myth will vary in accordance with the assumptions of any one time or place, and the form is independent of the meaning. The eschatological myth describes primarily what is and only secondarily what will therefore be in the future. The most appropriate mode of expressing religious experience is the myth. G. V. Jones asserts: "Any attempt to speak of God which renounces picture, myth, symbol or analogy, tends to result in a negative or apophatic theology in which the term 'God' makes little impression on the mind and little impact on the emotions or the imagination."[31] The purpose of the myth is to present that which lies beyond the descriptive power of words.[32] It cannot therefore provide a photograph of the world as it is, but it seeks a means of communicating an experience and a conviction. Mythological figures make a strong appeal to our imagination because they help us to rise above our frustrations. "Ultimately," we are told, "whatever its original character or intention, mythological language is symbolic, and if 'myth' is to be retained, it is as a symbol."[33] However, it is still not clear as to what is being symbolized by the eschatological myth. The mythological symbol passes beyond our common distinctions between natural and spiritual and between past and future. Yet Robinson has stated: "It is left to the form of the imagery employed (the sign-manual of apocalypse) to make clear that these ultimate occurrences cannot be conceived as *simply* historical, but must essentially be trans-historical in nature."[34] And Wilder adds: "The eschatological myth dramatizes the transfiguration of the world and is not a mere poetry of an unthinkable a-temporal state."[35] One of the central issues in the debate is clearly the real meaning of human history. Is it entirely relative and contingent or is it at least one means of expressing absolutely the truth of God? The observation of A. M. Hunter is relevant: " Unless the church is prepared to scrap its Hebraic heritage and adopt a Greek *Weltanschauung* to which time is largely irrelevant, we also must look at the world and history and God as Paul does." [36] The Biblical view of history must therefore be briefly examined.

Christianity has had to deal with two opposing views of time. Hellenistic influences emphasized the present, the timeless, the eternal now. Hebrew thought, however, considered history, the past and future, the critical turning points of time, the meaning of special events, and the divine purpose using the course of history to reach its own end.[37] Bultmann stands in the Hellenistic tradition when he writes: " Eschatology in a true Christian understanding of it is not the future end of history, but history is swallowed up by eschatology." [38] The transcendental imagery of myth does not deny the reality of the historical process, and Maurice Goguel is right in his affirmation: " The Christian conscience has always kept faithful to a dynamic conception of God which has its roots in the Old Testament and plainly is closely connected with an eschatological conception." [39] If, however, the temporal order is unable to show forth the victory of God, then his dealings in time that are proclaimed by Christianity and Judaism alike have been without point or result.

James Muilenburg has correctly noted: " In every philosophy of history it is the concept of time that is decisive and determinative." [40] Nowhere in the Bible do we find a philosophical discussion of the nature and significance of time, yet the Bible discloses a definite understanding of it. The measurement of time's extent is unimportant, but its immediacy and quality are that which make it notable. Dahl has pointed out: " [In Hebraic thought] . . . ' for ever ' does not mean time-*less*-ness, so much as time-*ful*-ness." [41] In the same manner early Christian eschatology seems to disregard the ordinary relations of time and space, but it is nonetheless solidly rooted in historical facts. For Christianity the calendar date is always secondary. The significance of any time is determined only by the working out of God's eternal purpose within and through it. James Barr has asked: "When we measure and state the time elapsing between two events, is this mere duration ('chronological time'), or does the reference to the two terminal events qualify it as 'realistic time'?" [42] The New Testament is directly concerned with time and history, but their meaning is determined only by the nature of historical events. From the Christian point of view these are eternal. According to Reinhold Niebuhr: "Eternity stands over time on the one hand and at the end of time on the other. It stands over time in the sense that it is the ultimate source and power of all derived and dependent existence." [43] Time and eternity are not in opposition, but both are necessary for full reality. In eschatology they are therefore present side by side, each throwing light upon the other. Christianity teaches that in Jesus, God has acted in the concrete past, and in him God continues to act in our present and will act in time yet to come. In the New Testament view, time has no independent existence or self-contained goal. The church is in time and beyond it. C. F. D. Moule writes: "Always at moments of Christian worship, time and space are obliterated and the worshipping church on earth is one in eternity with the church in the heavenly places." [44] Oscar Cullmann agrees with Bultmann that "in Primitive Christianity the connection of the historical events concerning Jesus of Nazareth with the nonhistorical account of the primal beginning and of the eschatological end is so close that the difference between history and myth is unimportant, not because Primitive Christianity possesses no historical sense, but because there exists here a positive theological outlook which transcends the contrast between history and myth." [45] That theological outlook is an awareness of God's purposeful acts in history.

The life, death, and resurrection of Jesus of Nazareth point to the meaning of all history, but the New Testament never suggests that this meaning has already been fully realized. Biblical faith always is thankfully aware of God's past deeds, but its dominant mood is one of hope and expectation of further and decisive divine activity. J. E. Fison has recognized: " Biblical eschatology only develops under a sense of the agonizing and acute tension caused by the contradiction between what is and what ought to be." [46] History and eschatology point to each other. History demands hope in God for its meaning, and hope in God has no support without reference to history. John Marsh is convinced that " Christianity, . . . by denying succession and affirming fulfillment as the relationship between this world and the coming one, enables history both to have an end and to have an event-relationship to the age that is to come." [47] It is Jesus Christ who provides the link between history and eschatology, between past and future. For the New Testament he is both the one who has come and the one who is yet to come again. Paul Minear has proposed: "It is our modern perception of time that induces us to separate so sharply the Christ who is from him who is to come, that leads us to focus our thought on the discontinuities between his present and future work rather than those between his work and the work of his adversary." [48]

If it is Jesus who provides the necessary link between what God has done and what he will yet accomplish, it is our experience of Jesus in the present that looks to both past and future. There is one continuing course of redemption which includes all tenses. Eschatology deals with the things that are final, not only in temporal sequence but also in truth and value. With regard to the sense of urgency that marks apocalyptic eschatology, H. H. Rowley suggests that it "may be born of our perception of the dire need of the world that is without God; it may also be born of our perception of the great purpose of God." [49] In that purpose time is an instrument. Past, present, and future are equally true and equally important because Jesus belongs to all three. The Christian disciple likewise is related to these three ages of time. According to W. A. Beardslee: "Early Christian eschatology was not only a confrontation of the individual 'will' with alternatives of ultimate destiny, but a confrontation of the whole structure of man's life in the world, and the proclamation of a gospel which claimed to set men free from that structure to live — if only in anticipation — by the powers of the new age." [50]

It is the individual who in his experience of Christ is enabled to comprehend all the ages of time and while living in the reality of the temporal to transcend it. Truth is apprehended by each man in his own time and place. On the other hand, the life of the individual has no meaning outside of its necessary relationship to the duties and tasks of the community in which it is placed. Only in some form of eschatology with its emphasis upon purpose and goal can we find a reconciliation of the tensions that exist between the individual and the group. In Christian eschatology both the individual and the community of which he is a part are under God's control and are the objects of his care.

Thus we can see that Christian eschatology has many strong theological foundations. It employs myth in order to express symbolically its understanding of the nature of that history which God has entered through Jesus and in which he will continue to be active in achieving his goal for each man and for all of his creation. We must agree with Moule: "It would be a gross oversimplification to arrange New Testament eschatology as an evolutionary tree." [51] It is far more than a matter of chronological progression. On the other hand, even modern science admits that at some point human history must come to an end upon earth. There are many reasons for fearing that this end may be soon, brought about by man's inability to control the discoveries that he himself has made. We must admit: "It is not possible for finite minds to comprehend that which transcends and fulfills history." [52] Yet we are not thereby released from the obligation to consider the truth that is available. The materials at our disposal are limited.[53] Moreover, they are capable of a number of varying interpretations. Yet they cannot be dismissed lightly or arbitrarily. E. G. Bicknell warns: "There is . . . the danger that a modern reconstruction of eschatology may omit elements of spiritual truth that are contained in the old descriptions." [54] That task must nevertheless be undertaken. N. Q. Hamilton declares boldly: "The preaching and teaching of a faithfully Biblical eschatology in its proper relations, and with the proper emphasis, could rediscover to the Church of our day a forgotten or misunderstood dimension of the Gospel." [55] A part of that reappraisal will be attempted in the pages that follow.

The eschatology of Paul has been chosen for study because of the fact that he has given us more eschatological statements than any other New Testament writer. In fact, he above all others has laid the foundation for all subsequent Christian eschatological thought.[56] In the generally accepted Pauline corpus there are 1,635 verses.[57] Of these, 518 or 31½ percent contain definitely eschatological thought and language.[58] There is a marked eschatological emphasis in every epistle, and in spite of some variations from one writing to another, the emphasis is surprisingly constant. The starting point for such a study must be these words written by Paul to express his own thought.[59] At the same time the words of Paul or of any other Biblical writer are not ends in themselves but imperfect vehicles for communicating truth. Barr has warned: "A valid Biblical theology can be built only upon the statements of the Bible, and not on the words of the Bible." [60] Behind the words of Paul lie certain basic conceptions and beliefs that constitute the center of his eschatology. It is this core that we seek to discover.[61] First, it is necessary to examine the general characteristics of Paul's eschatological thought before we study in detail the major categories of that thought. Finally we shall ask what is the significance of Paul's eschatology for our day.

Chapter I | PAUL'S IDEAS OF LAST THINGS

ESCHATOLOGY is only one part of Paul's theological thought, and as such, it shares many of the characteristics and influences of his doctrine as a whole. That he inherited directly or indirectly much of his belief and that to it he made important contributions of his own are equally clear, but it is not easy to determine how much he was influenced by what had already been taught or written and how much in his writings is due to his own creativity. F. V. Filson reminds us that in Pauline study "a tendency sometimes appears to regard any inherited idea of Paul as unimportant."[1] Yet it is impossible to evaluate Paul's position on any matter without knowing how much he has borrowed from his predecessors and how he has treated that material by omissions, alterations, and additions. Scholars are by no means agreed as to whether Jewish or Greek ideas lie at the center of his thought.[2] On the other hand, there can be no doubt that Paul was throughout his life a loyal and earnest Jew even though he was, of course, following his conversion also a Christian. However, the Judaism in which he was trained possessed its own characteristics, which are even now coming to be better known than ever before. Paul was a man of his time, and "the first-century milieu against which we are to place Paul was variegated and, above all, complex." [3] The truth that came to Paul from Judaism was retained as a means of interpreting the supreme fact of Christ. He was a Pharisee who had been found by Christ.[4]

Whereas in all areas Paul is heavily under debt to Judaism for help in describing the meaning of his Christian experience, it is in eschatology that he manifests his clearest dependence. The Jewish scholar H. J. Schoeps has declared: "That the doctrine of the last things forms 'the greatest block of Jewish material in the thought-world of Paul' is clear beyond a doubt."[5] There is a remarkable scholarly agreement that Pauline eschatology grows directly out of Judaism and the Old Testament, where we find clear statements regarding the consummation of God's purpose, the judgment, and the end of the world.[6] This borrowing is especially prominent when Paul discusses the future completion of the salvation begun in Christ and his imminent Second Advent. Accordingly, the most direct parallels to Jewish tradition are found in I and II Thessalonians, where the Parousia is a major issue.[7] The eschatology of the Old Testament has furnished Paul with both language and ideas, but Paul knows that the Lord of Old Testament prophecy is the Jesus who has come and who is still to come. Moreover, when Paul connects his eschatology with religioethical ideals he is drawing upon the insights of Judaism.[8] In Paul's day Jewish eschatology was not monochrome but contained at least two traditions regarding the coming Kingdom. In the earlier expectation, emphasis is placed upon the restoration by God of Jewish nationalistic sovereignty as the core of God's Kingdom. In the second type the future Kingdom is to be instituted only by God's supernatural action from without this world.[9] Accordingly, Paul displays elements from both forms of eschatology and employs terms that in Jewish usage had varying connotations. He is thoroughly acquainted with Jewish eschatology and uses it for his purposes, but he feels free to use only those elements which he finds relevant. Thus, his alterations of that eschatology may be even more significant than his borrowings.[10]

From ca. 200 B.C., Jewish eschatology was becoming more and more apocalyptic, and it is not surprising that Paul should therefore express his own views of the end frequently in apocalyptic language. In fact, according to Rowley, "The study of the eschatological teaching of Paul and of the other writers of Epistles reveals how far the ideas of apocalyptic eschatology had permeated the Church." [11] Apocalyptic arises from the attempt to systematize the predictive aspect of Old Testament prophecy and to interpret it by means of mythology. It thus has elements in common with the Old Testament and sharp departures from it. It is represented in literature that seems to have been known to Paul and used by him.[12] Typical apocalyptic figures are to be found in Paul's eschatological passages. There is, for example, a reference to the judgment fire in I Cor. 3:13; to the last trumpet in I Cor. 15:52 and I Thess. 4:16; and to the archangel's call in I Thess. 4:16. As we might expect, Paul's use of apocalyptic material is most demonstrable in the Thessalonian letters.[13] Especially to be noted in this connection are I Thess. 4:13-18 and II Thess. 2:1-12. B. Lindars makes an interesting observation that, contrary to his usual practice, "in his epistles to the Thessalonians Paul does not argue from biblical texts. His Old Testament allusions are for the most part either apocalyptic references or hortatory phrases." [14] Apocalyptic thought, in distinction from prophetic eschatology, is marked by a cosmological dualism that frees God from responsibility for this present evil age and connects him with a righteous age that he will bring about in his time. According to Schoeps, this doctrine became current about the middle of the first century B.C.: "The statement of Hillel in *Aboth* 2, 7 is one of the oldest witnesses to the use of the expressions: *olam ha-zeh olam ha-ba* ["This age"—"The coming age"]." [15] It is generally believed that Paul accepts this twofold division of time and builds his eschatological thought upon it, even though no such sharp division exists in the writings of the prophets.[16] We shall find that Paul does indeed start with the doctrine of the two ages, but that he proceeds to modify it in a fundamental manner.

It cannot be denied that Paul made use of apocalyptic materials to express his eschatology, but attention must be paid to the way in which he employed them. Thus, Johannes Weiss has declared: "He [Paul] does in fact show himself to be dependent upon the apocalyptic tradition, but he himself is not an apocalyptist." [17] The Jewish apocalyptic medium could not express perfectly the Christian hope. We may agree with Sydney Cave when he states that "much of the inconsistency of his [Paul's] teaching here is due to his attempt to express the new facts of Christianity in terms which belonged to the alien world of Jewish apocalypse." [18] If Paul offers no consistent picture of the coming end, it may well be because he has deliberately borrowed apocalyptic material to suggest theological truths but not to describe in detail that which lies beyond human description.[19] In any case, Paul approaches apocalyptic from the standpoint of Christian conviction, and he no longer regards God's action as a matter only for the future. The final end is to be judged in the light of the eschatological happenings within the primitive Christian community. Since apocalypses vary so much among themselves with regard to particulars, there is reason to believe that even the apocalyptists did not attach much importance to the details of their pictures. Finally, it must be pointed out that Paul differs from the apocalypses in many important ways.[20] He makes but little use of the apocalyptical sections of the Old Testament, and that by allusion rather than quotation. Moral values are central for Paul but are of secondary significance in the apocalyptic writings. Paul has altered the dualism of apocalypticism to include recognition of the struggle between flesh and spirit. Into the apocalyptic picture he has introduced the essentially new ideas of the event of Christ and the gift of the Spirit.

If, then, Paul is basically Jewish in his eschatological outlook, there would appear to be little room for Hellenistic influence. Yet the Judaism of Paul's day had already been subject to many ideas and terms that originated in Hellenism, partly through the Hellenistic Judaism of Alexandria. This is the truth behind the statement of W. D. Davies: "It is wholly artificial to make too sharp a dichotomy between the Hebraic and the Hellenistic elements in Paul's thought."[21] Moreover, Paul seems to employ some Hellenistic terminology, although not departing from basically Jewish teaching. W. D. Stacey has commented on Pauline thought as a whole: "Though Paul, as a Jew, resisted the thought of the Gentile world, the atmosphere he could not resist, and some of the language and thought of Hellenism penetrated his mind. Some Greek terms he borrowed deliberately to provide points of contact with his hearers."[22] It is no longer seriously proposed that Paul's language shows direct dependence on the mystery religions in the case of such terms as "salvation," "mystery," "perfect," "wisdom," and "gnosis." Yet Hellenism, like Judaism, provided Paul with some means of interpreting his thought and experience. Paul was willing to become all things to all men in order to win men to Christ, and he rejected no word or idea just because it was Greek. In the opinion of Barr, "The New Testament is notable for the limited and partial character of the criticisms which it made of Greek thought. . . . It is a distortion to suggest that an opposition to Greek thought is a key to New Testament interpretation."[23]

Although Paul does not share in the Greek philosophical dualism of an absolute separation between soul and body since he cannot think of the existence of spirit without a body, there is in his writings an opposition between spirit and flesh which is at least reminiscent of Greek thought. Leivestad notes: "There is an element of Greek idealism in the Pauline Epistles. . . . The visible is transient and unreal, it is delusive and deceptive; only the invisible is eternal and real. Matter is dead; the spirit alone is living." [24] To support this view we may note Rom. 8:11, "He who raised Christ Jesus from the dead will give life to your mortal bodies also through his Spirit which dwells in you." And also in II Cor. 4:18: "We look not to the things that are seen but to the things that are unseen; for the things that are seen are transient, but the things that are unseen are eternal." To such verses it will be necessary to return later, but at this point we do recognize in Paul an awarness of an unceasing struggle between two contrary orders of reality, an earthly and a heavenly. In this there is similarity to Greek thought. The two-age conception, which emerges in pre-Christian Judaism and which Paul takes over in order to amend it, may owe something to Greek sources.[25] Paul did confess that he was under obligation both to Greeks and to barbarians, and Caird finds: "In his conception of nature more than in anything else Paul was a debtor to the Greeks, and it was from them that he learned to view nature as 'one stupendous whole,' united by a bond of common frailty." [26] Paul's view of nature is a basic element in his eschatology. However, when Paul borrows a term or idea from Hellenistic philosophy or religion, he does so for his own purpose and does not often subscribe to the Greek understanding of it. Paul is neither an apocalyptist nor a Hellenist.

Ever since the recent discovery of the Dead Sea Scrolls it has become increasingly clear that the Essenes as a Jewish sect were well acquainted with certain Hellenistic ideas once thought to be incompatible with Palestinian Judaism. At the same time these Essenes clearly transmitted and developed Jewish apocalyptic tradition. The relationship between Paul, who knew both apocalypticism and Hellenism, and the Essenes is therefore a subject for attention. Millar Burrows maintains: "The whole life of the [Qumran] community was marked by its eschatological expectations." [27] This is true even though in the Scrolls there is no well-defined system of eschatology. The Essenes and the early Christians alike expected the final age to come soon because they were already living in the last times. Both groups had a developed Messianic hope and thought of themselves as the people of the new covenant in whom the new age was being ushered in. Although the apocalyptic element is most prominent in the War Scroll, all the Qumran literature reflects eschatology to some extent. It is constantly assumed that God is in control of all history and that his acts divide history into periods of time of which the last will be his complete triumph over all his enemies.[28] Although there is no elaboration of the future punishment of the wicked, there is a clear expectation of a final judgment for all. Matthew Black has summed up: "The general type of eschatology would appear to be that of an expected Kingdom of God (or New Creation) of eternal duration on the present earth, with Jerusalem (and the Temple) as its center." [29] In this area as perhaps in others there is parallelism between the Dead Sea Scrolls and the New Testament. F. M. Cross, Jr., has concluded: "The direct use of Essene or proto-Essene materials in Christian composition . . . can now be documented impressively." [30] If there has not been literary borrowing, we see at least two expressions of a common stream of thought.

The similarity in Christian writings to Qumran ideas is especially marked in the case of the apostle Paul.[31] In addition to general similarities already mentioned in which Paul shares, we find in the Scrolls an ethical dualism that has much in common with the struggle between flesh and spirit described by Paul.[32] Paul's reference to the "mystery of lawlessness" in II Thess. 2:7 suggests the "mystery of evil" which is mentioned in the Thanksgiving Psalms of Qumran. The Essenes speak of the present, preliminary age as the "dominion of Belial." Paul suggests the same thing in II Cor. 6:15. According to Cross, "The communal meal of the Essenes . . . must be understood as a liturgical anticipation of the Messianic banquet." [33] Paul writes in I Cor. 11:26: "As often as you eat this bread and drink the cup, you proclaim the Lord's death until he comes." At the same time, Paul differs from the Scrolls in many important respects. Even though he used some of the Essene expressions, he did so independently for his own end. Referring to surface similarities in a moral dualism, Davies states: "Paul stands in the essentials of his thought on these matters more in the main stream of Old Testament and Rabbinic Judaism than in that of the sect. There is no reason to suppose that in other aspects of his thought the case would be different." [34]

There can be no doubt that the teaching of Jesus and his concept of his own person and mission were eschatological. It seems highly probable, moreover, that in view of the influence of his first-century Palestinian environment his eschatology was to some degree apocalyptic. Albert Schweitzer is firmly convinced that "Paul shares with Jesus the eschatological world-view and the eschatological expectation, with all that these imply. The only difference is the hour in the world-clock in the two cases." [35] Yet in Paul the eschatology has become somewhat elaborated and interpreted. Lucetta Mowry declares: "Jesus' own reticence on matters of eschatology and his personal impact upon his followers are the ultimate element in the transformation in the Church's eschatology." [36] The life, death, and resurrection of Jesus constitute the major influence on Paul's thought. On the other hand, his knowledge of Jesus comes to him through the tradition of the early church. According to Hunter, three elements in that tradition are particularly prominent in Paul.[37] In the first place, Paul shares the conviction that the new age has been inaugurated because of the historic events connected with Jesus.

Secondly, although the Jews did not speak of the Parousia of the Messiah, Paul has much to say about it as do many other New Testament writers. Thirdly, Paul reproduces the conviction that there will be a final judgment somehow connected with Jesus' return to earth. Paul's debt to the apocalyptic ideas of primitive Christianity is seen most clearly in the Thessalonian correspondence.[38] He admits that in these and other matters he had been taught by those who were Christians before him. Yet the Pauline letters contain more than simply a reproduction of early Christian belief. To the tradition Paul has made significant additions of his own. Because his contributions are many and introduce some essentially new interpretations, it is possible to study the eschatology of Paul as a separate entity.

Paul's Contributions

The attempt to discover non-Christian influences in Paul's eschatological thought has not led us very far. It is much more fruitful to study how Paul builds upon his own insights into the meaning of the historic events connected with Jesus and his church.[39] Paul is in some measure an apocalyptist in the form of his writing, yet he finds important truth in the prophetic approach which aids him to interpret God's continuing activity.[40] In Schweitzer's view the Pauline eschatology is " a synthesis of the eschatology of the Prophets and the ' Son of Man ' eschatology of Daniel."[41] It is Paul, however, who creates the synthesis out of his own experience and reflection. Where necessary, he has departed fearlessly from conventional Jewish eschatology. He has proclaimed that the new age, the expected day of the Messiah, is already here for Christians.[42] Jewish pictures of the coming of the Messiah and the triumphant Day of the Lord are applied both to the first and to the second coming of Jesus. Paul realized that it was necessary to employ figurative language to express indescribable realities, but he attempted to make of his eschatological thought a logically consistent whole. He is convinced that he is dealing, not with ideas or preferences, but with facts.[43] Paul is well aware that Jesus has not yet returned to earth as Christians expected, and he is a pioneer among Christian writers in setting forth the true nature of the interim period in which the disciples await the final triumph of their Lord.

As a Christian, Paul believed that the longed-for Messiah had in truth come in the person of Jesus and that he had been killed and had been raised from the dead; but still the Kingdom associated with the Messiah had not arrived, at least in its fullness. Jewish eschatology knew nothing of a Messiah who had come into the world; and so Paul, faced with new facts, found the traditional forms inadequate and unsatisfactory and was forced to modify old views and set forth the full truth in fresh ways. Apocalyptic speculation is used only where it can make a positive contribution. Above all else it is Paul's assessment of the person and work of Jesus that underlies his eschatology. His religious experience stands behind his eschatology and at the same time causes him to turn also to other categories of theological thought as he draws out the implications of the fact of Jesus.[44] Because time has produced a fresh perspective, his eschatology is necessarily not the same as that of Jesus himself.

Paul builds upon familiar Jewish apocalyptic forms, but the significance of Paul's treatment is to be found, not in what he shared with others but in the purpose and the nature of his innovations. In his use of traditional materials he is creative. His insights show originality at point after point. New ground must be broken, and Paul is fearless. The truth is greater than man's mind, and Paul is free to discuss the whole range of God's purposes from before the creation of the world through the event of Jesus Christ to the glory of the everlasting.[45] Paul, then, is bound to no scheme or system derived from the past. He rejects mere apocalyptic speculations because he is interested only in the realities of the new life in Christ. Thus, for him, even the evils of sin, suffering, and death have a place in God's plan. Finally, it must not be forgotten that although Paul is a Jew and deals with Jewish materials, he writes in Greek and is convinced that God has called him to preach the gospel to the Gentiles, i.e., to interpret the Christian message to the Greek mind. It is here that Paul makes his most important contribution.[46]

Some Characteristics of Paul's Thought

Paul's eschatology is basically simple. Yet he does reflect a number of influences on his thought. He is moved by a variety of motives, primary and secondary. In the opinion of F. V. Filson, " Paul affirms principles but does not possess any clear detailed picture of the life to come." [47] Some scholars have found in Paul two unreconciled types of eschatology, one, a collective form rooted in Jewish apocalyptic and represented in I and II Thessalonians and I Corinthians, and the other, an individual approach emphasizing personal development and set forth in Philippians, II Corinthians, and Colossians.[48] Yet in Paul the individual and the corporate are not antithetic but complementary, and salvation is both a present experience and a future hope.[49] He is certainly not aware of expounding a system of eschatology, nor is he conscious of any lack of it. A few fundamental beliefs are allowed to throw light on the entire range of human experience, including some of man's most frequent questions about the future.

We do not possess all that Paul thought, preached, or wrote. His epistles assume or allude to the teaching that he had given earlier to his converts, but it is never repeated in full. Accordingly, there are gaps in our reconstruction of Paul's thought that were not present for Paul himself. In his letters he answers specific questions and speaks to particular situations; and in so doing he may emphasize one or another part of his total beliefs. Only the epistle to the Romans even suggests any deliberate attempt on Paul's part to express himself systematically or with fullness, and even in Romans there are gaps in human logic. Dahl reminds us: "The only kind of consistency we are prepared to recognize is that of abstract, systematic thinking, and of this there is little or none in biblical literature." [50]

Paul will not meet our preconceived desire for a complete exposition of eschatology. Because he was first of all a practical missionary he sees no value in a timetable of future events or a chart of heavenly places. On the other hand, his thought is richly varied, and it is impossible to reconcile all of his eschatological references. The discussion of the resurrection in I Cor., ch. 15, provides a clear example of apparent contradictions in Paul's writing. Yet Paul's emphasis is never on eschatological details, which he distinguishes sharply from underlying principles.[51] It is these central truths that provide the point of reference for every statement and supply coherence in his thought.[52] Therefore, Paul could never knowingly allow significant inconsistencies or obscurities to remain in writings that were missionary in purpose.

His words were not written as elements in an abstract or theoretical philosophy or theology. His only concern is with the religious health and growth of his readers. If Paul is more restrained and sober than other writers of apocalyptic, it is because his purpose has to do with the present life and with the future insofar as it throws light upon this moment. His interest in the life to come is ultimately practical. What he has to say specifically about any item and the amount of space given to it in his extant writings are determined not so much by his previous thinking or experience as by the religious needs of those addressed.[53]

Paul spends a remarkably small amount of time in developing detailed pictures of coming events such as are to be discovered in apocalypses generally. Traditional apocalyptic ideas are elaborated only in II Thess., ch. 2.[54] He makes scant use of apocalyptic sections of the Old Testament. The Book of Daniel provides little material for the expression of his views. Moreover, as H. A. Guy has indicated, "There is lacking in Paul much that was common matter in the apocalypses — vivid descriptions of the coming Day, speculations regarding the Resurrection, anticipations of the final fate of good and evil." [55] Such figures as the blowing of the trumpet and the descent from heaven with a shout are not important in themselves for Paul. They are used to stimulate the imagination so that the truths to which they point may become more immediately real. The facts with which eschatology has to do have been revealed to the believer by God, but to the human mind they are still a mystery. Paul E. Davies notes carefully: "The very fact that apocalyptic borrowed language and figures so readily is an indication of its poverty in any exact terms to describe the ineffable. The inconsistency of details shows that they did not take these details very seriously." [56] That which matters most to Paul is the certainty that God's purpose, made known in Jesus, will be fully accomplished.

Like Jesus, Paul frequently makes use of exaggeration and startling contrast to direct his readers' attention to what he has to say. He moves easily and rapidly from the particular to the universal, from the corporate to the individual, and from the present to the future. Many of Paul's statements, when isolated, become relative, and must be balanced with each other. Paul does not feel it necessary to reconcile such seeming opposites as the kindness and the severity of God (Rom. 11:22). If it is true that "Paul's Christianity glories in paradox," [57] the reason is the paradoxical nature of the message with which Paul has been entrusted. However, whereas in most eschatological writings, and especially in apocalyptic, the attitude toward this world and this time is condemnatory and negative, it will be quickly seen that Paul's utterances are chiefly constructive and positive. Again, eschatology has often disregarded or minimized the relevance of moral standards and activity; but in every part of Paul's thought moral motives are stressed. He makes it plain that there is an inescapable urgency about ethical duties. He holds that our present life is an integral part of all existence because God will be victorious in every time and place and state.

Goguel makes the striking statement: "The epistles [of Paul] contain the elements of a vast apocalypse, which begins with the revolt of Satan against God and even with the creation of the world while its end is the glory of God." [58] Paul, of course, never delineates this apocalypse even though it is potentially present in his letters. Rather, we may affirm that for Paul there is little or no thought that is consciously eschatological. He is concerned with the totality of Christian truth, and all life is for him judged by its goal and end. In the best sense of the word Paul is a theologian, and he sees that Christianity has innumerable facets. Other classifications than eschatology are needed to describe his thought. However, it is also true that, properly considered, all his teaching is eschatological. This is not to say that Paul's main religious interest was in eschatology,[59] but it was nevertheless an organizing center for the whole of his theological thought. Paul's ideas of last things relate to every part of Christian truth.[60] They are the leaven permeating the whole, but if they are considered only by themselves, there is the grave danger of abstracting an artificial collection of unrelated, disconnected elements that would mean little to Paul. C. H. Dodd is right in declaring: "In masterly fashion Paul has claimed the whole territory of the Church's life as the field of the eschatological miracle." [61] Eschatology is thus far from being a limitation or a confining influence. In fact, it provides the largest possible perspective for theological interpretation.[62] The death and resurrection of Jesus are set forth by Paul in an eschatological setting because only in this way can their true meaning be grasped. Paul experiences in his own life the living Christ. He knows that he and other disciples are part of the new creation. He is empowered by God's gift of the Holy Spirit. He sees the church spreading from Palestine to Rome. All these things are for him eschatological phenomena.[63] His very real life of suffering is both bearable and meaningful because of his certain hope of what will be. He writes, "I consider that the sufferings of this present time are not worth comparing with the glory that is to be revealed to us." (Rom. 8:18.) "When the perfect comes, the imperfect will pass away." (I Cor. 13:10.) "This slight momentary affliction is preparing for us an eternal weight of glory beyond all comparison." (II Cor. 4:17.) With such a foundation A. M. Hunter is justified in his conclusion: "Salvation as a future hope . . . was the very nerve of Paul's Christianity." [64]

The Development of the Eschatological Theme

If, however, it can be shown that Paul's eschatology was subject to change and development with the passing of the years of his missionary teaching and writing, the role of eschatology as a stable foundation for his theology must be reexamined. Moreover, it would be difficult to say much regarding Paul's eschatology in general if it must be subdivided into many different periods of growth. The question of the degree and kind of development in Paul's eschatological thinking as it is set forth in the extant letters is therefore crucial and has been described by J. A. T. Robinson as "one of the continuing debates of New Testament theology."[65] There are a few scholars who maintain that we can discover no development or change of emphasis.[66] Since in Paul there is no single system or plan of eschatology, variations of some kind are inevitable. Because Paul is not bound by one pattern into which all his thoughts must be fitted, there is room for some growth based upon experience and successive attempts at interpretation. A different form of presentation may be demanded by the particular immediate occasion of a writing or by some crisis in Paul's life. The emotional states of any writer will inevitably produce fluctuation in his expressed thoughts. Moreover, the Pauline epistles were written over a period of perhaps ten to fifteen years, and no one can remain unchanged for such a time.[67] There is no reason to suppose that Paul's eschatology was any more static than was his admittedly enlarging religious life. Some variations within his eschatological statements must be expected, and some of these may well represent a maturing of Paul's mind. The matter for investigation is the extent of these differences.[68] Only if they are numerous and significant will it be necessary to alter our characterization of Paul's eschatology.

R. H. Charles has contributed a detailed and notable analysis of the Pauline material.[69] He finds four stages in the development of Paul's eschatological ideas. The first period is that of I and II Thessalonians. Here alone we find the figure of Antichrist and the belief that the end of the age is being ushered in by the consummation of evil and the unbelief of mankind. The second stage is set forth in II Corinthians. The third period is seen in II Corinthians and Romans. Charles finds here a conscious change of view with regard to the time of the resurrection and a new concept that the conversion of the whole world will bring about the Advent of Christ. The fourth and final stage is the exposition of the cosmic significance of Christ in Philippians and Colossians (and Ephesians).

Another major study of this development is that of C. H. Dodd.[70] A central point in his discussion is the assertion that there is a major turning point about the time of II Corinthians. Dodd finds an identical pattern of development in three areas of eschatology. First, in I Thessalonians it is assumed that few Christians will die before the Advent. In I Corinthians most Christians are expected to die, but not all will do so (ch. 15:51). On the other hand, in II Corinthians, Paul has faced the fact that it is probable that he will, through the means of death, go to be with the Lord. In the subsequent epistles the thought of the imminence of the Advent fades into the background, and Dodd believes that thus the eschatological expectation is subordinated to the present reality of the life of the new age. In the second place, it is noticed that in the earlier epistles there is a depreciation of the present order. In I Cor. 7:31, Paul writes that "the form of this world is passing away," having dismissed any lasting concern for commerce, marriage, and human joy and sorrow. Even though in Rom. 13:1-10, Paul apparently ascribes positive values to the political institutions of the Roman Empire, the earlier epistles suggest that there is no value in the present order. The later epistles, however, are believed to recognize natural human goodness and to suggest that human institutions have a place in the Christian life because they have at least a relative value. Finally, whereas in I Thessalonians the final rejection of the Jews is proclaimed, in Rom. 11:13-32 Paul argues that their rejection cannot be final. The later epistles point to the universal triumph of Christ. Dodd concludes that these three changes have one common characteristic. They all provide a way of avoiding a certain harsh dualism that set "the things of the Lord" against "the things of the world," "this age" against "the age to come," "the elect" against "the rest of humanity." But the argument is not convincing. Charles and Dodd are both open to the charge that they depend upon the acceptance of a certain chronological sequence for Paul's letters which cannot be proved. Stewart generalizes: "Most of the schemes of development are precarious and artificial." [71]

Although not suggesting a course of development in all of the Pauline epistles, some scholars point to a special emphasis in one or another. For example, W. L. Knox has written: "The Second Epistle [to the Corinthians] is largely devoted to a complete revision of Pauline eschatology in a Hellenistic sense." [72] It will have to be determined later whether or not there is in II Corinthians a view of the future life unlike that which is set forth elsewhere by Paul. Another epistle that seems to introduce new ideas is that to the Colossians. Beare finds here a lessening of concern for the future consummation and a deepening of appreciation of those aspects of the coming age which Christians have already received from God.[73] Paul affirms in Col. 3:3, "You have died, and your life is hid with Christ in God." Beare sees reflected in such a statement a transformation in the Pauline eschatology in which the Jewish idea of a succession of ages has been virtually replaced by "the Hellenic conception of realms or orders of being, for which succession of time is irrelevant." [74] Again, the question of whether or not Paul at various times alludes to a timeless idealism as one way of suggesting the truth that is in Christ must be postponed for later consideration.

Most scholars admit some kind of a gradual development in the exposition of Paul's major eschatological concepts. Yet that development is very strictly limited. In essentials we find both consistency and continuity.[75] From his earliest letters to his latest there is a constant emphasis on the return of Jesus, the judgment, and the day of glory. At the same time there are admittedly changes of emphasis. Although Paul refers to the Parousia in I and II Thessalonians, I and II Corinthians, and Philippians, letters generally regarded as from the early, middle, and late periods of his missionary career, he seems to be less and less concerned about its date. Likewise, a careful study of the literature seems to indicate that there is a gradual shift from apocalyptic to nonapocalyptic eschatology, from some use of the traditional scenery to very little.[76] The pictorial elements appear with decreasing frequency as we move to the later writings. It may well be that Jewish pictures prove less and less effective in interpreting Christianity to the Gentile world and that Paul himself demanded other forms of expression.[77] In any case, however, the repetitions in Paul's thought are far more impressive than the variations that may be encountered from one letter to the next. The basic Pauline eschatological ideas or principles are to be found throughout all his writings, early and late. They are, for the most part, assumptions that Paul does not feel called upon to defend or elaborate, yet they form the core of his thinking.

Major Concepts

Although his eschatological ideas are expressed and applied in a wide variety of ways, they are essentially few in number and constitute the solid foundation on which he builds. It is the superstructure with which the reader first comes into contact, but it is the substructure that determines the strength of the building. Frequently these central Pauline beliefs are not directly stated but are presupposed in his argument. They must be reconstructed insofar as possible if we are to assess, classify, and compare the large number of sentences and phrases that are properly judged to be eschatological. We shall consider eight propositions.

These key ideas may be disclosed by a study of Pauline word usage. Although a single word may have several different meanings for Paul, a primary meaning can usually be established. It is also true that Paul does not shrink from employing two or three different words to express a single basic thought. Yet words are very important for Paul, and he uses them carefully and, for the most part, skillfully. He is aware of the meaning of word roots, and the many compound words that he employs must be examined for their roots as well as their prefixes if we are to discern Paul's intent in using them. There are approximately 279 different words (including compounds) used by Paul two or more times each that have a recognized eschatological meaning or which are primarily so intended by Paul. In addition, there are ninety-four words with clear eschatological meaning or intent that are found only once in Paul. Thus his eschatological vocabulary may be said to consist of more than 370 words. Some of these are used as synonyms, but a far larger number allow Paul to express himself with vividness and clarity. He is able to use words as a polished tool by which to convey his thought with precision.

First of all, Paul's language reveals the primary fact that for him time is not an illusion or a relativity but a concrete reality. In this respect he is loyal to his Jewish heritage. In both the Old and New Testaments time is the framework for God's redemptive processes, and therefore in the Bible there can be no antithesis between time and eternity. Time is the medium in which God acts, and so it cannot be spoken of abstractly. Even man's faith, his laying hold of God's power and love, must have a temporal basis. According to their nature, events impart varying value to time, but in Biblical and also Pauline thought there are only two kinds of time, that which is limited and that which is endless.[78] Therefore, everything that happens must take place within time.[79] There are six instances in the Pauline literature of the most common Greek word for time, *chronos*.[80] It is generally defined as indicating "a measurable period of time," as is suggested in the English word "chronological." In four of the six instances, Paul uses *chronos* to indicate a segment of human life. (Rom. 7:1; I Cor. 7:39; 16:7; Gal. 4:1.) The same word is used in Gal. 4:4 to refer to God's deed in the time that he controls: "But when the time had fully come, God sent forth his Son, born of woman, born under the law." In the final occurrence (I Thess. 5:1) Paul equates "times" with "seasons," represented by a second word for time, *kairos*. The latter is found eighteen times in Paul, with another four cases in Ephesians. In general, Greek usage of the word often means "the right, proper or favorable time, a fitting season, or opportunity." [81] Frequently, however, it has only the meaning of "time" and is an alternative for *chronos* (cf. I Thess. 5:1). Paul uses the word to fix the action of God or Christ (e.g., Rom. 5:6; I Cor. 7:29), but more often he suggests by it the crucial and limited nature of the present time for men (e.g., Rom. 13:11; Gal. 6:10; Col. 4:5). By both words, then, Paul points to the inescapability and the irresistibility of time for man, and he declares that God has chosen to act in this same medium.[82]

A third Pauline word for time is *aiōn,* which means "a very long time, an age" and which occurs in twenty instances, with six more in Ephesians. In nine places the word is found in a fixed, possibly liturgical, phrase signifying "for ever." In seven instances the word describes the particular time in which the early Christians are living. In the remaining three cases (I Cor. 2:7; 10:11; Col. 1:26) the word is found in the plural and indicates that limited periods or ages of history are a succession of the one time in which all existence occurs.[83] Paul agreed with late Jewish eschatology that this present age would, as a part of the succession of time, be surely followed by the age of God's triumph, which necessarily would be limitless and perfect. For Paul the word *aiōn,* unless it is specifically described otherwise, signifies the age to come, which is the one age above all others. The adjective *aiōnios,* formed from the noun *aiōn,* occurs eleven times in Paul; and although it basically signifies only "pertaining to a very long time or an age," it has come to mean, from a human point of view, "continuous or perpetual." For Paul it always points to that period of time belonging to God alone.[84] Thus, the adjective is found five times in the phrase "eternal life," which is everlasting only because it is a gift of the everlasting God. Once the word is applied to the comfort belonging to the coming age of God (II Thess. 2:16) and once to destruction (II Thess. 1:9). Three times it refers simply to the changeless reality deriving from God (II Cor. 4:17, 18; 5:1). In each instance the continuation of time is assumed, and there is no suggestion of its unreality or relativity. *Aiōn* and *aiōnios* do sometimes take on a moral or philosophical significance but only in a derived and secondary sense, since the present imperfect age is transitory, whereas the age to come is without end because God is without end.[85]

The second basic concept of Paul to be derived from his word usage is that God in Christ has revealed the unknown to those who will see. Eleven times Paul uses the word "mystery," *mystērion,* and there are six more occurrences in Ephesians. The word has been defined as "the secret thought, plans, and dispensations of God which are hidden from the human reason, as well as from all other comprehension below the divine level, and hence must be revealed to those for whom they are intended." [86] In Col. 1:26, Paul speaks specifically of "the mystery hidden for ages and generations," but here and elsewhere his emphasis is upon the fact that God has chosen to make known his secrets. Each time the word appears in Paul there is a sense of wonderment and awe because God has freely included man in the knowledge of his inner counsels. Since such information lies beyond the human mind, it is still considered to be a mystery; but because God has disclosed his nature and purpose in the life of Jesus, it is no longer secret. Dahl speaks of *mystērion* as "a detail of the eschatological plan, or the whole plan in its entirety."[87] In Paul's view, mankind now has the possibility for the first time of knowing the goal of all creation. Yet even so only mature Christians possess such understanding.

A third major Pauline idea is that God's purpose is not only revealed, but it is being fulfilled now and in time. One of the most important of all Greek roots for Paul is *tel-*, which signifies "end, goal, or purpose." Seven words formed from this root are used by Paul with deliberate effect. The noun *telos* occurs twelve times. It may indicate a definite termination or a fixed final day (e.g., I Cor. 15:24), and it may also point to an inevitable result (II Cor. 11:15) or the attainment of an inherent reason for being (Rom. 10:4). In each case it is God alone who determines the end, and man's only contribution is to recognize what God has established. The same root is found in four verbal forms that Paul employs twelve times. Furthermore, once (Col. 3:14) Paul speaks of *teleiotēs,* usually translated "perfection," but strictly signifying the full achievement of divine purpose. In seven cases Paul uses the adjective *teleios,* generally translated "perfect or mature." Twice the word refers to a deed or a condition (Rom. 12:2; I Cor. 13:10), and in the remaining instances it describes human beings. In each occurrence Paul assumes that the desired direction or standard to be reached has been given by God and cannot be determined by man. Thus, Paul's word usage makes it clear that there is a goal in every part of creation and that time is moving with a purpose. For Paul the last is related to the first because each point of time and process is from God. He is the master of what happens. The verb "to fulfill," *plēroō,* with three compounds, is used by Paul twenty-four times (with four more cases in Ephesians). The corresponding noun, *plērōma,* is found in eight places. Once again the basic idea is achievement of the full purpose intended by God for things and people and especially for Jesus (cf. Col. 1:19; 2:9). Fullness is therefore an appropriate expression for the nature of the Christian calling. God has set the goal, and he is working for its realization. In the meantime, everything is imperfect since it falls short of the standard that is God's intention for it.

A fourth central concept is that all history is a chronological progression. By definition eschatology is essentially concerned with the last events in a time series, and the inevitable tendency is to ignore or dismiss as unimportant all the time and the happenings that precede the end. Paul, too, regards the final events as the ground of meaning for all that comes earlier; but preceding events are not therefore without significance or value. He shows forth at all points a linear conception of time and has no place for a timeless idealism.[88] Even the unique, unrepeatable birth of Jesus is a fact of past history, an event in time. In Jesus we see God and time at their closest point. Thus, C. K. Barrett can write: " For Paul, though Jesus Christ is the divine intruder, his intrusion follows a pattern that could in a sense, and in some degree, have been predicted." [89] It is in Paul's graphic picture of the final events of history in I Cor. 15:22-28 that we encounter the clearest evidence of his acceptance of chronological progression. As the first-fruits Christ is raised, and then those who belong to him will rise in time to come. After Christ destroys all opposition, including death itself at the last, then Christ will subject himself to God and deliver the Kingdom to the Father. Paul has in mind here a definite time scale. But such an understanding is reflected everywhere in Paul. His vocabulary includes such paired opposites as " first-last," " old-new," " before-after." He emphasizes the place of the present in the course of time by words which mean " now," " today," " already," " near," " coming," " still "; and he recognizes that some things lie ahead in his expressions for " then," and " until." In the events of what we call past, present, and future there is an order of progression inherent in time itself (cf. I Cor. 15:23).

The progression is not easy or uniform, however; and a fifth Pauline conviction is that until the final event, which will come only when God brings it about, there is necessarily in all existence an unrelenting struggle between good and evil. Although Paul as a Jew believed that the world as created by God was good, he had been forced to admit that very early it had fallen from its original state. Somehow God's plan was being opposed, and there was rebellion at the heart of creation.[90] It was Paul's belief that this revolt had been taking place for a long time, but that in Jesus, God had acted to defeat it completely and quickly. He saw, however, that the evil forces are the same as they have been since the early days of creation. It has often been observed that Paul likes to speak in terms of tension and opposites. Nowhere is this more true than in his analysis of the reasons for the delay in the working out of God's plan. On the one hand, there are forces that hide the truth. The "hidden things" are "of men," "of the heart," "of darkness," and "of shame" (Rom. 2:16; I Cor. 4:5; 14:25; II Cor. 4:2). On the other hand, the work of God is to make manifest, to reveal, to make known, to uncover, and to point out. Typical is the statement of Rom. 1:19: "For what can be known about God is plain to them, because God has shown it to them." Altogether there are seventy-eight occurrences of verbs and nouns of this type, and in the vast majority of cases God is the expressed or implied subject of the action. The act of disclosure is described in the past or in the present or in the future because it is always in every time characteristic of God.

The act of darkening and the resulting darkness are attributed to evil forces, but the giving of light is the mark of God and the expected quality of faithful Christians. Christ is associated with the day, but evil is allied with night, which is also described as sleep, sin, and wickedness.

Evil corrupts the good creation of God, and so nature is referred to as corruptible and as exhibiting corruption. That which God gives in Christ is incorruption, and his life is incorruptible.[91] Evil is, in spite of wordly appearances to the contrary, essentially weakness; but God gives strength and power. Closely connected with sin, corruption, and weakness is death, about which Paul has much to say. Five different verbs that express the act of dying are used a total of fifty times, with one more in Ephesians. Two noun forms for death are found forty-three times, and two corresponding adjectives occur in forty cases, with four more instances in Ephesians. Death has marked all time since Adam and will be the last of all the forces opposing God to be vanquished. Thus, it is descriptive of all human existence until the final events.

The opposite of death is life, and again it is of primary interest to Paul. He uses the Greek verb " to live," with two compound forms forty-six times. Nouns for life and immortality are found in twenty-nine places. The act of making alive is ascribed to God or the Holy Spirit eight times. Nouns and verbs referring to the raising of the dead to life are discovered in forty-five cases. In the vast majority of instances references to life are in close proximity to references to death. Life is that which comes from God to overcome the effect of sin and rebellion against him.[92] Life is sometimes spoken of as a past event, and sometimes as a present experience, and sometimes a future hope; but always it is something that man receives in Christ and that he can never produce himself. When death meets life, the latter is bound to triumph. Yet the result of the working of sin and death is to put an end to any reason for being or continuing life apart from God. The Greek verb *katargeō*, used twenty-two times by Paul, has been defined by Dahl as " to deprive a totality of its autonomy over against God so that it ceases to have any effective existence." [93] So Christ will destroy every rule, authority, and power before the end (cf. I Cor. 15:24). Resistance to God brings about a void or emptiness that threatens every human being as well as things and forces. It is only " in the Lord " that our labor has ultimate meaning (cf. I Cor. 15:58). The purpose of God is to allow man to share in that which alone has significance because it remains and so truly is.

The Greek verb *menō,* " to remain," appears thirteen times in Paul, and seven compound forms add fifteen more instances. The noun *hypomonē,* derived from one of these compound verbs, means " patience " or " endurance " and is used in thirteen instances by Paul. In II Cor. 3:11 there is a sharp contrast between that which is being destroyed, *to katargoumenon,* and that which remains, *to menon:* " For if what faded away came with splendor, what is permanent must have much more splendor." Only that which is of God does not at some time wither and disappear. As the Christian in turn becomes aware of the stability and unchangeableness of God, he is enabled by faith to judge between the temporary and the eternal. The concept of abiding develops naturally into that of patient endurance. Instead of fleeing before the temporarily powerful hosts of evil, the Christian disciple stands firm and holds his ground.[94] He is confident and expectant. The strongest verb used by Paul (twelve times) to indicate total destruction is *apollumi.*[95] The related noun and two other words of the same meaning are found ten times in Paul.

The apostle does not shrink from considering the end of all that opposes God, but his principal emphasis is upon God's redemptive purpose. The verb " to save " is found nineteen times, and its synonym " to rescue " occurs in nine more cases. The noun " salvation " is used in fourteen instances. For Paul, " salvation " is a comprehensive term that describes the effect upon the whole of man's life when God's life enters it. It is constantly assumed that salvation is brought to man only by the life, death, and resurrection of Jesus. Because God's action in Jesus has great relevance for all history, Paul can say at one time, " we were saved," at another, " we are being saved," and at still another, " we shall be saved "; but in all cases there is only one process of salvation. There is no question but that God will be victorious. Yet that victory is not now finished, and a real and uncompromising battle continues with everything that resists God.

The consummation of God's plan is still in the future since this world is even now at least partially controlled by evil, but a sixth principle of Paul's eschatology is that this imperfect present time is a meaningful interim between two ages. Although from one point of view the work of Christ has been accomplished, and God need do nothing more for the world's salvation, the fruits of that work have not yet been fully ripened. The future will see more of God's victory than can be observed in the present. On the other hand, that future is by no means uncertain or unknown. Part of that which is yet to come may be experienced by the faithful Christian at the present moment, and the full promise of the coming age may be seized proleptically. In Rom. 8:37, Paul says of all Christians, " We *are* more than conquerors." It is in the present that we see the effects of the past and that we perceive in part that which is sure to come. It is also in the present that we must make our own decision as to which of the struggling powers from the past will assume the mastery in our lives. By our decision now we are helping to determine the nature of our own future. The past becomes the future only through the intervening medium of the present, and this is true even for the plans of God. The course of history is continuous, and the present differs from the past and the future only in being at another point on the time scale.[96] It is just because the present is subject to the same conditions of time that there is an extreme urgency about our choices and deeds. What happens now is neither of more nor of less importance than what has taken place and what will come to pass because all time stands under the judgment of God.

A seventh key idea of Paul is that the work of Christ and the work of God are one. Although Paul's faith is decidedly Christocentric and there are more references to Christ than to God in his writings, he remains a monotheist. Salvation has been provided by the historical Jesus, but it is God who sent forth his Son (Gal. 4:4). Christ died for us, yet in that death it is God who shows his love for us (Rom. 5:8). In Paul's view, Jesus is at the heart of our religion just because in him we see God most clearly and finally.[97] Thus Paul can apply titles of God to Jesus without jeopardizing in any way his monotheistic position. Similarly, Paul several times refers to the preexistence of Christ and many times to his heavenly glory. He has no interest in speculations regarding prehistorical or posthistorical states of Jesus, but he is seriously concerned with the question of how Jesus is made a part of God's eschatological plan. Paul is convinced that all history is focused in the brief life of Jesus of Nazareth. He sees Jesus as the fulfillment of Old Testament prophecy. Events of earlier Jewish history have prepared the way for his coming. In fact, Paul views the Old Testament as a Christian book because it points to the one who was to come and who now has come in Jesus. Moreover, from the time of his resurrection Jesus has been known and reigns as Lord. Through the church he is directing the completion of his mission, and he will continue to do so until the very last event (I Cor. 15:28). Except for this final rule of God alone, Jesus is also the key to the future. Accordingly, Paul ascribes to him both the preexistence traditionally associated with God and also heavenly exaltation. But Christ is not another God or a rival to him. He is the effective expression of God's purpose, the agent of creation and redemption. (Col. 1:15-20.) Whatever Christ has done, is doing, and will do is a part of the one divine plan.

The eighth of Paul's principles underlies all the others. God is in control of all history. Cullmann has reminded us that " Primitive Christianity knows nothing of a timeless God." [98] Rather, he is known to be personally involved in the whole span of time, from beginning to end. Even though God is greater than time, he has chosen to commit his purposes to it. Apart from time we can know nothing of him. In time, God and man are active together in spite of the fact that man is often working against him. Because Paul is unwilling to deny man's responsibility for his decisions and their results, he does not often speak of God's control of history; but that belief is always present in the center of Paul's thought. In Rom. 8:20 and I Cor. 15:27-28, Paul writes of God as one who subjects his creatures to his will within time.[99] In I Cor. 7:29 the RSV reads, " The appointed time has grown very short "; but the Greek is to be translated literally, " The time has been shortened." The inference is that God, as controller of history, has done the shortening.[100] According to C. K. Barrett, " It is not a rational coherence that Paul finds in history, but a personal and theological coherence." [101] Time and history are in the Pauline view subject to God, who created them; but they are also accepted by God as conditions for the carrying out of his plan. They are not unconditioned, independent entities but creatures whose importance rests in the way in which God has chosen to act in his creation.[102]

Chapter II | THE COMING OF THE LORD

As he writes to the Thessalonians, Paul is careful to deny absolutely any suggestion that the long-awaited day of the Lord has already come (II Thess. 2:1 f.). He gives full recognition to the importance of the present as the time that leads on to the future and that contains within itself for the Christian a foretaste of God's age. Yet he knows that the future is still ahead. The present is a mixture of imperfection and evil on the one hand and the working of divine power on the other. Nothing needs to be added to what God has already done in Jesus, but the effects of his mission are now only partially realized. His victory has been won, but the world does not yet know it. The committed Christian possesses the strength of Christ, but there are large numbers of people who are not Christians. Even the faithful disciple must admit that there is much to do. He is called, and he is on his way; but the goal is not reached. Although everything has been altered by the fact of Jesus' birth, death, and resurrection, that which God will accomplish in his time is far greater than that which is now.

In I Cor. 4:8, Paul rebukes the Corinthians with irony because they were acting as if they believed that the Kingdom of God had come: "Already you are filled! Already you have become rich! Without us you have become kings!" What has taken place in the past and what is now being experienced are in themselves incomplete, and their meaning is at least partly derived from what is yet to come. To ignore the future is to grasp only a fragment of reality. A. M. Hunter has observed: "For the Apostle, salvation as a future hope meant certain very definite things. It was the very nerve of his Christianity."[1] Paul regards history as involving at least three ages — the past, the present, and the time to come. The future is for him just as much a part of the procession of history as are the first two ages. He believes that there are some events that cannot take place until the end period. The age to come will produce a consummation that includes a final victory over death, the return of Christ, and the Last Judgment. For Cullmann "the time character of the future becomes especially clear from the fact that the eschatological drama, as it is pictured in the Apocalypses, including the New Testament ones, takes place in a thoroughly chronological progression."[2] In the detailed treatment in I Cor., ch. 15, Paul suggests that the resurrection of Christ occurs first, then that of faithful Christians at his second coming. The end is reached after Christ has destroyed all enemies, including death itself at the last, and has then delivered the Kingdom to God the Father. Such a happening is of course the end of history as we have known it, but it is also the beginning of the age to come. The end of the old world will introduce the new world of complete salvation. Only as the imperfect disappears can the perfect take its place (cf. I Cor. 13:10). Because it has only partly come, the new life is still hidden and awaits its fulfillment. Filson has noted in this connection: "It is only when assurance of a righteous future order is felt that the Christian can live in contentment."[3] The trials and sufferings of the present are without meaning unless there is more to history (cf. I Cor. 15:19, 30 ff.).

It is not surprising, therefore, that although Paul addresses himself to the present conditions and needs of his converts, he resorts again and again to the future tense in order to convey to them the full riches of their inheritance in Christ. That which God will bring to pass in his own time lies beyond the limits of human comprehension and expression, and so Paul sometimes employs familiar apocalyptic images and patterns to symbolize the revealed truth (e.g., I Thess. 4:13 to 5:10; II Thess. 2:1-12; I Cor. 15:20-28). Occasionally he dwells at some length on coming events, but he is much more interested in the assured principles than he is in detailed descriptions (e.g., II Cor. 5:1-10). Moreover, future happenings include a number of prospects. Paul discusses now one and now another aspect of what lies beyond. Perhaps his most comprehensive term for the final event is "the day of the Lord," but he is also mindful of the inevitability of judgment, of the joys of resurrection and the continuing life with God, and of the final crushing of all opposition to the divine plan. All experiences and events of whatever time are related to the future. Thus, even though we were reconciled to God through Christ's death and so are in a present state of reconciliation and are now justified, much more shall we be saved (Rom. 5:9 f.). We are now children of God, but far greater than anything we know in the present is the glory yet to be revealed in us (ch. 8:18). God, who gave his Son to death for our sake, will surely give us all things in time to come (v. 32). As Christians wait with patience for God to act, the Lord Jesus Christ will sustain them to the very end so that they may be guiltless (I Cor. 1:8). The sufferings of this moment are as nothing beside the eternal glory that will be given us (II Cor. 4:17). Much of eternal significance has already been done by God in the life of Jesus. God's own life has been made available to the disciple. Yet an even larger gift remains for the coming of God's own age.

Thus, hope is a necessary quality of the Christian for Paul. He uses the noun *elpis* twenty-five times, with three additional cases in Ephesians. The corresponding verb appears fifteen times, and he employs an alternate verb, *apekdechomai,* in six cases. In each instance the meaning is " confident expectation combined with eagerness." Paul admits (Rom. 8:24) that " hope that is seen is not hope. For who hopes for what he sees? " Hope has to do, rather, with the things that have not yet happened but that must occur because of the dependableness of God. Thus, Paul can speak of " the God of hope " (Rom. 15:13). Twice faith and hope are directly linked (I Cor. 13:13; II Cor. 10:15). The object of faith is variously described as righteousness, glory, salvation, and the Lord himself. Love hopes for all [good] things (I Cor. 13:7). With Paul, hope is by no means a word of flight, despair, or postponement. It is the basis of present action in view of facts that are no less real because they are future. Hope sees time as continuous and under the control of God. The only instance in Paul's writings in which the verb " to save," *sōzō,* is found in the aorist indicative, indicating an event that has taken place at some point in the past, is Rom. 8:24, " In this hope we were saved." Even the completed action of Christ is linked with the concept of hope.

A Future Salvation

Although God's act of vindication or deliverance has occurred in the past, the attainment of salvation belongs to the next age. Thus Paul teaches: " By one man's obedience many will be made righteous " (Rom. 5:19). It is generally assumed that justification is a Pauline figure for what God has done for us. It is important to recognize, however, that even justification has not yet fully come. To the Galatians, Paul writes: " We wait for the hope of righteousness " (ch. 5:5; cf. also Rom. 2:13). Paul's thought in Rom. 4:24 is much the same as he concludes that faith " will be reckoned [as righteousness] to us who believe in him." Since this present world is still marked by imperfection of all kinds, it cannot receive that perfect life and glory which in Paul's thought are derived from God alone.

According to Goguel, "Salvation is the state in which the elect will be when they belong exclusively to the new world." [4] When so defined, salvation is necessarily eschatological and all-inclusive. A detailed examination of Paul's use of the Greek verb "to save" supports this idea. As has been noted, there is only one instance in which Paul uses this verb in a past tense (Rom. 8:24). There are three instances in which the verb appears in a progressive present (I Cor. 1:18; 15:2; II Cor. 2:15), where there is a strong emphasis upon our experience now. In all of the remaining thirteen occurrences of the finite verb the tense or the thought is future. A typical case is Rom. 5:10: "Much more, now that we are reconciled, shall we be saved." In the one case in which the noun "savior," *sōtēr,* is used by Paul (Phil. 3:20) the thought is of future expectation. In Rom. 13:11, Paul can say, "Salvation is nearer to us now than when we first believed." Yet it is still to come. "The hope of salvation" is to serve as a helmet in the future struggles of the disciple (I Thess. 5:8).

In writing to the Christians at Rome, Paul states, "You have received the spirit of sonship" (ch. 8:15). Because this gift was made possible through the life of Jesus, it is true that Christians are now sons of God (Rom. 8:14; Gal. 3:26; 4:6-7.). But it is also true that this sonship belongs to the future. Although we are alive now, "we wait for adoption as sons" (Rom. 8:23). The revealing of the sons of God is still to come (v. 19). Such status does not belong to man by nature or right but is God's gift through Christ. Because of this mercy, men have been made heirs. They have been granted the right to succeed to that which belongs only to God. But that succession has not yet occurred in spite of the fact that it has been provided for. Twenty-eight times Paul expresses the idea of inheritance in one verb and three nouns, and always the direction of his thought is future. God's legacy to man has not yet been received and must be conditional. Paul's thought is most clearly expressed in Rom. 8:16b-17: "We are children of God, and if children, then heirs, heirs of God and fellow heirs with Christ, provided we suffer with him in order that we may also be glorified with him." Paul thankfully points to the offered privileges; but he is well aware that since man can do no more than respond to God's initiative, he must await the fulfillment in days ahead.

It was part of Paul's eschatological inheritance from Judaism to associate the gift of the Spirit with the last age. The prophecy of Joel (ch. 2:28 f.) was related to the general expectation of the Messianic age, and the connection of the Spirit with eschatology reaches far back into the Old Testament. The early Christians were convinced that the words of Joel had been fulfilled on Pentecost (Acts 2:17-21). So Paul writes, "We ourselves . . . have the first fruits of the Spirit." (Rom. 8:23; cf. also II Cor. 1:22; 5:5.) It is undeniably God's Spirit that we have received and not something less. However, the main crop belongs to the next age and can never be harvested in this world.

Paul believes that the work of God in Christ is complete and that what has been done will not be repeated. So he states, "The death he died he died to sin, once for all." (Rom. 6:10.) The effects of that death are even now being felt, but only in God's time will the revelation of his power and love be consummated. H. L. Goudge holds: "The Hebrews think, not like Neoplatonists, of a higher and a lower 'world,' but of a present and of a future 'age' of the one world which we know. St. Paul is altogether a Hebrew in this." [5] The principle of the succession of the ages by which when the one ceases the other begins was already a part of Jewish thought in Paul's day. The concept is reflected constantly in his epistles. Although Paul refers specifically only to "this age," there are many passages in which the other member of the contrast is directly implied.

Such a case is Rom. 12:2: " Do not be conformed to this world but be transformed." In Gal. 1:4 he describes the work of Christ as " to deliver us from the present evil age." When he tells the Corinthians that " the appointed time has grown very short " (I Cor. 7:29), he is referring to the ending of this age and the coming of the next.

On the other hand, the traditional apocalyptic scheme was upset by the facts of Christian experience. The Messiah had come in Jesus, and the Kingdom of God was proclaimed. Yet this world remained, and the believers were still in their physical bodies. Thus Paul is at times tempted to think of Christians, who stand between the resurrection of Jesus and the Parousia, as belonging to the two different ages at the same time.[6] The periods are seen as not mutually exclusive in the life of the Christian, but they must be carefully distinguished. At times Paul chooses to emphasize the richness of present Christian experience, but on other occasions he wishes to point out how much more God will give in time to come. Even for the believer, the present age is not fully divine, and the future for Paul always possesses a higher quality, i.e., the eternal. In the context of a series of sharp contrasts in Rom. 8:38 he writes of " things present " and " things to come " (cf. also I Cor. 3:22). Even present religious observances are to be seen as " only a shadow of what is to come " (Col. 2:17).

The age in which we live can never of itself produce the consummation. Even the glory of Christ could not be completely revealed in this earthly life, but full revelation belongs to the next age.[7] The Christian is called and justified now, but his glorification must come later. While we are in our physical body, we cannot receive our inheritance and our adoption. For Paul, glory, *doxa,* is a word with profoundly eschatological meaning. It signifies " brightness, splendor, or radiance "; but in Biblical usage it came to be applied to God alone. It is therefore that which will be revealed at the last day, the beginning of God's own age.

In Rom. 2:7 it is linked with honor, immortality, and eternal life. Paul states, " We rejoice in our hope of sharing the glory of God." (Ch. 5:2.) " The glorious liberty of the children of God " belongs to the end (ch. 8:21). Christian patience and fidelity are inspired by a hope which knows that God's reward cannot be immediate but will be given in his own day (cf. Rom. 8:24 f.; Gal. 5:5; Phil. 1:20).

Even though the eschatology of Paul was not directed toward some far distant time but was constructed in terms of the expectation of an imminent end, he made a sharp distinction between the present and the time to come.[8] He could not point to the decisive start of the final age, but he knew enough of God's revelation in Christ in the present to make that last age certain both in its coming and in its character. He asserts in II Cor. 1:22 that God " has put his seal upon us and given us his Spirit in our hearts as a guarantee." That guarantee pertains to all of the aspects of a completed salvation. God will give us all things (Rom. 8:32). The time of that gift is yet to come, but in the Pauline view its certainty is far more significant than its date.[9]

The Kingdom of God

The concept of the Kingdom of God also has its roots deep in the Old Testament. It is so bound up with Jewish history and belief that it had little meaning for the Gentile mind. It is, of course, at the center of the teaching of Jesus as seen in the Synoptic Gospels. In the Pauline writings, however, the term " kingdom," *basileia,* is found only eleven times. In eight instances we encounter the familiar phrase " the Kingdom of God." In two more cases the reference is clearly to God's Kingdom, and in only one verse (Col. 1:13) does Paul speak of the Kingdom of Christ. In Ephesians there is one reference (ch. 5: 5) to " the kingdom of Christ and of God." The Pauline use of the term is so very much less frequent than that of the Synoptic

Gospels that we are driven to ask the reason for the change.

The Jewish hope of the kingdom of God is for Paul inseparable from the revelation of God already made in Christ. K. L. Schmidt affirms: " It is on this decisive fact of the equation of the incarnate exalted and present Jesus Christ with the future kingdom of God that the christological *kērygma,* depends with its understanding of the mission of the Messiah as a *hapax* or *ephapax* event." [10] In this sense Christ has taken the place of the Kingdom in the thought of Paul and of other parts of the apostolic and subapostolic church. In the widespread application to Jesus of the term " Lord " in Pauline and later writings there may well be at least an implicit acknowledgement of the rule of Christ. In some places Paul admittedly speaks of the Kingdom as present and active.[11] He reminds the Colossians (ch. 1:13) that God has " transferred us to the kingdom of his beloved Son." That Kingdom is both contemporary and eternal. Again, at times Paul sees fit to stress its present aspect and at other times to see it as an eschatological reality. Guy is clearly right when he declares: " The sense in which he uses it [the term ' kingdom of God '] is generally future." [12] It speaks for him of a consummation that can come only from God and therefore in his time. That is why Paul only once mentions a " Kingdom of Christ " and why in his word picture of the end (I Cor. 15:25) he states that Christ " must reign [*basileuō*] until he has put all enemies under his feet." Then Christ will turn over the Kingdom to the Father to whom it belongs.

In Col. 4:11, Paul refers to " my fellow workers for the kingdom of God," but the stress is upon working together for God. There is no suggestion that we can work together with him in ushering in the Kingdom. Frame describes the Kingdom as understood by Paul as " the redeemed society of the future over which God rules, the inheritance of believers and the consummation of salvation." [13] In brief, it is the future sphere of the application of the fruits of God's redemptive activity. "Negatively," writes Schmidt, "it is opposed to everything present and earthly, to everything here and now. It is thus absolutely miraculous." [14] This is so because it is God's Kingdom and a part of his future age. The same view is presented by Paul when he writes, "The kingdom of God does not mean food and drink but righteousness and peace and joy in the Holy Spirit" (Rom. 14:17). It is not concerned with purely physical matters of eating and drinking, but it springs from the nature of God Himself.

Always for Paul "righteousness" is at the heart of God's being and doing. In I Cor. 4:20 we read: "The kingdom of God does not consist in talk but in power." Here, too, Paul is mindful of the sharp contrast between what belongs to men and what is of God. His power has been known, but it will not be fully felt until the end of time. So Paul continues, "God . . . calls you into his own kingdom and glory." (I Thess. 2:12.) The initiative is his alone, and it lies beyond the working of man. In this verse Paul equates kingdom and glory, and we have already seen that "glory" is a term that must relate to God's future revelation. It is one of his attributes that he will one day share with his children. Paul thinks of the Kingdom as the new covenant that God has made with his people through Christ. The covenant or will, *diathēkē,* has not yet been put into full effect; but the terms are known and the potential heirs are to wait with patience and faith. Highly significant, therefore, is Paul's use of the verb "to inherit," *klēronomeō,* in connection with the Kingdom. In I Cor. 6:9 f., Paul twice points out that the immoral will not inherit the Kingdom. In I Cor. 15:50, he declares, "Flesh and blood cannot inherit the kingdom of God." Finally, in Gal. 5:21, he states again that immoral persons shall not inherit the Kingdom. Although for Paul the Kingdom has some important present aspects, its major thrust is clearly toward the age to come. Yet the essentials are already revealed. The work of God in the life of Jesus does not need to be supplemented.[15] It is now and will be his Kingdom, but only in his coming age will it be completely established.

In the Jewish tradition of the Kingdom the individual was inescapably bound to the future of the community of which he was a member.[16] Accordingly we are not surprised to discover that for Paul the church is the New Israel and that he stresses the solidarity of Christians in union with their Lord. The final consummation is necessarily pictured in corporate terms. *We* are the children of God, and the glory is to be revealed to *us* (cf. Rom. 8:16-23). To the Philippians, Paul writes: "*Our* commonwealth is in heaven, and from it we await a Savior, the Lord Jesus Christ." (Ch. 3:20.) Particularly notable is the fact that Paul pictures the Parousia in terms of the company of the faithful. Toward the end of his life he is content to speak in more general terms, "When Christ who is *our* life appears, then *you* [pl.] also will appear with him in glory" (Col. 3:4). Earlier his language had been more specific while discussing the same hope. In I Thess. 3:13 he refers to "the coming of our Lord Jesus with all his saints." In the same epistle he declares (ch. 4:17) that the faithful who have already died and those who are still alive on earth will meet the Lord in the air and so be an integral part of his coming. The same event is mentioned in II Thess. 2:1, and in ch. 1:10, Paul suggests that at his coming Christ will, in fact, "be glorified in his saints." Thus, the future Kingdom as Paul sees it is not reward for the individual disciple or bliss for the chosen few but a consummation involving the whole body of the believers. The work of God is inseparable from the redeemed community.

The Day of the Lord

For Paul the end of the present age and the beginning of the new will be marked by three events: the (Second)

Coming of Christ, the resurrection of the faithful, and the Last Judgment. The last two are clearly dependent upon the first, which must be described as prior in time. Until Christ comes (again), we are still in this present age.[17] Yet the three events are so closely interrelated in Paul's thinking that they may be conceived as simply three aspects of one happening. To this extent we may agree with Bultmann's judgment: "The details in his [Paul's] picture of the cosmic drama have no theological importance." [18] The concern of Paul is with the full reality, and he is careful not to lose the proper perspective by undue concentration on particular circumstances. On the other hand, the Parousia is central in his whole view of the future.

Paul is firmly convinced that the supreme crisis in the world's history arises from the First Coming of Christ, the life and death of Jesus, now a past event, though with unlimited results for present and future. Because Jesus lived, it is possible for Paul to know the surpassing joy of being "in Christ" right now. F. C. Porter maintains strongly: "It is impossible to read his letters and still suppose that the physical descent of Christ, the shouting and sound of the trumpet of God, the bodily rapture of Christians into the spaces between earth and heaven, are original with Paul or of any essential importance to him." [19] If Paul does attribute so much significance to the past and the present for his understanding of Christ, we must reexamine what it is that Paul does say about the Parousia. J. A. T. Robinson admits the presence in large areas of New Testament Christianity, including the thought of Paul, of a confident hope of the Parousia. He states: "By the time of the earliest Pauline writings, the expectation is already there in as fully developed a form as it was ever to attain within the new Testament." [20] Objectively, Bishop Robinson's observation is true. In the Thessalonian correspondence we encounter unusually detailed word pictures of the Parousia, especially in I Thess. 4:13-18 and II Thess. 2:1-12. In all of Paul's letters, except Galatians, where Paul is understandably carried away by the demands of a current crisis, and Philemon, a personal note of only twenty-five verses, there is widespread reference to a (Second) Coming of Christ.

As has been noted, Paul states emphatically that the Day of the Lord has not yet come (II Thess. 2:1-3). In numerous places he refers to the coming of the Lord as an expected and fateful future event (cf. I Cor. 4:5; 11:26; I Thess. 1:10; II Thess. 1:7). He reproduces a primitive Christian prayer in I Cor. 16:22 by a Greek transliteration of the original Aramaic, *maran atha,* which is to be translated as " Our Lord, come! " In eight cases he uses with reference to Jesus a Greek word for " coming," *parousia,* which had already acquired a technical designation for the Second Coming of Christ. In half of these instances it is joined with the word " Lord," *kyrios.* There can be little question that Paul has in this area borrowed some descriptive material from Jewish apocalyptic writing. However, his basic understanding of the Parousia is not derived from any Messianic speculation. It may not even reflect the teaching of Jesus as reported in the Synoptic Gospels.[21] The ground for Paul's concept seems to be the Old Testament expectation of the Day of the Lord (Yahweh). The Greek term for that Day, *hēmera,* occurs in this special sense at least fourteen times in Paul's letters. In a few instances it refers directly to the Last Judgment associated with the Parousia (cf. Rom. 2:5, 16). Sometimes it is mentioned simply as " the day," or " that day." Five times the Old Testament phrase " day of the Lord " is taken over without change yet with the obvious understanding that to the Christian " the Lord " means Jesus Christ. The final step in the process is seen in the fact that in three verses in Philippians Paul refers to " the day of Christ." The Old Testament expectation of the Day of the Lord has now become both implicitly and explicitly an expectation of the

Day of Christ when he will act for God in the consummation of God's eternal purpose.

Whereas Paul does reproduce some apocalyptic material in connection with his discussion of the Parousia, the remarkable point is that he makes such little use of it.[22] His interest is not theoretical or imaginative but constructive. He wishes to make it plain that Christ must still win the final victory for God. According to Johannes Weiss, "It must once more be revealed to the whole world that Jesus is really the Messiah, the Son of God." [23] Behind the idea of the Parousia, Paul sees the primary truth that God's plan of action in Christ will triumph completely.

It is difficult to deny that Paul believed to the end of his life that the Parousia was imminent. At first he seems to have thought that it would arrive before his own death. Later, however, he may have admitted that he would die before the day of Christ, although still holding that it would be soon. In one of his last epistles he writes firmly, "The Lord is at hand" (Phil. 4:5). In keeping with the practice of apocalyptic writers generally, Paul does show some interest in the signs of the times and the chronological order of coming events. In II Thess. 2:3-8 he maintains that before the Day comes, the rebellion must first occur and the man of lawlessness must take his seat in God's temple. In I Cor. 7:26 he mentions the impending distress, an accepted apocalyptic sign; and in v. 29 he declares that the appointed time has grown very short. Finally in Rom. 13:11 f. he warns his readers that the day of salvation is almost here and the night is past. Yet these few verses are not expressive of Paul's deepest convictions. Even to the Thessalonians he states that "the day of the Lord will come like a thief in the night" (I Thess. 5:2). The violence and confusion of the end time will not be preceded by recognizable signs but will come when no one is expecting them. The last day cannot be manipulated by men because it belongs to God and to his Son alone.

There are at most only two places in all Paul's letters in which his expectation of the early advent of Christ is allowed to influence his teaching. When Paul is giving his advice on marriage, he urges his followers to remain in their present state because this world has at best only a few years more (I Cor. 7:26). In Rom. 13:11 f., Paul exhorts the Christians to stern moral effort because there is not much time left to turn from evil to good. In no other case does he suggest that an imminent Parousia is by itself a valid reason for adopting a particular form of conduct. The time of Christ's coming was for Paul of no real importance, but the certainty of that coming was a fundamental truth.

From a literal point of view it is obvious that Paul was mistaken in his expectation of an early return of Christ.[24] It is likely that he had already faced the problem created by the apparent delay of the Parousia. He felt compelled to write his first letter to the Thessalonians to explain that the believers who had already died before the Parousia would not lose out on the privileges to be enjoyed by the disciples still living on that happy day. To make his answer more convincing he deliberately drew upon standard apocalyptic pictures and applied them to Christ. The same problem raised by the delay of the Parousia may underlie Paul's explanation of the death of some Christians at Corinth as a punishment from God for an unworthy celebration of the Lord's Supper (I Cor. 11:29-32).[25] Nevertheless, Paul refused to be shaken in his confidence that Christ would bring in the successful completion of God's plan manifest in history. All life is to be lived in direct responsibility to God.[26] The fact that the risen Lord was invisible to physical sight and that the Kingdom he had won was not yet established did not in Paul's view in any way deny the basis for his future hope. And in turn, that hope was the ground for his present life in Christ.

According to J. A. T. Robinson, Paul is but part of the

general New Testament expectation of Christ's imminent advent which has misinterpreted the message of Jesus.[27] In his opinion Jesus held a genuinely Hebraic attitude toward time as *kairos,* whereas Paul and the rest of the early church thought of Jesus' work in terms of time as *chronos.* But the eschatology of Paul, including his understanding of the Parousia, is not to be explained by such a distinction. For him Jesus is a part of history, and history is composed of both *kairos* and *chronos.* Reinhold Niebuhr seems to be much nearer to an understanding of the Pauline position when he declares: " The symbol of the second coming of Christ can neither be taken literally nor dismissed as unimportant. . . . Against utopianism the Christian faith insists that the final consummation of history lies beyond the conditions of the temporal process. Against other-worldliness it asserts that the consummation fulfills rather than negates the historical process." [28]

The Final Conflict

Before the beginning of the age to come, God's own age in which he will rule absolutely, all opposition of whatsoever kind must be eliminated. Between the present and the future aeons there is a gulf not only of time but also of quality and essence. This world is imperfect and sinful, but the time to come will be perfect since it is of God. For Paul there was a new element in the picture, which the Jewish apocalyptic writers did not face.[29] What was the exact role of Jesus in the movement from one age to the next, and more particularly, what part does Jesus play in the subduing of evil? According to the pre-Christian " Damascus Document " (ch. 9:29), there is to be an interval of forty years between the death of " the Teacher of Righteousness " and the appearance of " the Messiah of Aaron and Israel." The conception of an intermediate Messianic kingdom before the end is found in some detail in several late Jewish apocalypses (e.g., II Bar. 30:1; II Esdras 7:26-30). Many scholars see in Col. 1:13 a reference to such an intermediate kingdom ruled by Christ: " He has delivered us from the dominion of darkness and transferred us to the kingdom of his beloved Son." The Jewish writer H. J. Schoeps asserts: " Paul was a theologian who thought in terms of the aeons, who saw a gulf between *malekuth ha-mashiah,* the kingdom of the Messiah, and *olam ha-ba,* the age to come." [30]

Of such a temporary kingdom of Christ there are at most only hints in the letters of Paul. We have noted above the reasons for identifying rather than separating the Kingdom of God and the Kingdom of Christ. However, Paul was most anxious to allow for the triumphant effects of the work of Christ in this world; and he was unwilling to yield those results to an unknown time far removed from the present. Yet he realized only too well that this world could never contain and reflect all the dimensions of God's victory. Regarding Paul's reference to " the Jerusalem above " in Gal. 4:26, Schweitzer comments: " He no doubt expects that this Jerusalem will in the Messianic time descend together with Paradise upon the earth." [31] However, Paul does not attempt any description of the Messianic Kingdom. A crucial verse is I Cor. 15:24: " Then comes the end, when he delivers the kingdom to God the Father after destroying every rule and every authority and power." In the context, the end and the Parousia are but two parts of one event, and no interval can be inferred. By the time of the Parousia every power hostile to God in this world has already been overcome.[32] Paul sees, then, the reign of Christ as taking place between the resurrection and the Parousia. To be " with Christ " is Paul's hope for the believer in the age to come (cf. I Thess. 4:17; Phil. 1:23). But this hope is directly joined with the present experience of being " in Christ." For Paul, therefore, the Messianic Kingdom of Christ is the present period of struggle in this world in which the power of Christ is ranged against the forces still opposing God. Since, however, the power of Christ is ultimately the power of God, Paul can also regard the Kingdom of Christ as of everlasting duration. Where Christ has triumphed, he " is all, and in all " (Col. 3:11). Any action of Christ in this world is not subject to possible loss or futility but will be subsumed in the Kingdom of God.

The evidence of I and II Thessalonians suggests that Paul has accepted one of the axioms of Jewish apocalyptic, namely, that evil will continue to grow until it has reached its climax of intensity and that only then will God bring the former age to an end and initiate the new age by direct intervention. The high point of sin is represented by the rebellion and the man of lawlessness (II Thess. 2:3, 9-10). The latter is a kind of counterpart to the Messiah, but he is for the moment being restrained (vs. 6-7). Paul strongly implies that when the restraint is removed the end will come at once. Charles recognizes that, according to Paul, " there can be no room finally in the universe for a wicked being, whether human or angelic." [33] The logic of this position requires either the final redemption of all persons or the destruction of those who refuse to repent. In the meantime sin and rebellion characterize this world. On the other hand, the redemption achieved by the death and resurrection of Christ must be such that it is sufficient for all time and all persons. It is truly " once for all." Since in the Pauline view personal beings include cosmic powers as well as the dwellers upon earth, the work of Christ must also be cosmic in its reach.

The unique reference in Col. 2:15 is thoroughly consistent with the rest of Paul's thought: " He disarmed the principalities and powers and made a public example of them." Christ has done all that the situation demands, but only proleptically can it be said that he has been victorious. The execution of the order for the suppression of all earthly opposition to God must be held until the end of the age. The passion of Christ has not in accomplished fact defeated God's enemies. "The rulers of this world" have not yet been overthrown, and the demonic "elements" are still exercising their power. It is quite possible even for believers to fall from grace and to be subject all over again to the dominion of evil. Referring to the Pauline concepts, Barrett writes: "Christians, including not least the apostles, are constantly in peril from demonic forces." [34] Thus in its present aspect the Kingdom of Christ involves an unremitting warfare against all forces and powers that continue to resist the will of God. It cannot be described as peace and harmony. The consummation of the victory of Christ must be viewed in a harshly limited perspective. Christ will in time put an end to the revolt of all cosmic powers. His conquest is dramatically symbolized by the forthcoming defeat of Satan, "The God of peace will soon crush Satan under your feet" (Rom. 16:20).

As Ragnar Leivestad has pointed out, "In this world death has always the last word." [35] The whole of the creation is dependent and therefore incapable of possessing life in itself. Without the gift of God it is doomed to corruption and death. In the Biblical understanding death is the opposite of life. Since life comes from God, death is God's chief enemy. Since God has chosen to grant to man the gift of life through Christ, death is also man's chief enemy. As seen by Paul, it involves far more than simply the cessation of biological existence; it relates to man as a totality. The powers of death are undeniably at work in this world. Paul is forced to admit, "Our outer nature is wasting away" (II Cor. 4:16). Moreover, these powers are not limited to the realm of the fleshly but threaten the spiritual order as well. It is therefore thoroughly understandable that Paul in his extended discussion of the end in I Cor., ch. 15, should state solemnly in conclusion, "The last enemy to be destroyed is death" (vs. 26). When this has been accomplished, the redemptive work of Christ will be done, and he can safely hand over the realized Kingdom to the Father.

The Renewal of Creation

The Old Testament is agreed that God is superior to his creation. He is able to express his redemptive purpose and fulfill his will in and through nature. Paul finds no reason to alter this traditional view. But it was also a part of Paul's Jewish inheritance to believe that through the primal disobedience of Adam nature, too, had lost the original perfection that had belonged to it as the handiwork of God. According to Gen. 3:17-18, God said to the sinful Adam: " Cursed is the ground because of you; in toil you shall eat of it all the days of your life; thorns and thistles it shall bring forth to you." Leivestad reminds us: " The idea of a cosmic disharmony and a cosmic reconciliation is to be found both in Jewish and Greek thought (e.g., Asc. of Is. 10:29; 7:9-12)." [36] It was a common view that when the new age dawns, nature will be restored to its lost perfection. Perhaps the most familiar Biblical prediction of this renewal is Isa. 55:12-13: " The mountains and the hills before you shall break forth into singing, and all the trees of the field shall clap their hands. Instead of the thorn shall come up the cypress; instead of the brier shall come up the myrtle." The words of ch. 65:17 were also influential: " Behold, I create new heavens and a new earth."

Since Paul observed evil all around him, not only among men but also in nature itself, there were two possible explanations to satisfy his faith. He might have turned to an otherworldly philosophy which would have denied the ultimate reality of this world and would have conceived of salvation as the means of escaping the severe limitations of a material environment. But as a Jew, Paul could not for a moment think in these essentially dualistic terms. The second possibility was to maintain that through the death and resurrection of Jesus the whole of creation was essentially redeemed. Admittedly, the idea of such a cosmic salvation raises many serious problems in itself.[37] However, for Paul and his Jewish and Christian contemporaries it was unquestioned that man and nature were alike created by God and subject to him. In this respect man and his environment were closely bound together. Likewise, the hand of God was to be seen in all parts of his creation. Dahl calls attention to the fact that " the term ' supernatural ' was almost unknown before the thirteenth century and is unknown in the New Testament, indeed in the whole Bible." [38] As Paul sees it, nature exists at all only because of that which comes to it from outside itself, the power of God.

Largely because of its Jewish backgrounds early Christian thinking refused to consider salvation as merely " inward " or " spiritual." It insisted on speaking of the redemption of man in his whole being. Likewise, nature was involved because no part of God's creation could be allowed to perish in meaninglessness. Accordingly, Paul's view of the effects of the cross is concrete and particular. E. Earle Ellis states bluntly and correctly: " Redemption for Paul is physical." [39] In Christ there is and will be a new creation, of man and of nature, but one that will fulfill and not deny the old. Nothing that God has made can be wasted. Paul is quite certain that the whole world will be saved. The purpose of God in Christ (Col. 1:20; cf. I Cor. 15:28) was " to reconcile to himself all things, whether on earth or in heaven." We are dealing here not with a pantheistic mysticism but with an affirmation of the totality of God's victory. This future consummation will mean, not the destruction of the physical world, but its transformation. One of the most searching and moving passages in all of the Pauline literature is the portrayal that he provides in Rom. 8:18-25 of the metamorphosis of nature at the last day so that it may be a part of God's new age.[40] In the fashion of a poet Paul sees the natural world as at present in labor pains, awaiting the birth of the new creation that will put an end to the sway of evil over the domain of the Creator. The particulars are in themselves unimportant. What does matter is that God is nowhere defeated and that redemption involves that which we experience through our physical senses.

The Sovereignty of God

Just as Paul holds firmly to the assertion that God has provided salvation for all time and for all his creation in the life, death, and resurrection of Jesus, so also Paul affirms that Christ will play a major role in the consummation of the end time. It might then appear that Paul has left little room for God in his emphasis upon the activity of Jesus Christ.[41] However, to stop here is to miss the central truth that Christ's only real significance is derived from his relationship to God. If in Paul's writings Christ is exalted, it is only in order thereby to give a more vivid picture of the sovereignty of God. If Christ has much to do both in the past and in the future, it is because God has chosen for himself to act in this way toward his creation.[42] Paul's understanding of the relationship between God and Christ is not easily comprehended, but certain propositions are clear. Nowhere does Paul assign to Christ the name of God.[43] However, in II Cor. 4:4, Paul states that Christ is " the likeness of God," and in Col. 1:15 he is " the image of the invisible God." Many of the attributes and functions characteristic of God in the Old Testament are unhesitatingly ascribed to Christ by Paul. Perhaps this is best illustrated by Paul's use of the term *kyrios,* " Lord." " Jesus is Lord " was probably the church's earliest baptismal creed (cf. Rom. 10:9; Phil. 2:11), and Jesus had already been addressed as " Lord " by the Aramaic-speaking Christians. But with Paul there is still further advance.

He applies to Christ a number of Old Testament passages that had referred to God as the Lord (*kyrios* in the Septuagint). Thus, Paul as a Greek-speaking Jew who had known the one God of Jewish faith as *kyrios* deliberately uses the same term as a title of Christ. D. E. H. Whitely has pointedly remarked: "Since *kyrios* speaks of Christ as sharing in the exercise of God's authority, it is not surprising that it should be closely connected with the Resurrection, the exaltation and the Parousia." [44] From the many verses that might be cited to support his observation we need mention only one for each of the three categories: Rom. 1:4; Phil. 2:9-11; I Thess. 3:13. In all cases the power of God is the essential ingredient, and Christ makes a basic contribution to man's salvation. C. A. A. Scott has summed up the matter well. "To say that for St. Paul Christ had the value of God may seem an inadequate thing to say. Nevertheless it must be the starting point for any positive statement upon the subject." [45] Whatever Christ does and reveals is an action and revelation of God.

So it is that Paul is never given to any extended discussion of the person of Christ; his interest, like that of the New Testament generally, is in the activity of Christ. At the conclusion of Paul's vivid depiction of the end in I Cor. 15:20-28 he declares unexpectedly: "When all things are subjected to him, then the Son himself will also be subjected to him who put all things under him, that God may be everything to every one." This critical verse apparently stresses the final subordination of the Son to the Father when the former's assigned task has been fulfilled. However, Paul is also restating his view that it is God who has given to Christ the authority to rule over all. When Christ has completed that rule, the end will come. The real point is not that Christ is subordinated but that he perfectly accomplishes the Father's will. Even the recognition of Jesus as Lord contributes to the glory of God (Phil. 2:11). The course of future events is in God's control alone and cannot even be imagined except in terms of the revelation given in Jesus Christ. The deeds of Christ do not limit or condition the sovereignty of God; rather, do they insure it. The conviction of Paul is succinctly expressed by C. K. Barrett: "Creation, and Christ himself, attain the ultimate purpose of their existence only when God is all in all." [46]

The end of the ages will include the reassertion of the sovereignty of God from which came the creation at the beginning of time. The future must bring the complete and conclusive victory of the Creator over all that has blocked his will. Goguel does well to insist: "God all in all [I Cor. 15:28] is something different and something more than God by himself." [47] It is only partly true to declare that according to Biblical eschatology the end will be like the beginning. As previously indicated, the end, *to telos,* means much more than just the termination of a process; it signifies also the purpose of the end seen in some degree in the whole course. The Biblical doctrine of creation stems from the purposiveness of the Creator and rejects every suggestion of aimlessness or chance. Salvation is cosmic because so is the creative activity of God. Neither sinful man nor imperfect nature is abandoned by God to destruction. Creation was followed by sin, but sin was met by redemption.[48] If God in the end will achieve all that he has willed, then it is of fundamental importance to ask what it is that he desires. For Paul that will has been clearly made known; it is to reconcile to himself *all* things through Christ (Col. 1:20). It is God's purpose to redeem whatever has fallen away from him — all nature and every personal being.

Chapter III | THE SPIRITUAL BODY

THE AGE to come will include, in Paul's thinking, the Day of the Lord, the resurrection, and the Last Judgment. The first of these is foreshadowed even now because Christ is leading the attack upon all expressions of hostility to God and he is reigning over the areas of achieved conquest. The judgment is in part already taking place through the inescapable fact of the moral order that is rooted in God's righteousness. But of these three future events belonging to the end it is the resurrection that has the most relevance for the present life of Christians, just because the all-important first step has been taken in the resurrection of Jesus Christ.[1] Paul is absolutely certain that Jesus has been raised from the dead and that therefore he lives as Christ. The solidly historical event of Jesus' resurrection has present and future implications of tremendous significance. Because Jesus rose in a time past, it is possible for Paul and for any Christian to be " in Christ." Those who are " in Christ " will take part in the resurrection of the Last Day. Therefore, Paul can declare: " If Christ has not been raised, your faith is futile and you are still in your sins." (I Cor. 15:17.) For Paul all of Christianity hinges on this one happening.

Paul nowhere suggests the manner of Jesus' resurrection. He makes no reference to the tradition of the empty tomb, but he chooses rather to accent the reality of Jesus' presence in reproducing the tradition of the resurrection appearances (cf. I Cor. 15:3-8). Although direct evidence is lacking in the epistles, there are many references to support the conclusion of Whitely: " St. Paul almost certainly believed that the earthly body of Christ was identical with the Resurrection body, and that the change from the one to the other, through the Crucifixion and Resurrection, was essential to our salvation." [2] Such a transition can be explained only as an act of God's might. In I Thess. 4:14, Paul states that " Jesus died and rose again," using the verb *anistēmi,* which usually implies self-direction. However, in every other reference Paul employs the transitive verb *egeirō* and asserts clearly either that " God raised Jesus from the dead," the usual formula of the primitive kerygma, or that " Jesus was raised," with the expressed statement or unexpressed implication that it is God's doing.

Because the resurrection of Jesus is essentially the manifestation of God's power in a unique manner, it is seen by Paul as a central eschatological event. Davies comments aptly: " We can not doubt that in the Resurrection of Jesus Paul saw the beginning of the end." [3] The resurrection is proof that the new age is here, but it also points to the future fulfillment for all believers of what is promised by the risen Christ. It is not in itself a new period of time, yet it does not belong to the present age.[4] Part of its uniqueness is derived from the fact that it refuses to fit into any established category. As Paul sees it, it is without any precedent; but it is a transformation of what has been, a resurrection and not an arbitrary creation — *de novo.* Since life is at the heart of God's creative act, the restoration of life necessitates the elimination of death. Death is the strongest enemy of all and so the last to be overcome (cf. I Cor. 15:26). If it is not vanquished, then Satan, closely allied with death in Paul's thought, is the master of this world. The resurrection is first of all a decisive victory over the hard core of enmity toward God. Accordingly, Paul always connects the new life with the raising of Jesus from the dead. Without the resurrection, there is no new life in this world because evil is still in control.

Moreover, the resurrection cannot be viewed as an isolated event. It is the opening round of the rising from the dead that is promised for the believers in God's age. Christ is " the first fruits of those who have fallen asleep " (I Cor. 15:20) . He is " the first-born from the dead " (Col. 1:18) . In the Pauline approach " the resurrection of man is connected organically with that of Christ." [5] The source is the same for both. " God raised the Lord and will also raise us up by his power." (I Cor. 6:14; cf. also II Cor. 4:14.) The barrier has been broken. Christians are in the resurrection period, but as yet only Christ is raised. Just as the death of Christ will never be repeated, so also is his resurrection final. He cannot die again because he shares the full life of God (cf. Rom. 6:9-10) . According to Cullmann, " The biblical hope of resurrection sees the destiny of the individual merely as a consequence flowing from the total work of Christ." [6] It must ultimately be a corporate expectation because it is indissolubly tied to the redemptive purposes of God. Generally speaking, Paul speaks of the death of Christ as accomplishing reconciliation and justification and of his resurrection as assuring our salvation and fullness of life (cf. Rom. 5:9 f. and many other passages) . There are exceptions to this usage, and frequently Paul wishes to set forth the crucifixion and the resurrection as a virtual unity of action. However, his intent to show that the resurrection of Christ is a key eschatological event that is solidly grounded in the past alters completely the meaning of the present for those in Christ and is the only sure basis for the hope of a life that is greater than physical death.

In his discussion of the life to come, Paul starts with the facts of his present experience of being " in Christ." He is carried away with the realization that he is possessed by his Lord, so that " it is no longer I who live, but Christ who lives in me" (Gal. 2:20). The quality of the life he now enjoys as a disciple has transformed everything for him, and he is well aware of the fact that this empowering presence of Christ would be impossible without the resurrection. But Paul also reasons, as J. S. Stewart has indicated: "The resurrection of the hereafter is simply God's seal set upon the life in Christ which the believer now possesses." [7] The relationship that begins in this world in an act of faith is essentially one with the nature of the life to come. As we will discover later on, this life is mediated by the Spirit, and so Paul can proclaim: "He who sows to the Spirit will from the Spirit reap eternal life" (Gal. 6:8). The life of the Spirit is the same whether in this age or the next. Moreover, Paul knows that life "in Christ" is qualitatively unaffected by any external circumstance. Nothing, not even death, can in any way "separate us from the love of God in Christ Jesus our Lord" (Rom. 8:39). If the Christian may participate in such a transcending companionship with Christ at this time, how much more lies ahead when the limitations of the imperfect world and the physical body are done away with.[8] An identification with the Lord, when it is true and complete, is a bridge by which the faithful may cross safely from this age to the next (cf. Rom. 14:8). But in God's age the possible expressions of that fellowship are infinitely greater than can be presently imagined. The committed disciple is already "in Christ," but in the time to come the relationship must be described as a "being with Christ." [9] Paul asserts, "If we have died with Christ, we believe that we shall also live *with* him." (Rom. 6:8; cf. II Cor. 13:4.) He admits to the Philippians (ch. 1:23; cf. Col. 3:4) that his personal choice "is to depart and be *with* Christ." Paul is convinced that the whole redemptive task of Christ was undertaken "so that whether we wake or sleep we might live *with* him" (I Thess. 5:10). What Paul calls "the power of his resurrection" is directed not toward the individual but toward the whole of mankind as the object of God's saving love.[10] Further than this Paul does not go except to add that in the perfect life with which we shall be filled by our resurrection there will be manifested something of the glory that is the property of God (cf. Rom. 8:18; II Cor. 4:17).

By his application of the terms " firstfruits " and " firstborn " to the resurrection of Jesus, Paul strongly implies that there is a balance of the crop to be harvested and that there are others to be born. Even though it remains mostly hidden, the new aeon has begun; yet there is a divinely established order of events by which Christ rises first and then those who are his (cf. I Cor. 15:23). Since that order is now initiated, we have seen the beginning of the general resurrection. On the other hand, the reason is not immediately apparent why the resurrection of one man should ensure that of others at some future time. Before we can accept the force of his argument, we must make sure of his assumptions regarding Christ and the recipients of salvation. Paul regards Christ as both a new Adam and a new Moses. The first Adam transgressed God's commandment and so brought sin into the world. With sin came death, which ever since has controlled the entire creation. The Law, which came through Moses, only made the situation worse. The commands of God were made more explicit, but man's inability to obey became only more evident. But in Christ an entirely fresh element is introduced. As the new Adam, he is the inaugurator of a new humanity. As the new Moses, he has brought into being a new covenant between God and man. He was free from sin in his earthly life and so had in himself nothing to do with death. The physical death that he underwent for man's sake was by the resurrection the scene of final victory. The Pauline view is briefly stated by F. W. Beare: " It is specifically in his Resurrection that Christ makes, in his own person, the beginning of the new creation." [11] Death, the last enemy to be destroyed and the center of the order opposing God, has been rendered powerless. The days of the worldly realm are strictly numbered.[12] In Christ, and especially in his rising from the dead, a new creation has appeared.

Man has now the possibility of being transformed. Among the faithful this possibility is in the process of being realized. In Rom. 8:29, Paul notes that those who are called of God " to be conformed to the image of his Son " are the means whereby he becomes in fact " the first-born among many brethren." The word " image " usually suggests an eschatological reality in the Pauline writings. Twice Paul uses an identical phrase to describe Christ as " the image (or likeness) of God " (cf. II Cor. 4:4 and Col. 1:15) . As he was created, man, too, " is the image and glory of God " (I Cor. 11:7) . However, according to the current doctrine of the Fall, that image was lost through Adam's sin. Paul, referring to the effects of the resurrection of Christ, remarks: " Just as we have borne the image of the man of dust, we shall also bear the image of the man of heaven " (I Cor. 15:49) . Paul agrees that only the future will bring about the redemption of the body (cf. Rom. 8:23) . Yet he sees that man is even now being altered. He can remind the Colossians that they " have put on the new nature, which is being renewed in knowledge after the image of its creator " (ch. 3:10) . The climax is reached in II Cor. 3:18: " And we all, with unveiled face, beholding the glory of the Lord, are being changed into his likeness from one degree of glory to another; for this comes from the Lord who is the Spirit."

Commenting on varying approaches to the question of the future life, W. L. Knox concludes: " There was indeed one essential difference between the Jewish conception, at any rate in its Pauline form, and the Hellenistic. The latter tended to confine immortality in its proper sense to the best and noblest of mankind." [13] It need not be added that no such qualification can be found in the Pauline view just because for Paul all life, including the resurrection, comes from God and in no way is subject to man's control. It is not a reward to be earned by good behavior, but is, like grace, a free gift (cf. Rom. 6:23).

In the resurrection something of God's age has been seen in the world's age. The result, however, is not an overlapping, a mingling of two different entities, but a vivid realization of the vast superiority of the one to the other. It is only the resurrection of Christ that has made it possible for us to comprehend the nature of the distinction. It is perhaps in II Cor. 5:1-10 that we find the antitheses revealed by the resurrection most clearly expounded. Those who are in Adam manifest the characteristics of this age, whereas those who are in Christ show the marks of the new aeon.[14] "The earthly tent we live in" is set over against "a house not made with hands, eternal in the heavens." "Naked" and "clothed" are similarly contrasted. So also are "what is mortal" and "life." "At home in the body" is regarded as the same as "away from the Lord," and so it stands opposite "away from the body" and "at home with the Lord." Finally we note the disparity between walking "by sight" and walking "by faith." Nowhere in Paul is there a more telling picture of each age. Mere worldly existence is in the light of the resurrection earthly, empty, mortal, fleshly, and restricted. On the other hand, to be with Christ means transcending the limitations of the flesh, putting on that which is eternal, and sharing life itself with the Lord.

The Time of Resurrection

Although the resurrection of Christ has begun the new creation, and present existence has been given another dimension for believers, Paul must admit that as yet only Christ has risen and that for all others the rising from the dead belongs to the future. He himself is striving to follow Christ "that if possible I may attain the resurrection from the dead" (Phil. 3:11).[15] There is nothing automatic about the future life; there is for Paul no natural immortality. He nowhere specifically refers to a resurrection of the unjust. The argument from silence is never conclusive and always dangerous, but there are enough specific references available to cause many scholars to conclude that Paul envisions only the resurrection of Christians. Charles is emphatic: "There could be no resurrection of the wicked according to St. Paul's view. . . . To share in the resurrection, according to the all but universal teaching of the New Testament, is the privilege only of those who are spiritually one with Christ and quickened by the Holy Spirit. Only two passages — John 5:28 f. and Rev. 20:12 f. — attest the opposite view."[16] The crucial verse for the understanding of Paul's mind is I Cor. 15:22: "For as in Adam all die, so also in Christ shall all be made alive." It is possible to interpret these words as a statement that in (or by) Christ all people will be raised to life, and in this case Paul holds to a general resurrection of all personal beings. However, the Greek represented by "in Christ shall all" is more naturally interpreted as a reference to "all that are in Christ." A parallel construction in I Cor. 15:18 and I Thess. 4:16 is translated in turn as: "those also who have died in Christ" and "the dead in Christ." Charles calls attention to the further fact that in I Cor. 15:22 Paul makes a characteristic pairing off of "all who are in Adam" with "all who are in Christ."[17] We may tentatively conclude that Paul looked for the resurrection only of those who were in Christ. Before we can be satisfied with these arguments, however, we must first examine the views of those who claim that Paul did expect the resurrection of all, Christians and non-Christians alike.

Schweitzer believes that Paul's failure to mention the resurrection of the unjust is due to the fact that it was too well known as a part of the final events of history to need any specific reference.[18] Such a judgment is obviously subjective. Weiss states candidly but unconvincingly: " We should be obliged to postulate for him [Paul] the doctrine of a general resurrection of the dead even though it were not expressed." [19] Somewhat more acceptable is the position that Paul's expectation of a universal judgment, for good and bad alike, to be conducted by Christ as God's agent, logically requires a universal resurrection to precede it. Whether or not, in fact, Paul did look for a future universal judgment must be determined later. For Filson the general references to God as one who raises the dead (e.g., Rom. 4:17; I Cor. 15:21; II Cor. 1:9) are sufficient evidence for the view that Paul looked for a general resurrection.[20] To others the Pauline hope appears to be one that makes no distinction between unbelievers and believers. They hold that only in the final judgment is such a difference significant. J. N. Sevenster considers that " there is no objection to applying the *gymnos* [" naked "] of II Cor. 5:3 to the state between death and resurrection for all men, believers and unbelievers." [21] The nature of this supposed interim state must also be considered later. It is the belief of Dahl that " a resurrection of the damned . . . must be faced as the necessary implication of the two unqualified *pantes* [" all "] in [I Cor.] 15:22." [22] That all have died in Adam and that all will be made alive in Christ is a possible interpretation, but in view of other factors seems unlikely.

There is very little positive indication that Paul thought of a universal resurrection. As we shall see, he is not at all concerned to describe the ultimate fate of non-Christians. The truth is briefly expressed by Whitely: " St. Paul has simply not told us what will happen to those who are not Christians; he has not even told us for certain whether in the end there will be any such." [23] The lack of reference to a resurrection of the non-Christians does not prove that Paul denied its possibility, but it does indicate that Paul's primary concern is for the future of believers. About this he has much to say although again his words are not clear-cut. Ideally, in terms of Paul's inherited doctrine of two ages, the time of this world should be brought to a close by the extension to all who are in Christ of the resurrection of their Lord. If the Parousia had not been delayed and Christ had returned to end the age before any Christians had died, there would have been no problem. In fact, however, many Christians had already died before Paul wrote (cf. I Cor. 11:30; 15:6; I Thess. 4:13). It was therefore necessary for Paul to say something regarding the present state, before the Parousia, of those Christians who had died and gone from this earth. There are, apparently, two conflicting answers that he provides. According to Davies, "What we find in I Cor. 15 and II Cor. 5 is the juxtaposition of two different views; first, that the Christian waits for the new body, till the Parousia and, secondly, that immediately at death he acquires the heavenly body." [24] Is Paul unable to decide between these two different positions, or does he really hold only to one? Or is his thought such that it can be accommodated in neither and demands a larger statement?

We turn first to a consideration of the position that after his death the believer remains in an intermediate state until the Parousia does take place. Two passages seem to bear especially on this question: II Cor. 5:1-10 and Phil. 1:21-23. Scattered verses elsewhere supply further material for study. T. F. Glasson is authority for the statement that "in the apocalyptic literature, it is difficult to find much evidence before the first century A.D. of the view that the righteous passed to heaven immediately after death." [25] He points out that the exception is the Similitudes of Enoch (chs. 37 to 71), whose provenance and date are admittedly doubtful. If Paul does teach that the Christian dead are in an intermediate state, it must be largely a product of his own reflection.[26] Nevertheless, in I Cor. 15:23, Paul seems to stress the order of eschatological events. Christ is the first to rise from the dead, and at his coming those who belong to Christ, will rise, but not before that time.[27] The Day of Christ will bring about the decisive transformation. At that moment, according to I Cor. 15:51, " we shall all be changed." In I Thess. 4:15-17, Paul points out that on that day those who are still alive will be caught up with those who have died to meet the Lord in the air.

For Schweitzer the fact that death is the last enemy to be destroyed before Christ turns over the Kingdom to the Father is proof that the general resurrection will be the final event of the transformation of the natural into the supernatural world.[28] The critical nature of the Parousia is thought to make impossible the earlier occurrence of any of the final events, including resurrection. This is seen to apply more particularly to the " spiritual body," which Paul regards as the mode of passing from death to life (cf. I Cor. 15:44). Presumably Christ has the only " spiritual body " existing now. Cullmann asserts: " The putting on of the *sōma pneumatikon* . . . really depends on the return of Christ to earth and the recreation of matter itself." [29] Since for Paul the concept of " the body " has strong overtones of corporateness and solidarity, it may well be impossible for Paul to think of the " spiritual body " as given to an individual at the time of his death. " The body " as a symbol of the fellowship of Christ's own people would indeed be relevant for the Parousia. Essentially this is the position of R. F. Hetlinger: " The Parousia remains significant for the Christian who dies before it, not because he must wait naked until that Day, but because the work of Christ in his Body can only be perfected then." [30] Moreover, in I Cor. 15:44, Paul is careful to demonstrate that there are two bodies — one physical and the other spiritual. In v. 50 he deduces that the physical body, which is perishable and composed of flesh and blood, cannot inherit the Kingdom of God. The material elements of the two bodies are not identical; therefore the passage from one to the next requires that special act of God which is associated with the Parousia.[31] Christians who die before the end have not yet been resurrected, according to this argument; and therefore they must be in some kind of interim state.

It is to be noted that on nine occasions Paul uses the verb " to sleep " to indicate death. Such an application is found with some frequency throughout the Greek Bible and in Greek secular literature as well. It may suggest that death is not final and that it is a condition of weakness that man himself cannot overcome. Inasmuch as " those who have fallen asleep " are distinguished from those " who are alive, who are left " in I Thess. 4:15, Paul may believe that the dead in Christ have their own special existence before the Parousia.

It is generally agreed that, for whatever reason, we do not have in the epistles much information about the particulars of the supposed intermediate condition. It is only in connection with the Parousia and Last Judgment that Paul becomes at all specific about the dead, and this fact would seem to explain Paul's reticence about an intermediate state as due to his expectation of the imminent return of Christ, probably during his own lifetime.[32] Nevertheless, some scholars have discovered in the Pauline writings a few indications of the present state of the Christian dead. In referring to I Thess. 5:10; Phil. 1:23; and II Cor. 5:8, Cullmann declares: " Those who have died and who die in Christ are in a new state; they are raised up to Christ and are ' with him.' " He then concludes, with no evident support: " But they still remain in time, they are waiting." [33] In Cullmann's opinion, Paul believes that the dead in Christ belong to a period between the resurrection and the Parousia in which there is a continuing tension between the present and the future. However, the possible basis for such a supposition is so small and so uncertain in its interpretation that the conclusion appears unjustified.

Hetlinger's approach is striking: " Although baptism and not death is the decisive moment for the Christian, he does enter at death upon a significantly new stage of that embodiment in Christ which will be consummated at the Parousia." [34] The implication of this exposition is that for Paul there must be two resurrections; first, that which occurs for the individual disciple at the moment of his death when he is freed from the limitations of his physical body and continues in a new form his fellowship with Christ, and second, the general resurrection of the Last Day when this age is succeeded irreversibly by the time of God's complete triumph.[35] And yet again the positive evidence is not sufficient for such an elaboration. It is far from clear that Paul ever considered the possibility of two resurrections.

Commenting on Paul's hope that after our death, when we have lost our physical body, and before the Parousia, when presumably we shall receive our spiritual body, "we may not be found naked" (II Cor. 5:3) in some intermediate state, which is neither one thing nor the other, Albrecht Oepke suggests: "It is arguable whether what Paul wishes to avoid is the temporary loss of the body by believers prior to the Parousia or the final destiny of unbelievers for whom there will be no heavenly body." [36] In this view "nakedness" lies ahead, not for the Christian, but for the unbeliever. Accordingly, we are not dealing with an intermediate state for the faithful or even two resurrections. Ellis arrives at the more sober conclusion: "The idea of an intermediate state . . . must be understood . . . in terms of an altered or suspended time factor for the dead and not as an anticipated fulfillment at death of the Parousia consummation." [37] Paul's problem is how to describe the immediate future of the faithful departed without at the same time infringing upon the prerogatives which he assigns to the Last Day.

Thus, the attempt to find in Paul the basis for a doctrine of an intermediate state for the Christian dead is not convincing, and we are ready to assess the alternative position that the resurrection takes place for the believer at the time of his death. But first, the arguments for a later resurrection may be directly answered. For example, Paul's use of the verb " to sleep " already generally employed by non-Christian writers as a figure of speech for the harsh reality of death, provides no basis whatsoever for the supposition or the characterization of an interim period after death. At the most Paul is stating that those who die in Christ before the Parousia will be included in the events of the end. The key passages of II Cor. 5:1-10 and Phil. 1:21-23 fail, upon close examination, to provide any real allusion to an interim.[38] More especially, the reference in II Cor. 5:3 to " nakedness " has no such implications; Paul is thinking of something completely different. Sevenster has stated: " When Plato and Philo write about the being *gymnos*, their interest is entirely concentrated on the contrast between body and soul, but for Paul the central point lies in the stage of the communion with Christ." [39] Moreover, a thorough study of Pauline thought must reveal that for him the reality of present communion with Christ, the state of being " in Christ," is so profound and so pervasive that nothing can interrupt it, not even a hypothetical interim period. It is precisely that intimate relationship which, when once established, remains unaffected by any other circumstance (cf. Rom. 8:38 f.). It becomes quite natural, then, that Paul should reject any intimation of an interim for the departed. We must agree with the emphatic statement of Davies: " There is no room in Paul's theology for an intermediate state of the dead." [40]

There are positive indications that Paul was convinced of an immediate resurrection at death. Paul's rather extended treatment of the change from the physical body to the spiritual body in I Cor. 15:45-49 points toward the idea of an instant rising from the dead, but the thought is undeveloped. In II Cor. 5:1-8, however, the concept has become explicit. If and when we die, we *have* (a present tense of timeless fact) a proper body prepared by God himself.[41] Whereas Paul knows at firsthand that the believer may be " with Christ " even in this life, he also affirms that those who die in Christ are " with him " at once after their death and before the Parousia. To be away from the physical body is to be " at home with the Lord " (II Cor. 5:8). To depart this world, by death, is to " be with Christ " (Phil. 1:23).[42] Thus, Paul in several of his later epistles, instead of mentioning a resurrection to glory, speaks, rather, of a final revelation of the glory that the Christians who die already possess (cf. Col. 3:4).

The Resurrected Body

It is in I Cor., ch. 15, that Paul presents in a more detailed manner than elsewhere his views of the resurrection, and it is here that he demonstrates how the physical body of this world can be succeeded by a spiritual body designed for the life to come. What Paul has to say about the resurrection, therefore, depends directly upon what he means by the term " body," *sōma*. *Sōma* is a specifically Greek word without any true equivalent in the Old Testament. It is a word that Paul may have chosen deliberately so that within the context of Biblical theology he might fill it with his own meaning. In the Septuagint it is used to translate at least twelve different Hebrew words. In the unquestioned Pauline letters *sōma* is found eighty-six times; it is as frequent as " flesh," *sarx,* and it is much more prevalent than psyche, *psychē*. In his splendid study of *The Body,* J. A. T. Robinson states unreservedly: " One could say without exaggeration that the concept of the body forms the keystone of Paul's theology. . . . For no other New Testament writer has the word *sōma* any doctrinal significance." [43] Since Paul never considers man except in positive or negative relation to God, he uses the word " body " to describe man as God has created him and as he will save him at the end. The physical body of flesh with which man was made has become corrupt through sin. But man's resurrection, the climax of his salvation from sin and death, will require a spiritual body. The body is a constant reminder to man of his dependence upon his Creator and Redeemer. At the same time Robinson remarks: "*Sōma* . . . does not mean simply something external to a man himself, something he *has*. It is what he *is*." [44] Thus what "body" means to Paul is a product of his own theology and is not determined by any fixed significance of the word.

Nevertheless, there are those who would insist on a fundamental Jewish influence in Paul's usage even though the word *sōma* has no Hebrew equivalent. According to Davies, "There can be no question that in those earlier passages where Paul deals with resurrection he is thoroughly pharisaic. This is evident in I Cor. 15." [45] So it is that Paul discusses resurrection and not immortality. The only Pauline uses of the word "immortality," *athanasia,* occur in I Cor. 15:53, 54, and in both of these instances it is specifically stated that "this mortal nature must put on immortality." Eternal life is entered only through resurrection and not by any natural process. Moreover, Paul's employment of the word "body" for both physical and spiritual existence gives to the latter a characteristically Hebraic materiality and objectivity. The later Christian creedal phrase, "the resurrection of the body," frequently misunderstood in a non-Hebraic culture, is derived from the language of Paul. On the other hand, *sōma* symbolizes to others the fact that Paul is more than a Hebrew. He is a Christian writing to a Greek-speaking world. Thus Stacey maintains: "The very existence of *sōma* in St. Paul makes the theory that he suffered no Greek influence, not even an indirect one, untenable." [46] Paul does not claim, in Hebraic fashion, that the physical body will be resurrected. That which is raised is a spiritual body (cf. I Cor. 15:44). Paul distinguishes, in a Greek manner, between the perishable and the imperishable, between the mortal and the immortal. In brief, Paul's concept of the resurrection body is something entirely new and yet is dependent upon those who had written of the future life before him.[47]

As we have seen, the term " body " also suggests to Paul a corporate relationship. The resurrection body is something prepared by God for those who are in Christ so that in that body they may be with Christ. Thus it is inseparable from the fellowship of the disciples with their Lord and so with one another. This truth is well stated by Robinson: " The doctrine of the resurrection of the body is the doctrine of the redemption and replacement of one solidarity by another — the body of the old mortality by the Body of Christ. It is an assertion that no individual can be saved apart from the whole." [48] Salvation cannot be said to be realized until the universally related events of the end.

The meaning of the " spiritual body " for Paul can be understood only after we have first investigated his concept of the " physical body " (I Cor. 15:44). It is perishable and mortal and related to dishonor and weakness (cf. I Cor. 15:42 f., 53). Its temporary nature is especially emphasized. At the last day " the creation itself will be set free from its bondage to decay " (Rom. 8:21). In the present age " our outer nature is wasting away " (II Cor. 4:16). The adjective, " physical," is found in Paul, apart from I Cor. 15:44, 46, only in I Cor. 2:14, where, departing from the RSV, we should translate: " A purely physical man does not receive the things which come from the Spirit of God." Obviously, the physical suggests to the apostle something severely limited and in sharp contrast to the spirit. The corresponding noun, *psychē,* denotes physical existence and so, derivatively, individuality.[49] Paul uses it only thirteen times and never applies it to the life to come. Only in I Thess. 5:23 does he link it with spirit and body in connection with the Parousia. He does seem to limit the existence of the psyche to this present life. Charles makes the important observation: " The soul is never conceived as the bearer of a higher spiritual life by St. Paul." [50] Furthermore, the psyche is inextricably bound up with the flesh. Our physical bodies are "flesh and blood" (I Cor. 15:50), a contemporary Jewish phrase to emphasize man's creatureliness and objective reality. Altogether Paul employs "flesh" seventy times, and of this total thirty-six instances stress simply man's physical concreteness, whereas the remaining thirty-four refer to man's worldliness, weakness, and sin. Robinson, mindful of these elements, holds that "*sarx* stands for man, in the solidarity of creation, in his distance from God." [51] "Flesh" means the outward, observable, and living man, but it also signifies man as hopelessly sinful and unable to help himself. Paul writes in Gal. 6:8: "He who sows to his own flesh will from the flesh reap corruption." The physical body is also marked by corruption (or perishableness).

Paul seems to make the point particularly plain that the present material body, composed of flesh and controlled by the psyche, can have no part in the resurrection or the coming Kingdom (cf. I Cor. 15:50).[52] It is not the flesh that is raised, but a body. Flesh would appear to be a form of hostile power from which man must be released before he can share in the true life of God. This is what Robinson is stressing when he asserts: "Death is significant, not for the entry into the new solidarity, but for the dissolution of the old." [53] Inasmuch as death frees us from the physical body of flesh, it is a happy and necessary prelude to a higher gift. We can be "at home with the Lord" only when we are "away from the body," that is, freed from the encumbrance of sinful flesh (cf. II Cor. 5:8). Accordingly, there are some strong reasons for supposing that Paul reflects a kind of Greek dualism of flesh and spirit and presumes that the spirit enjoys unhindered activity only completely apart from the flesh.[54]

If Paul's views are accurately described in this manner, then he has come a long way from the traditional Jewish expectation of the resurrection. Likewise, the spiritual has been far removed from the normal experiences of this world, and the age to come is idealized by pious imagination. It is the belief of W. L. Knox that " Paul shows no objection in II Cor. to abandoning the resurrection of the dead in favor of the immortality of the Soul." [55] Nevertheless, the Pauline conviction is more faithfully represented by resurrection than immortality. The passage from one world to another is never explained by any suggestion of a division of the self. Insofar as the physical body and the flesh stand for the concrete reality of our being, their transformation in death cannot result in something that is less concrete. For Paul our present weak and sinful physical bodies do not constitute the totality of our being even though they are admittedly powerful in determining how we live. But on the last day, all, the survivors and the dead, will be changed (cf. I Cor. 15:51; Phil. 3:21). In the meantime the fundamental question is the true relationship between the spirit and our flesh.

Whereas the word *psychē* is found only thirteen times in Paul, the word for spirit, *pneuma,* is found in 110 instances. According to Stacey: " Paul's knowledge of the Holy Spirit set the basis of his anthropology." [56] If the psyche or soul meant little to him, the spirit was central in his thought, as it was for early Christianity generally. In his discussion of the spirit, as in that of the body, Paul makes many fresh contributions. In I Cor. 15:44 ff., Paul shows that by the resurrection man ceases to be physical, and becomes " spiritual." Plato and Philo alike believe that it is the psyche which becomes naked at the moment of death.[57] According to Paul, man's essence cannot be so limited and must include spirit. Moreover, that spirit cannot be defined, as it was in some forms of Greek philosophy, as a divine element imprisoned temporarily in an evil human body. There is ceaseless interaction between the two. The higher side of man's nature, which Paul calls spirit or mind or heart or the inner man, is in danger every moment of falling under the power of the flesh.

On the other hand, Charles points out that for Paul even in this present world "the presence of the Spirit is essential to man's spiritual life." [58] It is precisely in this realm that God is already actively triumphant. Man in this age consists of both flesh and spirit, and his plight is to be explained in large measure from the fact that between the two constituent elements a paralyzing and destructive conflict is raging (cf. Rom. 7:14-24). Thus Leivestad is compelled to conclude: "There is with Paul an anthropological dualism which cannot be explained away." [59] Something of this may lie behind Paul's reference in II Cor. 12:2-3 to the fact that his own transcendent mystical vision of being caught up to the third heaven may have been "in the body or out of the body." Paul isn't sure which it was, but that it could have been either is significant. Because the flesh represents the stronghold of sin and all its consequences, it must be subdued by the spirit, and the more it is defeated, the more the spirit may enlarge its activity. Paul adds, "But if Christ is in you, although your bodies are dead because of sin, your spirits are alive because of righteousness" (Rom. 8:10; cf. II Cor. 4:7 ff., 16 ff.). In the opinion of Leivestad, "The moral struggle is a struggle to make the Spirit lord of the flesh." [60] Obviously, in this world the battle is enjoined but is never brought to a conclusion. The most that can be expected is the possibility that the spirit may assert its rightful control over the flesh.[61] However, the hope of the Last Day is defined in Rom. 8:11: "He who raised Christ Jesus from the dead will give life to your mortal bodies also through his Spirit."

The giving of life to mortal (physical) bodies by the spirit may be understood as a symbol of the victory to be won by the spirit in the end over the entire world of matter. Charles makes the apt statement: "Though the flesh is in antagonism with the spirit, there is no such antagonism between the body and the spirit. Nay, rather the body is indispensable to the completed well-being of the latter." [62] And so the question of how the conflict between flesh and spirit in this life is resolved in the resurrection is to be answered by the Pauline doctrine of the body. Niebuhr is forced to admit: "We are still confronted with the formidable difficulty of asserting what seems logically inconceivable, namely, that eternity will embody, and not annul, finiteness." [63] The spiritual body that Paul believes will succeed the physical body suggests the manner in which finiteness will be incorporated into eternity. The resurrection, in which Paul tells us all persons will be changed, is a major portion of the complete and final transformation of the whole of creation. Moreover, it is the concept of the body that preserves human individuality and personal identity within the framework of the fellowship of all the faithful. Finally, it is the body that provides the opportunity for the spirit to be manifested recognizably, concretely, and in particularity. "That which is spiritual" has for Paul no connotation of a mere ideal, however exalted. If the spirit can be known and can be effective even now through the flesh, how much more when the flesh has been cleansed of all rebelliousness and foolish pride and has been renewed in the age to come?

In I Cor. 15:25-50, Paul is concerned to show that there is a vast difference between the earthly body and the resurrection body. Certainly, the dying physical body does not of itself bring forth its spiritual successor.[64] Yet between the two there is some likeness. Paul writes in II Cor. 5:4: "While *we* are still in this tent, *we* sigh with anxiety; . . . that *we* would be further clothed." The continuity between the one stage and the next is provided by personal experience. On this matter Stewart's conclusion is correct: "The real point at issue, as Paul saw very clearly, was the continuance of personal identity." [65] Something essentially unchanging is identified with the physical body now and will be with the spiritual body after death. As Paul attempts to depict the resurrection in I Cor. 15:42-44, he presents a series of four antitheses: perishable — imperishable, dishonor — glory, weakness — power, physical body — spiritual body. For each antithesis we find the same pair of Greek verbs: *speiretai* ("it is sown") — *egeiretai* ("it is raised"). For these verbs, which are in the passive voice and without any specified subject, there is no grammatical antecedent that can supply the subject. Accordingly, for the first antithesis the RSV translates: "What is sown — what is raised," but for the remaining three the impersonal "it" is utilized. Paul is here stating that the individual is "sown" in a physical body for this life and that he will be raised in a spiritual body in the coming life.

Thus there are two common terms found on both sides of the four antitheses: (1) the individual, unexpressed but necessarily implied by the form and context of the verbs and, (2) the body. It may be concluded that in Pauline usage the body signifies, in addition to its corporate aspects, the whole human personality. It may take different forms, but its essence is always greater than any particular manifestation of it. Dahl has justifiably declared: "The resurrection body is somatically identical with this one." [66]

There is no available evidence as to the nature of Paul's thought regarding the fate of the unbelievers at their death. However, it may well be that he believed them to be disembodied beings who had lost by death their physical bodies and who, as unbelievers, could not be given a spiritual body. Christians, however, could not be disembodied.[67] As a Jew, Paul was unable to imagine personal existence except in terms of a body, but as a Greek he could not conceive of the earthly suddenly becoming heavenly. Yet in the resurrection "the perishable puts on the imperishable, and the mortal puts on immortality (I Cor. 15:54)." Paul does not speculate on the way in which this is done; he is concerned only with the principles and the assured results. The corruptible is succeeded by the incorruptible, and since this is a statement of principle, there is no reason to suppose any interval of time. The function of the physical in providing a body for our present life is taken over by the spiritual in the new age. But there is no hiatus.[68] At all times God provides the believer with a body in which his life is lived and by which he may express himself.

The questions of Paul's contemporaries are not unlike those of later centuries: " Some one will ask, ' How are the dead raised? With what kind of body do they come? ' " (I Cor. 15:35). Our inquiring minds want to know: What does the future body look like? Of what is it made? The " spiritual body " of I Cor. 15:44 has been interpreted to mean a body composed of spirit in the same way that the " physical body " is made up of flesh. The assertion that " flesh and blood " can not inherit the Kingdom implies that " spirit " can do so. It would seem to follow that the body of the future must be fashioned of pure spirit. However, Paul propounds no theory of the precise nature of the resurrection body, and he never attempts to depict the circumstances of the life to come. He makes no claims to answer the philosophical question of substance. What matters to him is the functioning of the new body.

H. Clavier has summarized Paul's position: " The essential characteristic of the *sōma pneumatikon,* according to Paul, is not to be or not to be a body composed of spirit, but an organ of the spirit, ordered by the Spirit." [69] It is a question of dominant energy and directive force. The spiritual body must be such that it will be able to meet the demands of the spirit and transmit its life-giving energies, but the composition necessary to achieve these ends is determined by God alone. Of such a body Paul may well have had some knowledge in the appearance of the risen Christ to him (cf. I Cor. 15:8).[70] Paul puts no stress upon the fact that by death the physical body is discarded, but he does call attention frequently to the hope of the new body much more as a higher gift than as a liberation from bondage. It is the positive aspects of spiritual life that count for most. Derivatively, Paul can apply to the resurrection body the Greek term for incorruptibility, *aphtharsia;* but he intends thereby not to ascribe to the spiritual another quality but to point out that it is beyond the process of death that governs the flesh. Its indestructible nature provides it with the opportunity of doing what the physical can never do, that is, of manifesting the glory that originates in God and that is radiated by the risen Christ. Christians may be glorified with Christ in their resurrection body because they have been united with him (cf. Rom. 8:17). At the end of our present life we will, in our resurrection body, share "an eternal weight of glory beyond all comparison" (II Cor. 4:17). Only in such a body will we appear with Christ in glory at his Parousia (cf. Col. 3:4).[71] The spiritual body, is, then, of a higher order; but it is not in any sense important in itself. It is the way chosen by God to bring man to his fulfillment in the final age. The glory continues to belong to God, but in the spiritual body man can live fully the life of God.[72]

Eternal Life

The resurrection comes as a gift of life and is not a product of death. Nevertheless, Paul considers what the future life means negatively with regard to the present under the conception of salvation. It means for Paul in the first instance a liberation from hostile forces. Dahl has reasoned: "Since sin, death, and corruption form a dynamic totality together, the only salvation worth the name is a real deliverance from all three." [73] But if death is overcome, its opposite, life, is established. The conqueror of the powers that oppose God and threaten man is now revealed as "the law of the Spirit of life in Christ Jesus" (Rom. 8:2).

Twenty-seven times Paul uses the word for life, *zōē;* forty-three times he utilizes the verb " to live," *zaō,* and seven times he applies the verb " to make alive," *zōopoieō,* to God or the Spirit.

For Paul " life " is a qualitative term in most instances. It speaks of a meaningful existence and is the positive assertion of that which death destroys. We are not surprised to discover that in five cases Paul prefixes the adjective " eternal," to " life " because it is eternal life of which Paul speaks, whether or not the quality is specifically mentioned.[74] On three occasions Paul refers to " the life of Jesus " or " his life." It is clear that he understands life as the existence that belongs to or is granted by God. As previously noted, the resurrection of Christ can be attributed only to the power of God. In fact, Christ is living now by that same power (cf. II Cor. 13:4).[75] Even in the case of Christ, Paul is determined to demonstrate that eternal life is the gift of God and that belief in the resurrection is by no means acceptance of a theory of natural immortality. Immortality does not belong to man as man; it is put on when God resurrects the believer. The life that God imparts has the quality of the eternal; it is not eternal life as such that God grants. The life of God signifies for the Christian increasing companionship with Christ and of necessity an existence that is everlasting because it is lived in the final age of God.

In the Last Day the Lord Jesus Christ " will change our lowly body to be like his glorious body " (Phil. 3:21). This transformation is, however, not without some preparation. Even in this world the disciple has begun to know the life that God gives. Paul can remind his converts, " So death is at work in us, but life in you " (II Cor. 4:12). And " Christ . . . is our life." (Col. 3:4.) Everyone is to " lead the life which the Lord has assigned to him " (I Cor. 7:17). Each has an inescapable responsibility to his Creator. In describing the internal conflict that the Law creates in man,

Paul recognizes that there is an " I " that hates the evil and wants to do the good (cf. Rom. 7:15, 18 f.) . He calls it the " mind " in Rom. 7:23 and 25. In Rom. 7:22 he confesses: " I delight in the law of God, in my inmost self (*kata ton esō anthrōpon*) ." Using the same phrase, he discloses: " Our inner nature is being renewed every day " (II Cor. 4:16) . This inmost self or inner nature is the reality by which God can give to each one a unique responsibility and by which he can hold the individual accountable to the divine judgment. It is also the explanation for the continuity that exists in the body in its two forms. The " inward man " is potentially at least the " new man " and belongs teleologically to the age to come. Paul is not a philosophical dualist, but there are actualities even in the present age, as well as in the coming age, that cause him to confess: " We look not to the things that are seen but to the things that are unseen; for the things that are seen are transient, but the things that are unseen are eternal " (II Cor. 4:18) .

Chapter IV | A DAY OF JUDGMENT

THE COMING AGE, in Paul's view, meant, first of all, the return of Christ in triumph. Secondly, it involved the resurrection in a final, corporate sense. The third event of the end time was the Last Judgment. Paul does not suggest that these three occurrences will take place in this particular chronological order. Rather does he point to the many ways in which the three are tied together so as to constitute one happening by which God's age is to begin and upon which it is built. Nevertheless, until the Parousia there can be no resurrection realized for the entire body of the faithful; and the resurrection obviously makes possible the accomplishment of God's judgment upon all (cf. I Thess. 4:16 f.). In this sense the Last Judgment is the final element in Paul's hope for the future. In the remaining chapters we shall be concerned with how this hope alters our present life in Paul's thinking and also with the effect that our relations with this age may have upon the future.

Perhaps in no other area of eschatology does Paul exhibit such a direct dependence upon Jewish thought as in the theme of the judgment of God. The whole Bible is dominated by this principle. As creator, God is the judge at the beginning of the world. The Old Testament sees him as judge at every turning point of history. According to both Testaments, God will become judge when this world and human history are brought to an end by him. Representative of the Biblical understanding of God are the familiar words of Ps. 96:13: " For he comes to judge the earth. He will judge the world with righteousness, and the peoples with his truth." God is sovereign; he is working out his purpose in history. Therefore, he can be depended upon; and he is trustworthy. The life that he has formed must possess these same characteristics, and so the Jew looked to God's revelation of the standard by which man is to be guided individually and corporately.

In the tradition of the prophets, stress was laid upon the fact that whole nations are controlled by this judgment. From the time of Jeremiah and Ezekiel the role of the individual was more clearly seen. But behind all else was the conviction that God is not mocked and that his will is the ground of existence. The same view is repeated by Paul, deepened by the further truth of Christ, in whom, as " the image of the invisible God," " all things hold together " (Col. 1:15, 17). From this faith in the essential consistency of life arose the two ideas of reward and punishment. If God is a judge in fact, he must grant their just deserts to the righteous and to the wicked. At first, punishment and reward were conceived in external and material terms, and only gradually was it recognized that redress might assume an internal form. When compensation was limited to this world, there was no choice but to assess every misfortune as punishment for wrong and every blessing as recompense for right conduct. However, with the recognition that this world has lost the perfection of God's creation came the growing realization that punishment and reward can be only partially given in the present and that their completion must be reserved for the world to come. Particularly strong was the view that the righteous were to be vindicated and blessed in the Messianic age. In the rabbinic tradition every divine commandment implied a reward for keeping it and a punishment for breaking it.

As a result the Jewish mind was much concerned with what was thought to be the law of merit and penalty. Of this conception Filson writes: "This retribution of God follows the sinner through life and is constantly operative in history." [1]

Such was Paul's inheritance, and the degree to which Paul reproduced it serves to distinguish all the more sharply the specifically Christian elements in Paul's view which were transmitted from the primitive church or which arose in his own interpretation. A study of the special vocabulary used to express his ideas of retribution is most illuminating. To begin with, Paul holds firmly to the dependableness of the righteous God whose unyielding opposition to all evil and to every failure to accept his will is depicted as "wrath." Over against this wrath is the "fear" of man. To express the firmness of the divine order Paul employs two different Greek expressions for "necessity" and "constraint." The verb "to sow" points to man's freedom to choose and to act, and the "seed" is that which man does. On the other side, we find a large number of Pauline words that make it clear that man cannot escape the effects of his deeds as God has determined the effect. Such words are: "to reap," "to bear fruit" and "fruit"; "to hire," "to recompense," and "wages"; "to get again," "to receive back," "to give back," "to repay." Others are: "to deem worthy," "to account worthy," "worthy," and "worthily"; "to avenge," "avenger" and "vengeance." Twice Paul uses negatively of God the noun meaning "respect of persons" (or partiality), and then describes God's role as judge. For this purpose he uses many other words, such as: "righteous judgment" and "to judge" with eight compound verbs using the same root and three derived nouns. The adjective meaning "disapproved" occurs five times, but on fourteen occasions we discover the same root, without the negativizing alpha privative, in the form of the verb "to approve" (or "deem worthy") along with nine occurrences of related words brought in to describe one central doctrine. Many of these words are encountered repeatedly. Thus, the very bulk of the references is a strong indication of the importance that Paul attributed to the concept.

The word " wrath " is met with in Romans, Colossians, and I Thessalonians a total of sixteen times. In one instance it is used to refer to the human emotion of anger, but in all other cases it is applied to God. In secular use the term was clearly descriptive of an undesirable passion, but its Biblical meaning is entirely different. In later Judaism and the New Testament there is a careful avoidance of any anthropopathic description of God. Unlike man's anger, God's reaction to evil is not sudden or unexpected. It is, rather, one aspect of his immutable nature. According to Barrett, " Wrath is God's personal reaction against sin." [2] We would expect, therefore, that this wrath would be manifest at all stages of history. In I Cor. 10:1-10, Paul mentions a number of events connected with the exodus and the wilderness wanderings of the Jewish people. He regards them as providing examples and warnings for the later Christians. R. V. G. Tasker notes that in the Old Testament accounts of almost all of these historical examples the wrath of God as his necessary opposition to sin is specifically cited.[3]

Since God must always resist evil powerfully and unrelentingly, his antagonism to it has become a part of his creation. Strictly speaking, his wrath is constant and so timeless. It belongs to the past and to the present as well as to the future. However, in almost all the Pauline usage it has a strong eschatological tone. The climax is the picture of " the day of wrath " (Rom. 2:5). Jesus is the one who " delivers us from the wrath to come " (I Thess. 1:10). The end will include the unrestricted operation of the canons of existence derived from God's righteousness. Because of this Caird argues persuasively: " He [Paul] will never speak of the wrath as though it were a personal attribute of God. It works, rather, as an impersonal principle of retribution." [4]

Two of the most difficult to understand of all the Pauline passages are Gal. 3:13 and II Cor. 5:21. In both, the sinless Christ is said to have been made sin or a curse in the course of his redemptive death. The intent of Paul is to indicate that Christ's identification with mankind was so complete that it involved experiencing the wrath of God, which is always directed against human sin. In this manner Paul could hold the apparently illogical position that God, whose love for sinners is expressed supremely in Christ's death (Rom. 5:8), can also extend his wrath toward Christ as he bears man's sins upon the cross. In the opinion of Tasker: "The *locus classicus* in Scripture for the manifestation of the divine wrath to the heathen world is Rom. 1:19-32." [5] Extreme moral degradation is explained as the result of God's law governing human behavior. He has decreed that those who practice evil deserve to die. In Rom. 2:5 ff. eternal life is set opposite wrath. In Rom. 5:9, salvation, as distinguished from the preliminary justification, is detailed as deliverance from the wrath of God.

The final expression of God's wrath is the Last Judgment, but it cannot be reserved for the future any more than for the past or the present alone. Romans 1:18 reads in the RSV: "The wrath of God is revealed from heaven against all ungodliness." However, it is just as correct to translate: "The wrath of God is (continually) being revealed." As long as evil exists, this will be the situation. Bicknell sees Paul's references to God's wrath as expressing "the reaction of God's holy love against all that is evil." [6] For Paul the love of God is more significant than any other part of his self-revelation. His hatred of sin is unalterable and cannot be ignored. but it is only part of the divine nature. He chose to create that which was good, and when evil entered in he chose to redeem. For Paul the heart of the Christian message is expressed in I Thess. 5:9: "God has not destined us for wrath, but to obtain salvation through our Lord Jesus Christ." The summary of Whitely is helpful: "The wrath of God . . . is an *effectus* which is ultimately under the control of an *affectus;* and this *affectus* is His love." [7] Yet God's wrath clarifies the choice that the disciple must make: "Hate what is evil, hold fast to what is good" (Rom. 12:9).

Even the love of God flows from his righteousness, which is thus for Paul the word that most fully describes God's nature. Man can be justified only through the outpouring of God's own goodness.[8] No one can escape the judgment of God (cf. Rom. 2:3), but it is not an arbitrary or whimsical exercise of power. What God is and what he asks of man have been revealed. He cannot render other than a "righteous judgment" (Rom. 2:5; cf. II Cor. 1:5). The rules for human life are extensions of the divine life. Right and wrong matter to God because he himself is righteous. Niebuhr has marked the positive result of this fact: "When history confronts God, the differences between good and evil are not swallowed up in a distinctionless eternity." [9] Once more, Paul presents us with few particulars. He refuses to engage in speculation about the unknown, and so he has little to say about the tangible rewards for the righteous or the afflictions of the evildoers. Filson comments: "Paul was more concerned with the fact of divine punishment on sin than with the concrete delineation of the nature of that punishment." [10] The wrath of God is evidence that he has not turned his back on the world's struggle to achieve the good against iniquity. Rather, he is in the midst of the battle, guiding his forces to victory.

The Hebrews expected God's judgments to be expressed here and now in this world, and they maintained that God's control of men and nations is to be observed as much in history as at the end of time. Accordingly, Paul, like the Fourth Evangelist, marks the present operation of the forces of judgment, even though there will be a great Judgment Day at the beginning of the next age. Most of Paul's ideas concerning judgment are addressed to the living as a guide by which to prepare for what lies ahead. On the other hand, Kennedy affirms: "Those who have refused to surrender to the love of God, established in the Cross of Christ, have thereby, in the apostle's estimation, pronounced their own judgment." [11] Once more it is evident that the wrath of God is not a personal expression of God's feeling toward an individual because, under the rules and in view of man's gift of free choice, each man brings upon himself the divine judgment. When Paul writes in a vein such as that of Rom. 8:6, it is difficult to tell whether he is referring only to the present or in reality to what will eventuate: "To set the mind on the flesh *is* death, but to set the mind on the Spirit *is* life and peace." This is especially true in Rom. 6:23, where one of Paul's words for "recompense" or "wages" appears: "The wages of sin *is* death, but the free gift of God *is* eternal life in Christ Jesus our Lord." It is quite possible to interpret these, and many similar verses, as statements of a present reality as well as of an ultimate effect of what is now seen.

According to Tasker, "The doctrine of the wrath of God safeguards the essential distinction between Creator and creature." [12] For Paul and for the rest of the Judeo-Christian tradition, man's chief sin is pride, the attempt to vaunt himself against his maker. How frequently the readers of the epistles are rebuked for their tendency "to puff themselves up" with nothing but emptiness! Moreover, we are informed by Ellis: "It is not in Greek anthropology, but in Hebrew eschatology that the meaning of *gymnos* ["naked"] and *ekdyō* ["to put off, as of clothing"] in II Cor. 5 is to be found. . . . In the Old Testament—nakedness (or being stripped) and shame often denote the guilty under the glaring light of God's judgment." [13] Thus, when Paul offers the assurance that we will not be " unclothed " or " found naked," he is really, according to this view, thinking of the position of the Christian with regard to the Last Judgment. It is only as we are " in Christ " that we can have any hope at that time.

Although Paul uses the simple verb " to judge " thirty-three times, and employs the compound that signifies " to condemn " only five times, Filson can state of his writings: " The majority of references to judgment carry the idea of condemnation, more or less clearly." [14] Wherever God is the judge and man stands before him awaiting a decision, there is no reason on the face of it why he should not be found guilty and dealt with accordingly. Thus we can understand Paul's purpose in admonishing the Philippians: " Work out your own salvation with fear and trembling " (ch. 2:12). The same root for fear stands behind Paul's words to the Gentile Christians at Rome: " Do not become proud, but stand in awe " (ch. 11:20). Quoting the Psalms, Paul charges that both Jews and Greeks are sinful because " there is no fear of God before their eyes " (Rom. 3:18). " The fear of the Lord " and " the fear of God " are not for Paul merely expressions of a blind subservience to a sovereign ruler. He has in mind the fact that man cannot presume upon his maker by claiming any virtue or any right. The love of God in Christ does not annul his wrath, but it does give an entirely fresh perspective to the judgment.

The Coming Judge

Beginning with Amos, the Old Testament prophets had developed a doctrine of the Day of the Lord as a day of judgment. When prophecy ceased in Israel, the apocalyptists took up the teaching; and, according to Stewart, " Apocalyptic literature had depicted the terrors of judgment in lurid colors and with an excessive wealth of detail. . . . Paul's treatment . . . is characterized by a noble dignity and restraint."[15] Whereas there are a few traditional phrases relating to the events of the Parousia and the resurrection in I and II Thess. and I Cor., ch. 15, there are no such particulars in Paul's references to the Last Judgment. As Kennedy remarks, "He writes concerning the Day of the Lord, not with a theoretical but with a practical interest."[16] The truth about God's judgment is partially proclaimed by a reminder that we live in a world of moral law, of the operation of cause and effect in the area of character and conduct. This for Paul is an undeniable present reality. God is continuing to reveal his judgments in the ordering of the history of individuals and of nations. In order to protect this belief against the charge of obvious inequalities and injustice in this world, rabbinical thought stressed more and more the idea of a real judgment to be pronounced immediately after death. Paul, however, saw the situation in a much larger perspective. What happened to the individual was only a very small demonstration of the sentence to be passed on the whole body of mankind.

The constant and unvarying working of the principle of recompense that applies to each man is represented by the present tense of the verbs describing the act of judging. But even the continuative present is not adequate to depict the end result of all history and of all human lives. Only the future tense (or some other construction requiring a future interpretation) will suffice. (Cf. Rom. 3:6; I Cor. 5:13; II Thess. 2:12.) Its futurity points to its inevitability as well as to the fact that it transcends all experiences of this or of any other single period of time. Niebuhr has asserted in this connection: "There is no achievement of partial realization in history, no fulfillment of meaning or achievement of virtue by which man can escape the final judgment."[17] The wrath of God means an unyielding and ultimately thoroughly effective resistance to evil which guarantees full salvation for the believers. As thus conceived, wrath must be an eschatological term and must be joined to a " last day," a symbol of the full establishment of God's rule.[18]

The Day of Judgment is far more than the termination of an automatic evolution of history. It is the final and authoritative evaluation of history by the Lord of history, who is working within it but who also stands above it. It is true that one might assume a doctrine of automatic progress from the KJV of Rom. 8:28: " We know that all things work together for good to them that love God." The same type of interpretation is found in the recent Phillips translation: " We know that to those who love God, . . . everything that happens fits into a pattern for good." To such an interpretation of this verse there are two objections. The first is textual and syntactical.[19] The second is contextual. Paul nowhere thinks of history in terms of automatic process. It is for him a coproduct of the exercise of man's divinely given free will and the immanent activity of God, largely sustained through his Holy Spirit. The natural creation is too much filled with evil to allow Paul to state that even for those who love God everything turns out for good. In this case the coming of the last day would be determined only by the forces in history itself, whereas Paul knows, with Jesus, that its coming will be completely unknown to man just because it is fixed by the mind of God.

The correct interpretation of the thought of Paul and therefore also of Rom. 8:28 is provided by the RSV: " We know that in everything God works for good with those who love him." The wording of the New English Bible is equally sound: " In everything, as we know, he co-operates for good with those who love God." He does work within history with those who accept his will, but he is the master and judge of history because it is not self-sufficient and must answer to him.

What man does in history, however, is in Paul's view the basis for the judgment he must receive from God. Barrett has indicated: " When the judgment is held, national privilege, and an attitude of moral superiority, will be irrelevant." [20] The Jews, who may boast of their special relationship with God, are still to be assessed by their performance (cf. Rom. 2:17-27). The Gentiles, who may know something of God by their conscience and the evidence provided in nature, are evaluated in terms of their acceptance or rejection of God's demands (cf. Rom. 1:19-32). In brief, each life, regardless of its supposed status or number of special privileges, is to be tested by its results. Paul's position is clear and his formulation is explicit: " He [God] will render to every man according to his works " (Rom. 2:6). He continues: " It is . . . the doers of the law who will be justified " (ch. 2:13). Negatively phrased, those who disregard the moral law have no possibility of entering into the Kingdom (cf. I Cor. 6:10). The principle of retribution has been instituted by God and therefore is a part of his purpose. Paul urges his converts to make no mistake by assuming that they will escape through mercy or special favor: " God is not mocked, for whatever a man sows, that he will also reap " (Gal. 6:7). This belief is simply expounded by Filson: " God holds each servant responsible for the faithful performance of his task, and he will reward each one according to his individual labor." [21] Although the recompensing must be left in God's hands alone and man cannot name his reward, Paul teaches that the payments will vary in accordance with the quality of the deed. No favors are granted, and no one is exempt. He warns: " We must all appear before the judgment seat of Christ, so that each one may receive good or evil, according to what he has done in the body." (II Cor. 5:10.) There is one standard for all because God shows no partiality.

The suggestion that service is an opportunity and a duty that is not in any way commensurate with the principle of payment or reward is foreign to Jewish thought generally and but little reflected even in the teaching of Jesus. Paul cannot deny that one's life record is to be brought before God and that it is in some manner related to the enjoyment of salvation. Obviously, Christians as a class will, no more than the Jews, be exempted from the application of the law designed for the regulation of all men. What becomes, then, of Paul's greatest single contribution to Christian thought, the doctrine of justification by faith and not by works? To the Galatians, Paul wrote: " By works of the law shall no one be justified" (ch. 2:16). It is the conviction of Whitely that " St. Paul's teaching on justification by faith is concerned less with how man receives the gift than how God gives it, which is simply as a gift, due to His love alone, and not to anything which we are or do." [22] Thus it is that not even our faith, as a channel for the reception of God's grace, can be regarded as involving any merit on our part. From beginning to end our salvation rests wholly in the divine love. Yet the mercy of God is not a contradiction of his justice. Side by side in Paul's interpretation we encounter his proclamation of God's free gift in Christ and his insistence upon the direct relationship between our earthly deeds and the last judgment, i.e., upon the law that links our actions to their results. Whitely discovers no inconsistency in the placing of these two statements in close proximity in the Pauline exposition of the gospel, and he concludes: " For him these ' doctrines ' are not conflicting answers to the same question but are concerned with different questions altogether." [23] We shall examine Paul's teaching regarding the relationship between faith and conduct in a later chapter. Meanwhile, we have need only to state that in his discussion of the nature of justification Paul is dealing with the source of salvation, whereas in his many references to man's accountability to the heavenly judge he is speaking of man's response to all that God has done and particularly to the revelation given in Christ. Some may regard this situation as further evidence of the paradoxical nature of Christian truth. Others may be led to admit that Paul's care is not with logical consistency but with fidelity to what he has been allowed to know. And regarding the basis of the last judgment he had no doubts.

Although God must judge according to a man's works, Paul is quick to add that the internal conditions of the heart, thoughts, and motives will also be assessed. He unquestionably had come to know of the teaching of Jesus which had made it clear that external actions proceed from the inner person and that therefore the state of mind is as meaningful as the deed. On the day of judgment, Paul specifies, the Lord " will bring to light the things now hidden in darkness and will disclose the purposes of the heart " (I Cor. 4:5; cf. Rom. 2:16) . Nothing is beyond his searching examination. A man's deeds are an expression of his true nature only insofar as they correspond to what he is in his inner being. Therefore, Paul asserts that what God judges is the real person apart from all appearances, impressions, and mere opinions, whether of the individual himself or of others.

The idea that the judge of the world is God is deeply rooted in Hebrew tradition. It is usual for Paul to refer to the Last Judgment as presided over by God (cf. Rom. 14:10) . He asserts: " Each of us shall give account of himself to God." (Rom. 14:12.) On the day of wrath it is God's righteous judgment that shall be revealed (cf. Rom. 2:5; 3:6) . Only he can know the thoughts of a man's heart and so possess all the facts for making a just evaluation. The standard by which men are to be judged is of his institution. Judgment is basically the final assertion of the sovereignty of his will. In all of this Paul is not departing from the beliefs of his ancestors. It is all the more significant, therefore, that Paul also assigns an important place to Christ in the judgment. With that future event Paul connects the (Second) Coming of Christ. In I Cor. 1:7 f. " the day of our Lord Jesus Christ " is described as the time when the faithful may be presented guiltless. Paul's hope is that the Philippians "may be pure and blameless for the day of Christ" (ch. 1:10). He advises the Corinthians not to "pronounce judgment before the time [of judgment], before the Lord comes" (I Cor. 4:5). In the preceding verse he has confessed that "It is the Lord who judges me." Thus, Paul can speak of "the judgment seat of Christ" (II Cor. 5:10). He tells the Colossians that "from the Lord you will receive the inheritance as your reward" (ch. 3:24). The Lord is also an avenger in cases of wrongdoing (cf. I Thess. 4:6). Paul is able to ascribe a judicial function to Christ only because it is part of the task that God has entrusted to him. The judgment remains in God's control, and it is in Rom. 2:16 that we see Paul's real meaning. There he mentions "that day when, according to my gospel, God judges the secrets of men by Christ Jesus." God will judge through Christ. Moreover, since the criterion of the divine evaluation is the revelation given in Christ, he will be there when the sentence is passed.

Will All Be Saved?

Tasker declares: "The New Testament is very far from asserting that the Christian is automatically, as it were, removed from any manifestation of the divine anger." [24] Paul is no exception to this generalization. The salvation that Christians may know through the grace of God does not include any promise of freedom from the final judgment. In Rom. 14:10, Paul is condemning the practice of one Christian judging another Christian, a brother; and he drives home his point by noting: "We shall all stand before the judgment seat of God." The reference is clearly to all believers. In at least two instances Paul strongly implies that judgment for Christians may also involve punishment. Thus he warns: "If any man's work is burned up, he will suffer loss, though he himself will be saved, but only as through fire." (I Cor. 3:15.) The same thought is expressed in I Cor. 11:32: " When we are judged by the Lord, we are chastened so that we may not be condemned along with the world." Such references have caused Guy to assert: " Paul appears to have in mind chiefly Christians when he speaks of the Judgment." [25] In this case Paul stands firmly in the tradition of Amos, who declared to the people of Israel: " You only have I known of all the families of the earth; therefore I will punish you for all your iniquities " (Amos 3:2). Christians are the ones who have received God's revelation in Christ and therefore are held the more responsible to it. On the other hand, the faithful will be saved from the wrath of God (cf. Rom. 5:9). They are not destined for wrath but to obtain salvation (cf. I Thess. 5:9). In brief, Christians are not necessarily free from the necessity to stand before God's bench. Furthermore, those who have done wrong will be punished. However, as long as the disciples remain " in Christ," they share his life and so are not subject to the principle of wrath. The trouble arises when the believers fall from grace.

There are some indications that Paul expected a universal judgment for all men, believers and nonbelievers alike. The principle of recompense appears to apply everywhere. Each human being knows that he will be treated according to his works (cf. Rom. 2:6). It is part of the doctrine of the wrath of God that it is built into the structure of all existence. In Dan. 12:2 there is an undeniable suggestion that resurrection will take place for the sake of judgment: " And many of those who sleep in the dust of the earth shall awake, some to everlasting life, and some to shame and everlasting contempt." Accordingly, there was in Judaism a growing belief in a great and universal judgment upon all men. Some of these convictions Paul must have shared. The reason why he does not develop them, however, is succinctly stated by Wood: " The whole subject of God's final dealing with evil men lay out of the center of Paul's religious attention." [26] Paul was writing to provide direction and assistance for Christians, and he had no time for other concerns.

If all men regardless of their belief or lack of it are to appear before God for judgment on the Last Day, there remains the possibility that at the end all will be saved. Referring to the death of Christ, Paul points out: " One man's act of righteousness leads to acquittal and life for all men " (Rom. 5:18) . He continues: " God has consigned all men to disobedience, that he may have mercy upon all." (Ch. 11:32.) It may seem proper to conclude that in Paul's view all men, after trial, will in the end be saved. However, Filson is unable to discover any basis for a supposed universalism in Paul, and he claims that the passages that suggest an easy universalism that saves all without condition demand some other explanation.[27] It is not Paul's intention to state that no human beings will be lost forever. He has no desire to make a pronouncement about the fate of each individual, whether it be acquittal or condemnation.[28] He is determined to make clear the principles involved and to speak positively and constructively about the sure fulfillment of God's promises.

Paul is convinced that there is no other way by which to be saved than by the gift of God in Christ Jesus (cf. I Cor. 3:11) . Calling, election, and predestination are fundamentally terms to expound the initiative of God without which there can be no redemption. They are, therefore, not limiting concepts, as it is frequently argued, but inclusive expressions. Most of the sentences commonly used to support the theory of a theological universalism in Paul are, rather, formulations of God's purpose to save all his creation. It must be admitted parenthetically that the strongest argument for such universalism is the fact that Paul did teach that God's desire is that no man should be cut off forever. In Col. 1:20, which is typical of many passages, Paul depicts the plan of God as through Christ " to reconcile to himself all things." All men, without distinction, are the objects of his mercy. Commenting on the full sweep of the Biblical story, Dodd has asserted: " The coming of Christ . . . marks a crisis in God's dealings with the human race, in that down to that time His purpose proceeded by successive stages of exclusion . . . but since His resurrection it proceeds by way of inclusion, until in the end no member of the human race is left outside the scope of salvation." [29]

The future of those who had never heard the gospel did not form part of Paul's practical interest except for his own kinsmen. In Rom., chs. 9 to 11, Paul discusses at unusual length the question of why God has apparently rejected Israel. The theory that the rejection of the gospel by the Jews is really a device by which the Gentiles may be converted and that the conversion of the Gentiles is another device by which the Jews will be provoked into accepting Christianity and so all will be saved is undoubtedly a product of Paul's mind. Its importance lies, not in its faith-produced program of what lies ahead, or in its ingenuity, but in its soundly based vision. Charles makes the observation: " In Rom. 11 the Apostle proclaims the inner and progressive transformation of mankind through the Gospel, culminating in the conversion of the entire Gentile and Jewish worlds." [30] Paul recognizes that God wants all his creation to be reconciled to him, Gentiles and Jews alike, namely, the totality of mankind as Paul was accustomed to describe it. No human being can set limits to the accomplishment of God's purpose. Only God determines the extent to which he will allow man's rebellious free will to thwart his will.

There is not much more evidence for Paul's views of the future state of those who reject the gospel than there is for his opinion regarding the fate of those who have never heard of Christ. Most of what Paul does have to say in this matter is found in I and II Thessalonians, his earliest writings, which, more than any other, are indebted to Jewish apocalyptic literature. It is stated in II Thess. 1:9 that those who do not know God and those who do not obey the gospel "shall suffer the punishment of eternal destruction and exclusion from the presence of the Lord." In II Thess. 2:10 we read that those who refuse to love the truth are to perish. There are other passages that are less vivid and forthright but that suggest the same belief. Paul holds it to be true always that "the wages of sin is death" (Rom. 6:23). He states in I Cor. 1:18: "The word of the cross is folly to those who are perishing." "Those who are perishing" are mentioned also in II Cor. 2:15 and ch. 4:3. The intention is to say that if their present course is not altered, they will be lost. Of "the enemies of the cross of Christ" it is said that "their end is destruction" (Phil. 3:18, 19). Furthermore, in I Cor. 15:51, where the usual text is translated: "We shall not all sleep, but we shall all be changed," there is an interesting textual variant, supported by several important manuscripts, which is to be rendered: "We shall all sleep, but not all shall be changed." Thus, there is some support for the view that Paul expected the annihilation of the persistently wicked. The verb translated as "perish," *apollymi,* means "to be destroyed without hope of restoration." [31] Paul uses two different nouns to denote "destruction," *apōleia* and *olethros.* Referring especially to the passages in II Thessalonians, Charles explains: "In this harsh forecast of the future the apostle has hardly outgrown the narrow intolerance of Jewish eschatology." [32]

However, most scholars feel that Paul is not thinking about the annihilation of the unrighteous. In II Thess. 1:9 he links "eternal destruction" with "exclusion from the presence of the Lord." In the opinion of Filson the wicked are seen as doomed to a meaningless existence because the recompense principle continues to operate. He declares: "It fully satisfies Pauline usage to understand *apōleia* ["destruction"] as meaning utter ruin, complete spiritual disaster, the final loss of all that makes existence valued and desired." [33] The reference in Rom. 11:32 to God's intent to have mercy upon all is not an assertion that his mercy will in fact be received by all. Paul is not a universalist, and although God's purpose in the incarnation is "to reconcile to himself all things" (Col. 1:20), the accomplishment of that purpose is another matter. There is also the question of election and predestination as they are set forth in Rom. 8:29 f. and ch. 9:17-21. Hunter admits: "It is true that to say that some people are eternally elected to salvation implies, in logic, that others are eternally rejected. In logic, yes; but Paul is here splendidly illogical." [34] Logically, Paul's eschatology demands one of two alternatives: the final salvation of all men or the destruction of the unalterably wicked. However, once again, logic, a category of the human mind, is not his concern. In the developing rabbinic tradition the resurrection was regarded as essentially a reward for the righteous. Paul recognizes that there is some truth in this position. Only in Christ can the resurrection occur. Only in Christ can eternal life be given. The conclusion of Barrett is pertinent: "Men are related to God, and participate in the last things . . . only in virtue of their relation with Christ." [35] Paul has no desire to proclaim annihilation for the unconverted. However, those who refuse the offer of God in Christ cut themselves off from salvation and align themselves with its opposite, which is death. The drawing of this conclusion is not Paul's task because it belongs to God.

The Triumph of God's Will

The principle of recompense is at work in all creation, but it is also dependent upon and derivative from God. It has no independent existence and is complemented by the revelation of God's mercy. He is eternally opposed to evil, but its destruction is not a primary goal. Another note is sounded by Paul S. Minear: "The primary purpose of judgment is not to vindicate man's sense of justice or his claim to reward but to vindicate God's purpose in the face of human transgression." [36] The purpose of God is positive and redemptive. Thus, Paul describes the effect of Christ's death as "reconciliation." It is liberation and deliverance. God's will is conveyed to man as a "calling," a communication asking for a response. The events of the last day are parts of one purpose: "That God may be everything to every one" (I Cor. 15:28). Although the ultimate victory of God is the necessary climax of the gospel, the stress is significantly not upon the crushing of evil but upon the full extension of the good. Dodd has pointed out carefully: "The ultimate unity of all things in God is secured not by the mere suppression or destruction of hostile elements, human, sub-human, or super-human, but by bringing them all into harmony with the will of God as expressed in Christ." [37]

In II Cor. 2:15 f., Paul marks the contrast between those who are perishing, a fragrance from death to death, and those who are being saved, a fragrance from life to life. Since he relates salvation to the calling of God, it is tempting to suppose that the opposite of election (to salvation) is predestination to perdition. But for Hunter the counterpart is "unbelief—a self-incurred thing." [38] Defiance of the divine commands remains a real choice for man, and there is nothing to deny the possibility of perverse human wills that unswervingly refuse to yield to God's purpose. For Paul the expression of human free will, even in rebellion, was an expression of the will of God, who had granted it in creation, and not a restriction or denial of God's power. A strong indication of Paul's view of the reality of man's choice is found in his admission that even a Christian may fall from grace (cf. Gal. 5:4). Believers will not automatically be saved on the Day of Judgment. The kindness of God is extended to the Gentiles provided they continue in his kindness (cf. Rom. 11:32). The Colossians are advised to "continue in the faith, stable and steadfast" (ch. 1:23). Tasker adds: "Many of the Corinthian 'Christians' in particular failed to see that Christianity was very different from the Greek mystery religions. It was not an *opus operatum* rendering them permanently secure."[39] For the believer and the unbeliever alike God's gift of free will provides both the possibility and the obligation to make meaningful decisions and to choose between viable alternatives.

Thus, before all men there lie two ways. On this fact Caird comments: "The Christian must choose between the dominion of the elemental spirits and the dominion of Christ, and those who voluntarily re-enter the one are thereby severing their connection with the other."[40] The choice is real, and its results are binding. Paul attributes to evil no suggestion of illusion or unreality. It remains a force and factor in our present existence, and it must be overcome by a struggle instituted by God and shared by the faithful. However, the other side of the picture is the dependable nature of God. The retention of the concept of reward or pay is a means of indicating that God can be relied upon. The consequences of choosing him provide the only firm foundation for the future. The faithlessness of unbelieving Jews does not nullify the faithfulness of God (cf. Rom. 3:3). Paul affirms: "The Lord is faithful (*pistos*); he will strengthen you and guard you from evil." (II Thess. 3:3.) He writes: "He who calls you is faithful, and he will do it." (I Thess. 5:24.) On three occasions Paul uses the Greek phrase, *pistos ho theos,* "God is faithful," and so describes him as the source of our calling and of our strength (I Cor. 1:9; 10:13; II Cor. 1:18). That "God is faithful" means to Paul that he is worthy of our faith, of the offering of our whole being, including our free will that we have from him.

In Rom. 11:22, Paul points to both the kindness and the

severity of God, and he does not attempt to reconcile their obvious differences. It is enough for him to report God's hatred of sin and his love for all men even though they do evil. Judgment and grace are equally revelations of God's nature. The consummation, therefore, must involve judgment, even for the believers; but in one sense that judgment begins now as we make our decisions. If we remain firmly " in Christ," there will be nothing to fear. At the beginning of what has been called " the greatest chapter in the Bible," Rom., ch. 8, Paul does not claim that there is no judgment for those who are in Christ but that there is no condemnation for such. If we allow him, the Lord Jesus Christ will sustain us to the end, guiltless in the last day (cf. I Cor. 1:8). Provided that we agree, he who begins a good work in us will complete it at the time of judgment (cf. Phil. 1:6; 2:13). Regarding the last judgment, Paul can show confidence and joy, not because of any trust in himself, but because of the faithfulness of God, who is both judge and savior.

Chapter V | THE WORLD WITHOUT CHRIST

ACCORDING to Jewish eschatology, the life of man is related to two eras, the present age and the age to come. A third period is presupposed and occasionally directly mentioned, the beginning time or the age of creation. Paul accepts this overall pattern, but the life of Jesus has necessitated for him a major modification. Paul believes that the Messiah has appeared, but in much Jewish thinking the Messiah's arrival was to mark the opening of the age to come. On the other hand, it was only too evident to Paul that the age to come, as he had been taught to understand it, was not yet here. He knew that the future time, in which God's rule was fully established, would be entirely different from the present age; and yet he still observed the evil and imperfection associated with the latter. In order, then, to fit the life of Jesus as the Messiah into a scheme of the succession of ages, Paul, in effect, created two new epochs. He saw history as resting upon two activities of God, creation and redemption. It is creation that initiates the historical process, but redemption becomes operative with the sin of Adam. Therefore, for him, the present age, the time of evil, is also the period of God's plan of salvation, which comes to its climax in Jesus Christ. It is Christ who cuts in two this era of man's sin and God's salvation. The world before Christ is the age of the history of Israel's rebellion. But the world since the birth of Jesus is the era in which salvation is offered to all men. Yet again, this time of Christ is not yet the age to come because in it some men are his faithful disciples, whereas others fail to believe and to follow him and so are not in the way of salvation.

The thought of Paul, therefore, includes five ages rather than the three of traditional Jewish eschatology. These are: (1) the age of creation, (2) the age of the Fall and of time before Christ, (3) the present age which rejects Christ, (4) the present world of which Christ is Lord in fact, and (5) the age to come. (1) and (5) are essentially unchanged from their source in Jewish usage. However, that which is the present age for the Jews becomes for Paul a combination of (2), (3), and (4). The life of Jesus is an authoritative event by which all history must be viewed, past, present, and future. It is only Christ who can demonstrate the true significance of the history of Israel. In the present he is the inescapable standard by which men judge themselves and so are judged. The present is either a time in which Christ is accepted or a time in which he is denied. There are no alternatives. Paul remains sufficiently Jewish in his outlook to regard (1), (2), and (5) as occurring in a chronological order. However, because of the judgmental nature of the fact of Christ, (3) and (4) must overlap and are for the most part concurrent. On this point we can see the truth of the remarks of Barrett: " Paul sees history gathering at nodal points, and crystallizing upon outstanding figures. . . . As far as the experience of mankind is concerned they need not be chronologically distinguished." [1] In Paul's view Christ has brought a new, qualitative dimension to the present age.

From Adam to Christ

The concept of a goal requires the institution of a process by which the goal is to be approached, and the idea of a termination demands a beginning. All eschatology, therefore, assumes a starting point. T. W. Manson has explained one of the axioms of eschatological thought: " The two epochs [*Urzeit* and *Endzeit*] correspond because the purpose of God, which runs through and determines the whole process, is one and homogeneous throughout. The end answers to the beginning because all things are in the hands of God who sees the end from the beginning." [2] For Paul too, all five ages are rooted in the plan of God and through him are linked closely together. If the end is the final triumph of God's rule, the beginning is also the expression of his will. Paul is thoroughly in accord with the viewpoint of Genesis in its repeated assertions that what was created was good. There is no reason to suppose that Paul was not at one with contemporary rabbinical teaching regarding the original perfection of the physical universe. It finds few direct reflections in Paul's own doctrine simply because it was so well known and so widely accepted that Paul had no need to elaborate upon it. In Rom. 8:12-22, Paul tells us that the creation was subjected to futility as a part of God's plan and that it is groaning in travail while awaiting in hope a liberation from the bondage to decay and a participation in God's own glory to be given at the last day. Of these verses Mowry has written: " Paul looks forward to the return of the world to conditions as they existed in Paradise before the Fall." [3]

The significance that Paul attaches to the Fall points to the harmony which existed before the Fall between all nature and the Creator. It is true that because of sin this harmony has been lost and that in its place have come corruption and death. Nevertheless, Paul's view of nature's original perfection is revealed in the fact that " ever since the creation of the world his [God's] invisible nature, namely, his eternal power and deity, has been clearly perceived in the things that have been made " (Rom. 1:20). Even in its later, fallen state, natural creation can still reflect enough of the glory of its maker to provide a compelling reason for the Gentiles to believe in God. Moreover, nowhere in Paul do we find any hint that nature is essentially bound up with a dualism of good and evil. Goguel has noted: "There are not existing from eternity two conflicting principles but the dualism is the result of a disorder which came into the world."[4] The material world is in Paul's understanding essentially, originally, and potentially good just because God has created it. Unless nature were so conceived, it would not be possible for Paul to include its renewal in his picture of the last age. But the end was to be like the beginning.

All human history begins for Paul, as it must to every one who accepts the Genesis narrative, with Adam, the first man.[5] He is created in the very image of God. He has become a "living being" (I Cor. 15:45). At the same time he possesses a physical body so that he is "from the earth, a man of dust" (ch. 15:47). He stands at the head of this age. As it will be noted in the case of Abraham, that which stands first in the Biblical story is regarded by Paul as chronologically prior to that which is described later. Thus, Adam's purity, derived from the image of God which he bore, precedes his fallen state, which is the result of his misuse of free will to vaunt himself against his Maker.[6] By his sin Adam lost the divine image, and he put a serious obstacle in the way of God's purpose for creation. His rebellion is spoken of as a "trespass" (Rom. 5:15), literally, "a falling away from." Paul seems to refer to the belief, widespread in the Judaism of his day, that Adam was an ideal man before the Fall.[7] Paul undoubtedly accepted the myth as literal history, but in any case, Adam is every man for him because the experience of Adam has affected all the rest of mankind. Paul states, without elaboration, that "sin came into the world through one man and death through sin" (Rom. 5:12). He adds: "One man's trespass led to condemnation for all men." (V. 18.) The image of God is obscured in all. Corruption has entered into every part of man's nature. According to Dahl, " Man is ' flesh ' before the Fall as well as after. But before it the *direction* of his ' flesh ' is upward — it is part of the Light; afterward its direction is downward, earthward, backward." [8] The Judaism of the period had a well-developed doctrine of the Fall in which Paul had received early instruction. Barrett states: " When we turn to the writings of Paul the Christian we find that this sense of disastrous consequences, both personal and cosmic, derived from Adam, is still present." [9]

It is from Adam, after the Fall, that we receive our fallen humanity. And so Paul refers to " our old self " and " the sinful body " (Rom. 6:6). The " old nature " is something that has to be put off (cf. Col. 3:9). Our inescapable involvement in this " original sin " is set forth briefly in I Cor. 15:22: " In Adam all die." Davies reminds us: " A marked feature of Judaism in the centuries preceding the Christian era was the growth of speculation about the Fall and about the First Man." [10] To this inheritance Paul adds the perspective furnished by the coming of the second or last man. But for him Adam is both a historical figure of universal significance and also a representative of all mankind, corporately and individually. The original perfection of creation and the original righteousness of man were quickly destroyed in the sin of Adam. Ever since that time the world has been marked by evil and death. Our physical descent from Adam is manifested in what Paul describes as " this body of death " (Rom. 7:24). He is emphatic in asserting that in the Law, which was brought into the world through Moses, sin found a stronghold and a seemingly invincible base of operations, but he is also careful to indicate that death was in the world as the result and companion of sin, even in the period from Adam to Moses (cf. Rom. 5:14).

In spite of the doctrine of the Fall, Judaism continued to insist upon the role of individual freedom. Each man was confronted by two tendencies, of good and of evil, the *yetzer ha-tov* and the *yetzer ha-ra;* and each man was to make his own choice. With much of this emphasis Paul was in agreement. According to Davies, "For Paul every man sins both because of his own submission to the yetzer and also because of the sin of the first man." [11] He noted first that all men sin, and secondly that all men die (cf. Rom. 5:12). Since both sin and death are bound up with Adam, it is a short step to deduce that they have a common cause and that they are interrelated. Sin and death are repeatedly mentioned together by Paul (cf. Rom. 6:23; 8:2; I Cor. 15:56). Since all men have sinned, for whatever reason, sin is universal in time and scope. As rebellion against God it is contrary to his purpose, and so Paul regards it as having assumed the proportions of an external and objective force that has gained control of this world. C. A. A. Scott has concluded: "'Sin' is not for him a synonym for a sinful status; it is a power invading, attacking, subjugating men from without, and using for this purpose the flesh or physical constitution as its instrument." [12] Sin produces not merely a physical death in which biological life comes to an end but also a spiritual death. The subject is much upon Paul's mind. The Greek word for "death" appears forty-three times in the undisputed epistles. In a number of these instances it is contrasted with life, which is the gift of God, and is the expression of all that is completely opposite to the divine.

Although Paul clearly believed that the story of Adam was to be accepted as literal history, it was also for him a symbolic and representative narrative. It is with Abraham and Moses that we enter more directly upon the stage of history, and from here on we discover solid evidence for arriving at Paul's view of the events of the past. The interpretations that are made of what has already happened will throw much light upon how Paul regards that which is yet to take place. Amos Wilder remarks: "Paul gives substance to his expectation of the renewal of the creation and of man by appealing back to David, to Moses, to Abraham, to Adam, and to the creation itself." [13] Details of this history are frequently found to contain an important revelation. Indications of chronological order or extent in historical narratives are treated with care. In Gal. 3:17 there is a reference to the period between Abraham and Moses as " four hundred and thirty years." This is taken by Barr as proof of Paul's exact knowledge of Old Testament chronological schemes because Paul " quotes the figures precisely as they were transmitted in the Greek and Samaritan tradition." [14]

It is especially in the Epistle to the Galatians that we see abundant manifestations of Paul's regard for history. In the first two chapters he defends his apostleship by relating carefully those events in the life of the early church in which he had played a part. That he is well aware of the necessity for accuracy in his report is demonstrated by the unusual vehemence of the parenthetical remark in Gal. 1:20: " In what I am writing to you, before God, I do not lie! " In chapters three and four he defends his apostleship by showing how his teaching is derived from Israel's own history, especially in the story of Abraham. He points out how these past events were both the means and the promise of God's purpose and plan. Even though God had justified Abraham by faith, the Law was added through Moses " because of transgressions " (Gal. 3:19). It was of limited duration but had a role to play, albeit negative. Thus, the Law is described as " our custodian until Christ came " (ch. 3:24). The historical period from Abraham to Christ is pictured by the figure of a legal heir who cannot receive his inheritance until the time designated in the will (Gal. 4:1 f.). The correctness of Paul's specific interpretations is not an issue here. However, his judgments are significant because he finds a discernible pattern in history. We can share the view of Bultmann: " Paul conceived the total past as a unity invested with a special meaning." [15] In

Paul's understanding all history, but particularly that of Israel, when properly read, discloses the activity of God by which he is directing it to his end.

If Paul saw Adam as the first of men and the start of the present age, he viewed Abraham as the father of Israel according to the flesh and also as the first man to exhibit the principle of faith. In contemporary Judaism many legends were gathered around his name, and he was the inspiration for much theological argument. Of all Old Testament figures only Moses is mentioned more often in the New Testament. In part Paul agrees with the accepted Jewish evaluation of Abraham, but in part he is forced by his Christian convictions to formulate a fresh approach. He freely calls Abraham " our forefather according to the flesh " (Rom. 4:1). His remarkable deeds, sparked by his obedience to the call of God to journey from Mesopotamia to Palestine and his willingness to sacrifice his son, were too well known to be overlooked. His physical descendants were as the stars of the sky in number. And Paul can boast as a Jew: " I myself am an Israelite, a descendant of Abraham " (Rom. 11:1). Genesis 15:6 was a standard text for discussion in rabbinical schools and so was thoroughly familiar to Paul. The usual interpretation was to point to the quality of Abraham's faith as the good work by which God was able to justify him.

Paul's conclusion was completely different, however; and in Rom. 4:1 ff. and Gal. 3:6 ff., he maintains that no one, including Abraham, can ever be justified by good works. Abraham's faith is an absolute trust by which God's free and undeserved gift of justification is accepted. Following this account of Abraham's justification by faith, and without reference to works in Gen. 15:6, is the recital of God's promise to Abraham in Gen. 17:4: " Behold, my covenant is with you, and you shall be the father of a multitude of nations." Since the account of the justification appears earlier in the text than the statement of the promise, in

Paul's thinking the promise was chronologically later. In Gen. 17:10 ff., the covenant is said to include the command to institute circumcision. To traditional Judaism circumcision has been the necessary sign of the physical descent from Abraham, which means membership in God's chosen people. Paul, however, makes much of what he holds to be the fact that the promise and circumcision are later than Abraham's faith. His exegesis may not be convincing, but his theological purpose is clear. He believes that circumcision is no more than a sign or seal of Abraham's prior justification by faith (cf. Rom. 4:10 ff.). It follows that the terms of the promise have to do with the expression of faith and are without reference to physical descent. Thus, Paul declares: "Not all are children of Abraham because they are his descendants." (Rom. 9:7.) The next point is equally important: "This means that it is not the children of the flesh who are the children of God, but the children of the promise are reckoned as descendants" (v. 8). Those who follow Abraham by showing faith in God are the sons of Abraham (cf. Gal. 3:7). In this manner Christians, whether Jew or Gentile, are heirs of the promise (cf. Gal. 3:29; 4:28). Not even circumcized Jews can on that ground be rightly called children of Abraham (cf. Rom. 9:8).

With Abraham the principle of faith, as the channel for God's grace, is introduced into the world. By it God is able to save Abraham, but Paul does not say that any other Old Testament figure is so justified. It is not until the coming of Christ that faith is effectively revealed (cf. Gal. 3:25). Apparently, in the interim between Abraham and Christ, faith is only a potential, which became obscured and hindered first by circumcision and then by the Mosaic Law. Yet Abraham does manifest saving faith, and it precedes the giving of the Law through Moses. When it appears fully in Christ, it is not a new provision but the final implementation of something seen long before. God's plan of redemption is to be observed throughout history, and it does not manifest itself suddenly and without preparation. Such a conviction does not deny that from Abraham to Christ faith lay dormant. Barrett declares: " Abraham's faith . . . did not put an end to the evil powers that had been admitted to the creation, and to authority within it, by Adam's unfortunate and blameworthy act." [16] Adam's disobedience brought a hostile evil force into man's environment so that all men are affected. Abraham's faith, because of its personal character, offered an example and showed the way but could not alter other men's decisions. Only with Christ does faith become a power to do battle with evil.

Differing from the general usage of the New Testament, Paul pays less attention to Moses than he does to Abraham. Nevertheless he shows himself to be fully aware of the central place that Moses held in the Judaism of that time. Without doubt Paul regards him to have been the founder of the religion of his race in its definitive form. In several instances Paul provides evidence of his acquaintance with the many legends that the reputation of Moses had called forth (cf. II Cor. 3:7; Gal. 3:19) . Moses is the deliverer through whom the exodus from Egypt is successfully accomplished (cf. I Cor. 10:2) . It is, however, as the lawgiver that Moses interests Paul the most. Many of his judgments regarding the Mosaic Law are positive and laudatory. It is not contrary to the promises of God but is included in his plan of redemption (cf. Gal. 3:21) . The intent of the Law is found in the commandment to love one's neighbor, which is, in fact, the law of Christ (cf. Gal. 5:14; 6:2) . Paul concludes: " The law is holy, and the commandment is holy and just and good." (Rom. 7:12.)

Yet Paul states that with Moses the Jewish people entered a period of enslavement (cf. Gal. 3:23) . Barrett has noticed: " Paul works back from Christ to Moses, understanding Moses in the light of Christ, not Christ in the light of Moses." [17] Accordingly the Law of Moses can be judged a custodian to help to bring us to Christ in the realization that we are transgressors of the Law and unable to help ourselves. But for those who don't know Christ, the Law has become a snare and a barrier against God by appealing to man's pride. Because of legalism it is necessary to die to the Law in order to live to God (cf. Gal. 2:19). Paul asserts: "All who rely on works of the law are under a curse." (Gal. 3:10.) Sin and death entered human existence with Adam. Barrett's reminder is important: "The Law . . . was addressed to a race, which, ever since the time of Adam, had been under sentence of death." [18] Yet Paul concludes: "Sin indeed was in the world before the law was given, but sin is not counted where there is no law." (Rom. 5:13.) Moses began the time in which the true nature of sin is known through the impossibility of keeping the demands of the Law. Moreover, sin is increased as the commandments are multiplied. The effect is such that Paul exclaims: "The power of sin is the law" (I Cor. 15:56). His attitude toward the Law is both positive and negative, but the latter is more central in his thinking. Moses is one of the greatest of the patriarchs, but the period from Moses to Christ is one of almost unrelieved darkness.[19]

The events of the exodus are often in the background of Paul's thought. In I Cor. 5:6-8, the Christian life is described against the pattern of the first Passover. In I Cor. 10:1-10 the crossing of the sea, the cloud, the manna, the water from the rock, and the sins of the people in the wilderness with the resulting punishment are all recalled. Paul knows that these happenings are firmly rooted in history, and that fact is a part of their significance; but they are also episodes in the story of God's unified plan. Davies says of Paul: "He obviously regards the great deliverance at the Exodus and its accompaniments as the prototype of the mighty act of God in Christ." [20] Just as Adam was "a type of the one who was to come" (Rom. 5:14), so also the chastisements of evil behavior in the wilderness are

" warnings for us " (I Cor. 10:6). Paul concludes his account of the wilderness wanderings by asserting: " These things happened to them as a warning "; and then he adds significantly: " But they were written down for our instruction " (I Cor. 10:11).

This typology of Paul is not a discovery of a detailed prediction of the future in certain historical events, nor is it the finding of some exact correspondence between a past happening and one that was to occur at a later date. It is, rather, the insistence that the unity of history is revealed in the continuing activity of God. His purposes have been fully declared in Christ, and therefore a veil lies over the minds of all who read Moses until it is taken away by Christ (cf. II Cor. 3:15 f.). In the light that Christ supplies it can now be seen that the Mosaic Law was written on tablets of stone, and the glory that accompanied its coming was of very temporary duration. Mindful of its effects Paul calls the Law a "dispensation of death" (II Cor. 3:7). In sharp contrast the new covenant in Christ is written with the Spirit on tablets of human hearts and is accompanied by a glory that never fades. Thus, all of history is the scene of God's action; but the world before the coming of Christ is imperfect and incomplete. Its meaning is to be found only as it is placed in the perspective of Jesus the Messiah.

The Unredeemed World

On seven occasions Paul uses the expression " this age." In Rom. 12:2 he urges: " Do not be conformed to this world." In the remaining instances there is reference to the controlling powers or wisdom of our present existence. In Gal. 1:4, " the present evil age " is a condition from which Christ came to deliver us. " This age " is obviously regarded as standing in opposition to " that age," the time to come which will be completely in God's control, although these two ages are explicitly distinguished only in Eph. 1:21. " This age " is not obedient to God, and because it wants to ignore its creatureliness and behave in an independent and self-sufficient manner, it is evil. Disciples are called to be " children of God without blemish in the midst of a crooked and perverse generation " (Phil. 2:15). The area not yet controlled by Christ is " the dominion of darkness " (Col. 1:13). Paul also talks about " the present time," *ho nun kairos,* on four occasions. This includes sufferings, which, even though they are severe, cannot be compared with the glory of the time to come (cf. Rom. 8:18). Paul employs still one more phrase of similar meaning, " this world," in three different passages. In I Cor. 3:19 he describes " the wisdom of this world " as foolishness with God. In I Cor. 5:10 " this world " is said to contain immoral people, and in I Cor. 7:31 we are told that " the form of this world is passing away."

This objective evidence all points in one direction. Although the rulers of this age " are doomed to pass away " (I Cor. 2:6), they are still very influential. Elias Andrews has written: " At first sight the apostle Paul appears to be a confirmed pessimist, and he *is* so far as this present world or age is concerned." [21] The current aeon is dominated by sin and death because only where Christ rules have the effects of Adam's disobedience been overcome. Man's present condition is therefore one of perishableness (cf. I Cor. 15:42). Paul considers the state of the world to be tragic, and he is sure that it is already condemned by God (cf. I Cor. 11:32). Porter observes: " Paul can still speak of this world and of its rulers and even its god. The present world is the place or time of the power of evil. The Christian is not to be conformed to it." [22] This age is in bondage and has surrendered to the elemental spirits (cf. Gal. 4:3). It is composed of the things that are seen, which are transient, and so its time is limited; but the end is not yet, and in the meantime its existence and its powers are real. Christians, by virtue of their union with Christ, no longer belong to this world even though they continue to live in it. To his fellow believers Paul is able to say truthfully: " He has delivered us from the dominion of darkness " (Col. 1:13). A portion of the old world has therefore been destroyed, but it is equally important to acknowledge that an even larger portion still remains, forceful and threatening.

The world is essentially that which God has created. The word appears thirty-six times in Paul's letters. Sometimes there is in the term a reference to creation, and sometimes it describes the totality of space and objects; but in the majority of cases it pertains to a realm or order of being that stands over against God. Typical is the twofold occurrence of " worldly affairs " in I Cor. 7:33 f. as the counterpart to " the affairs of the Lord." It is in this sense that Paul utilizes the phrase " this world " as a synonym for " the present time " or " this age." An originally material and spatial concept has become a term for an era in which God's saving power is not known, because the creation has revolted against its creator. The world is therefore to be judged by God (cf. Rom. 3:6). The folly of the wisdom of this world is exposed by the divine wisdom (cf. I Cor. 1:20). In this dominion of darkness Christians are the only lights (cf. Phil. 2:15). The rest of mankind have identified themselves with the world. Whitely affirms: " For St. Paul the ' spiritual ' like the earthly, and like Man himself, was part of the created order and was capable of acting against God's will." [23] Sin has badly obscured the image of God in which man was created, and it has penetrated into his innermost being.

In II Thess. 3:2, where Paul alludes to wicked and evil men, there is the simple but profound statement that " not all have faith." Some do not believe in Christ because they haven't yet heard of him (cf. Rom. 15:20, 23 f.). Some choose not to follow him because of their own selfishness. But the result is the same in either case. Dinkler has summarized the situation: "The nonbeliever has no part in the new creature. He remains in the old aeon. . . . Two aeons — the old aeon of subjection to the demons and the new aeon of salvation and of the new creation — lie side by side, and both fill out the dimension of time and reality." [24] The Christian and the non-Christian thus live in two different realms which are to be sharply distinguished even though they are contemporaneous. Since the disciple is one who has put on Christ and severed all connection with "the elemental spirits of the universe," he is not to live as if he "still belonged to the world" (Col. 2:20). Paul plainly supposes that those who have not believed in Christ and who still obey the elemental spirits are the children of this world in spite of the fact that "Christ died for the ungodly" (Rom. 5:6).

Without Christ all men are subject to the dominant force of death, sin, and the law (cf. I Cor. 15:56). The first two have been present since Adam and the last since Moses. Basically sin is rebellion against God but it has also become a personal power that holds men in bondage because "all men sinned." As rebellion it includes guilt, but as a hostile force it produces man's cry for help. Death is an intruder into God's creation which has ruled ever since its introduction along with sin. It holds a special position in that it will be the last enemy to be destroyed on the Day of the Lord (cf. I Cor. 15:26). Presumably the other enemies are more easily vanquished. Leivestad declares: "Death . . . is not only the divine punishment of sin, but a diabolical power, hostile, not only to men, but even to God." [25] The early church's concern with the problem of the death of many believers before the expected Parousia points to the fact that acceptance of Christ does not release the Christian from the necessity of facing biological death. According to Ellis, "In the midst of moral-psychological renewal the Christian remains, in his mortality, under the death claims of the old age." [26] Paul then describes even that perfect life of discipleship in which Christ is resident within and ruling as a life lived "in the flesh" (Gal. 2:20). It must be true that the flesh is therefore not necessarily and essentially evil. The believer is asked to surrender himself so completely that "the life of Jesus may be manifested in our mortal flesh" (II Cor. 4:11).

Until their death Christians must "live in the world" and "in the flesh" (cf. II Cor. 10:3; Phil. 1:22, 24). At this point Paul's thinking is decidedly Hebraic. "Flesh" for Paul is the substance given by God for man's life upon the earth. It is in itself morally indifferent since it is only an instrument. Although it is not inherently evil, it is marked by weakness. Davies maintains: "*sarx* . . . has become the basis from which sin attacks man; has, in short, passed under the dominion of sin; it was a corrupted not a corrupting element."[27] Frequently when Paul uses the word "flesh," he has in mind, not what it was originally or in essence, but what it has now become, the agent of evil, the seat of selfish desires that work against the divine demands. The flesh is thus the scene of the unavoidable conflict between good and evil. Because sin has gained temporary control of the flesh, God must work through the spirit to redeem the flesh. Stacey acknowledges: "The unusual intensity of Paul's experience of both *pneuma* and *sarx* gives rise to a contrast between them that is without parallel. . . . No antecedents can be found to explain the contrast between *pneumatikos* and *psychikos* in Paul."[28] In this development Paul is neither Hebrew nor Greek; he is expressing his own convictions in a new way. The "purely physical" is roughly equated with the flesh in its present corrupted state. The "spiritual" is that part of reality where God is still in control and thus the seat of his activity for liberating the flesh from its bondage to sin. In this age, however, sin, death, the physical, and the flesh are indissolubly linked together.

To express the reality of sin and death for the individual, Paul sometimes makes use of the word " body." Thus, the body is called " sinful " and " mortal " (Rom. 6:6, 12). Its deeds may be evil (cf. Rom. 8:13). It is lowly and made of flesh (cf. Phil. 3:21; Col. 2:11). The basis of Paul's thought is seen in I Cor. 15:44, where he asserts: " If there is a physical body, there is also a spiritual body." This is not an expression of philosophical dualism but of religious conflict. The physical body cannot be the source of salvation but it is nonetheless a part of its object. What Paul calls " the outward man " must share the fate of this present age. Even Christians are faced with actual danger. Thus, Barrett has warned: " Neither the efficacy of the sacrament, nor the anticipation of the eschatological future, alters the fact that men in this world have mortal bodies, conditioned by the present age, not the Age to Come; and in these bodies sin is ever at hand." [29]

Paul sees sin to be so widespread and so firmly entrenched in all the world that he often refers to it as a demonic power, a personal being at war with God. The exact nature of Paul's belief in the existence of independent evil spirits is a matter of much debate. The suggestion is sometimes made that Paul at times turns to highly rhetorical language to make his point or that he consciously and deliberately reproduces some bit of mythology. However, Cullmann speaks for the majority of scholars when he declares: " It will not do to transfer this conception of the angels and powers to the periphery of the Pauline theology." [30] The large number of references to hostile powers in the Pauline writings seems to indicate that they were important in Paul's thinking. In II Thess. 2:3 ff. he pictures " the man of lawlessness," " the son of perdition," who is connected with the climax of evil. He tells the Galatians that before they became Christians they " were slaves to the elemental spirits of the universe " (ch. 4:3; cf. Col. 2:8, 20). He mentions " the god of this world " (II Cor. 4:4) and " the rulers of this age " (I Cor. 2:6). Frequently, these rebellious forces appear in lists using a wide variety of names: angels, principalities, powers, the astrological terms " height " and " depth," rule, authorities, thrones, and dominions (cf. Rom. 8:38 f.; I Cor. 15:24; Col. 1:16; 2:10, 15).

This Pauline view is also reflected in Ephesians, where we read of " the prince of the power of the air " (ch. 2:2) and " the world rulers of this present darkness, the spiritual hosts of wickedness in the heavenly places " (ch. 6:12). The Christian would seem to be surrounded by vast numbers of hostile, invisible beings who are responsible for much of what happens in the world. Cadbury declares: " The conflict of the spirits of good and evil is not a poetic drama. The actors are not mythological. It is the real decisive battle in the world's history." [31] The rulers of this age crucified Christ, but they didn't understand the wisdom of God which will surely bring about their downfall (cf. I Cor. 2:6 ff.). The " governing authorities " in the political order may not be the emperors and kings but the invisible powers who control them (cf. Rom. 13:1-5). The law has served as the handmaid of sin, and so Caird states: " The demonic forces of legalism, both Jewish and Gentile, can be called ' principalities and powers ' or ' elemental spirits of the world.' " [32] Paul is struck by the enormity of evil among men, and he finds a major source in the work of antagonistic supernatural beings. The effects of their operations are everywhere apparent.

Whitely has pointed out: " St. Paul is more concerned with the all-pervasive large-scale effects of the demonic-complex as a whole than he is with the activities of ' individual ' evil spirits." [33] To admit the existence of evil powers is not to yield to them any ultimate authority. The preexistence of Christ means that he is before all things and that in him all things were created, including thrones, dominions, principalities, and authorities (cf. Col. 1:15 ff.). At times Paul refers to a victory of Christ over all these opposing forces as already won (cf. Col. 2:15). At other times, however, Paul points to a current struggle whose outcome is sure but not yet reached. Confidently, Paul affirms: "The form of this world is passing away." (I Cor. 7:31.) Yet this world is still with us. Leivestad has noted: "Paul, it seems, thought of some kind of mighty angelic powers, . . . astral spirits with a cosmological function, probably as rulers over certain domains of the created universe. But Paul's attitude towards them is strongly polemical." [34] He builds upon the foundation of angelology in the Old Testament and includes subsequent developments.[35] In most of Paul's direct references to angels there is an unfavorable connotation. All the supernatural beings are probably thought of by Paul as some form of angels, of whom Paul believes only a small number are now obedient to God.

The only personal names given to devils in the New Testament are Satan and Belial. The first of these occurs eight times in the Pauline literature, and the only New Testament occurrence of Belial is in II Cor. 6:15. Paul nowhere employs the term *diabolos*. In his view Satan is the archenemy of God, the foremost opponent of the Kingdom and the personification of all evil. He is the head of all the anti-Christian forces. In II Cor. 6:15, Paul asks the purely rhetorical question: "What accord has Christ with Belial?" Obviously there is nothing between the two except unending struggle for the mastery. In dealing with a matter of gross immorality in the Christian community at Corinth, Paul instructs the congregation to deliver the offender "to Satan for the destruction of the flesh, that his spirit may be saved in the day of the Lord Jesus" (I Cor. 5:5). Whatever may be the specific meaning of the passage, there is within it an acceptance of the view that Satan is the ruler of the kingdom of death. He is constantly working to hinder the spread of the gospel. The physical affliction that Paul had to bear while engaging in his missionary activity, his " thorn in the flesh," is described as " a messenger of Satan " (II Cor. 12:7). The power of Satan is subject to no moral restraints, and so Paul observes on the basis of his own sad experience as an apostle: " Even Satan disguises himself as an angel of light " (II Cor. 11:14). Paul's personal plans were sometimes impossible because of Satan's hostility. So he writes to the Thessalonians: " We wanted to come to you — I, Paul, again and again — but Satan hindered us " (I Thess. 2:18).

This world has become a battleground in which Satan and all his subservient forces are engaged in a bitter and decisive conflict. According to Grundmann, " As in the case of death's dominion, all his [Paul's] references to demons and to Satan are meant to give actuality to his teaching about sin; they are not the outcome of dualistic speculation, but the testimony of one who sees sin as it really is." [36] How Paul conceived of Satan is relatively unimportant, but the continuing opposition to God's will which Satan symbolizes is a central part of Paul's theological thought. The present age without Christ is the age of Satan.

Chapter VI | THE TIME IS NOW

THE AGE before the birth of Christ and the present age which has not believed on him are differentiated by the fact that in the former, saving faith, glimpsed in Abraham, has not yet been revealed, whereas in the latter, a positive or negative decision cannot be avoided. On the other hand, these two ages have much in common, for they are in effect both without Christ. In each the rule of sin and death is unchecked, and in neither is God's salvation heeded. Yet the faith of Paul is rooted in the fact that "when the time had fully come, God sent forth his Son" (Gal. 4:4). His life, death, and resurrection have completed the divine plan, and all subsequent history must be different because of these events. This conviction is clearly indicated by Dodd: "It is in the epistles of Paul that full justice is done for the first time to the principle of 'realised eschatology' which is vital to the whole kerygma. That supernatural order of life which the apocalyptists had predicted in terms of pure fantasy is now described as an actual fact of experience." [1] Those who are in Christ are no longer a part of this present evil world because "he has delivered us from the dominion of darkness and transferred us to the kingdom of his beloved Son" (Col. 1:13).

The work of Christ means for those who are his disciples, negatively, release from bondage and forgiveness and, positively, entrance into a new age. The promises of God given to Israel have been fulfilled. Our only ground for hope in the future is the experience we enjoy in the present because of what God did once for all in Christ in the past.[2] For Paul the cross of Christ is the center of all history, the culmination of the scheme of salvation begun after the Fall, the source of present power, and the positive assurance of God's final victory. Paul proclaims that Jesus Christ " gave himself for our sins to deliver us from the present evil age " (Gal. 1:4). It is inconceivable that this self-offering, in accordance with God's will, should be ineffective among those who have faith.

For the believers, therefore, the old age has gone, and the last things are at hand. Schoeps suggests: " The eschatology of Paul . . . is distinguished from all forms of Jewish speculation by the fact that in consequence of the Resurrection of Jesus from the dead it considers the eschaton to have already begun." [3] Paul sees the present time in which Christ is allowed to rule as the last stage before the end. This means that from one point of view it is the commencement of the end itself; but from another it is proof that the end is not yet. In the opinion of Cullmann: " It is not ' a new time ' which is created after Christ, but a new division of time." [4] It seems more in keeping with Paul's thought to describe this period as the age of the Lord. It has its own special characteristics. The presence and power of Christ provide the central element not found in the earlier ages, but the role of Christ as the agent of God points toward the one more age to come. The quality of this age is thus that of Christ himself.

Goguel believes that " even if there had been no fall, the creation would not have been completed without the appearance of the second Adam, who had to be the bridge across which it would pass from the carnal level to the spiritual level." [5] Whether without the Fall there would be this gulf between the carnal and the spiritual is a matter for serious discussion, but there is in any case abundant evidence that Paul conceived of Jesus as the Second Adam. Barrett makes the significant comment regarding Paul's writings: " In every passage in which Adam is named, there is specific reference to Christ." [6] Paul concentrates on two areas of the Christian life, justification and resurrection; and in both there is a direct link between Christ and the believers. Because of their solidarity with the first man, Adam, all men have been enslaved by sin; but they may be saved through their solidarity with the Second Adam. So Paul declares: " One man's act of righteousness leads to acquittal and life for all men " (Rom. 5:18) .

On the basis of the same principle of solidarity Paul turns to the resurrection and concludes: " As in Adam all die, so also in Christ [as the Second Adam] shall all be made alive " (I Cor. 15:22) . The comparison is explicit in I Cor. 15:45-49. The first Adam, or the first man, is set over against the Second Man, or the Last Adam. The first was " a living being," but the second " a life-giving spirit." The first was " from the earth, a man of dust," but the second " from heaven." According to Jeremias, " In later Rabbinic literature we never find the Redeemer described as the last Adam." [7] Paul, however, did make that identification because his understanding of the new life brought by Christ demanded it. The preexistence of Christ showed that the Last Adam comes before the first. It is Christ who gives life to Adam and to all other men. Adam by his sin repudiated the image of God in which he was made, but Christ is that image (cf. Col. 1:15) . He is called simply " the man," above all others, in Rom. 5:15 and I Cor. 15:21. He is the head of the new, and true, humanity, as Adam was of the old.

It is in the light of Paul's concept of the Second Adam that we can best understand his words in II Cor. 5:17: " If any one is in Christ, he is a new creation; the old has passed away, behold, the new has come." In this new humanity the distinction between circumcision and uncircumcision has been transcended (cf. Gal. 6:15). Walking with Christ involves newness of life and spirit (cf. Rom. 6:4; 7:6). Righteousness, peace, and joy mark the life of the disciple; and these are also features of the Kingdom (cf. Rom. 14:17). Robinson asserts: " St. Paul . . . never derives any *moral principle* from the belief in the Second Advent; the whole quality of the Christian life is based directly upon the fact that Christians *have already been* translated into a new order of existence." [8] Paul sees this experience as including " the things that are above " (Col. 3:1). It is a renunciation of " things that are on earth." Dinkler agrees: " This means that he who believes in Christ *is* a new being, that for him the Christian era of Salvation *has* come, the past *is* ended, and forgiveness *has* graciously been bestowed." [9]

What the death of Christ upon the cross discloses is not the power of the " principalities and powers " by which a righteous man is made to suffer and die or, on the other hand, the lack of power or concern of a good God, who must remain aloof while evil flourishes. Rather, the crucifixion is for Paul the strongest possible demonstration of the love of God (cf. Rom. 5:6). Against such a force the present age is powerless. Neither suffering nor persecution " nor anything else in all creation, will be able to separate us from the love of God in Christ Jesus " (Rom. 8:35, 39). Schweitzer has reasoned: " Since Paul's conception of redemption is eschatological, it is natural to assume that it is problems of eschatology which force him to the assertion of a redemption which is realizing itself in the present." [10] Salvation is properly to be reserved for the future, since it conveys the thought of completion and finality; but the righteousness of God, very closely related to his love, is being revealed unceasingly now that Christ has come (cf. Rom. 1:17). Thus, his love is effectually at work in the age of the Lord. God's might has been released for the accomplishment of his purpose. Barrett points out: " The Gospel itself is the operation of God's power working toward salvation. . . . This proleptic enjoyment of salvation in the power of the Gospel, which at once announces and anticipates it, is a most important key to Paul's thought." [11] The faithful must know that they belong to a movement that is advancing toward its divinely established goal.

As Christ is the Second Adam, so also is he the New Moses. The function of the old Law was primarily negative, to convince man of his own helplessness, and its time was strictly limited. After declaring that Abraham's offspring was Christ, Paul adds that the Law was given "till the offspring should come to whom the promise had been made" (Gal. 3:16, 19). From the time that the Law had been granted it was ever drawing closer to the end of its function. Paul reports that when Moses returned to his people with the tablets of Law, he "put a veil over his face so that the Israelites might not see the end of the fading splendor" (II Cor. 3:13). Inasmuch as the law has increased transgressions and has at the same time deceived man by contributing to his pride, it has become an ally of sin and death and so an enemy of God. Schweitzer admits: "That the Law comes to an end when the Messianic reign begins is for Jewish thought self-evident. But Paul represents it as already invalidated by Jesus' death." [12]

Paul believes that the Christian must die to the Law as also to the elemental spirits of the universe (cf. Gal. 2:19 and Col. 2:20). Before faith was revealed in Christ, men were confined under the Law and kept under restraint just as they were enslaved to the elemental spirits (cf. Gal. 3:23; 4:3). The Law was weakened by the flesh, and the elemental spirits are weak and beggarly (cf. Rom. 8:3 and Gal. 4:9). Thus, for Paul, the cosmic forces and the Law alike belong to the old age done away by Christ. According to Gutbrod: "For Paul the negation of the law follows from the cross." [13] Because Christ died, a man is justified by faith and not by works of the Law (cf. Gal. 2:16). If the Law had been sufficient, then the cross is purposeless (cf. ch. 2:21). Yet it is also true that from Moses to Christ the Law is binding. It is consistent with the promises of God and not contrary to them (cf. ch. 3:21).

But the day of the Law is over. Fully aware of the fact that *telos* means both termination and goal, Paul can state: " Christ is the end [*to telos*] of the law " (Rom. 10:4). He has concluded and also fulfilled it, in accordance with God's plan. Gutbrod summarizes: " Only when a man lets himself appropriate the righteousness of God in Christ, is the Law abolished for him. . . . The relationship with God now rests no longer with man himself. Thus the Law as the road to salvation is now barred; Christ has stepped into its place." [14] Justification could never take place by the Law, but the new and sufficient way of justification by faith in Christ has stripped the Law of even its limited and subsidiary function. In this whole approach Paul is speaking of the Mosaic Law and its accompanying interpretations and also of the legalistic principle by which men offer their individual acts of obedience to law as credit for their salvation. For Paul the Mosaic Law is also one of many expressions of God's just demands upon mankind which remain unchanged from one age to the next. Yet even here it has been replaced by the law of Christ (cf. I Cor. 9:21), which is the law of love. And love is one of the marks of the Kingdom.

Life in the Spirit

Contemporary Judaism, which had fully recognized the role of God's Spirit in creation and in the history of Israel, taught that in the coming age God would send his Spirit upon all men (e.g., Joel 2:28 f.). It is the conviction of Paul, and the whole early church, that through Christ the gift of the Spirit has been made. According to B. Lindars, the earliest Christian use of the phrase " to give the Holy

Spirit " is I Thess. 4:8, " God, who gives his Holy Spirit to you," which he believes is a quotation from Ezek. 7:14.[15] Later examples are I Cor. 12:7; II Cor. 1:22; 5:5; Rom. 5:5, and many verses in ch. 8. The pouring out of the Spirit is regarded as another way in which God's promise has now been fulfilled. Thus, for Robinson, the new creation which the coming of the Spirit has made possible " is not a fresh start, but the old made new — not a *nea* but a *kainē ktisis.*" [16] The presence of the Spirit means the reassertion of the divine control inherent in the original creation.

Moreover, Paul sees the present activity of the Spirit as constituting the heart of Christianity. Rhetorically, he asks the Galatians: " Did you receive the Spirit by works of the law, or by hearing with faith? " (ch. 3:2) . And then he proceeds to rebuke them for returning to legalism and questions again: " Having begun with the Spirit, are you now ending with the flesh? " (v. 3) . Faith and not the Law has enabled the Spirit to come among them, and the Christian calling involves a movement away from the flesh to the spirit. As the Last Adam, Christ has been called " a life-giving spirit " (I Cor. 15:45) . Those in Christ have in fact entered into that life which he bestows, and at the same time Paul states simply: " The Spirit gives life " (II Cor. 3:6) . Thus, the sharing of Christ's life is a testimony of the Spirit. Charles asserts: " This new creation is due to the entrance of God's spirit into man, which henceforth becomes a divine immanent principle within man, dwelling in him." [17]

The status of the believer is presented in no more exalted terms anywhere than in I Cor. 3:16: " Do you not know that you are God's temple and that God's Spirit dwells in you? " Christians are the sons of God who are led by his Spirit (cf. Rom. 8:14) . The Spirit alone makes possible all Christian worship and belief (cf. I Cor. 12:3) . The righteousness, peace, and joy that belong to the Kingdom and that are experienced in the fellowship are "in the Holy Spirit" (Rom. 14:17). In commenting on the Pauline view, John Knox has declared: "The age of the Spirit had not, strictly speaking, arrived, but the life of the Spirit had already begun."[18] The quality of what is now known belongs also to the future age; only the quantity will change. The resurrection itself will take place through the same spirit that now dwells in the believer (Rom. 8:11). Cullmann interprets: "It is the action of the Holy Spirit which testifies that from now on we are living in the last age of time. This last age is a fragment of the future, the only part of the coming age which exists in the present age."[19] It is therefore the Holy Spirit who raises most acutely the issue of the meaning of the present and the future in the life of the Christian.

The resurrection of Christ began a new period of time characterized by the active presence of the Spirit and a renewal of life. It introduced the rule of Christ as Lord. Paul proclaims that Jesus Christ was "designated Son of God in power according to the Spirit of holiness by his resurrection from the dead" (Rom. 1:4). He pictures the incarnation as a humiliation that led to the cross, but this perfect obedience was followed by an exaltation (the Greek term used, *hypsoō,* is a symbol for resurrection in John's Gospel) accompanied by the granting to Christ of the name "Lord." The confession of Jesus as Lord and belief in the resurrection of Jesus are set side by side in Rom. 10:9. It follows that Jesus must therefore be reigning now. In the opinion of Robinson: "However vivid its expectation of Jesus, the Church remained content to express its certainty about the future as part of its conviction of the present and continuing sovereignty of Christ, already enthroned as history's Lord and history's Judge."[20] Christ's Lordship means power and authority. He will never be more a king than he is in this time. Whereas most references by Paul to the Kingdom (of God) convey a sense of future expectation, the only instance in which he speaks of a Kingdom of Christ emphasizes its present reality.[21] It is strongly implied that this rule consists in large measure of a campaign to overcome all of the enemies of God (cf. I Cor. 15:24 ff.). The battle will continue until complete victory is won at the end. Goguel has stated: " When Christ re-appears at the end of time he will destroy all the hostile powers, but his victory will only be a consequence of the fact that he has become Kurios." [22] From this point of view the Second Coming of Christ is only the conclusion of the rule begun at the resurrection and continuing now. As the resurrection was joined inseparably to " the Spirit of holiness," so the reign of Christ in his Kingdom is carried out through the same Spirit. With this fact in mind Paul declares in II Cor. 10:4: " The weapons of our warfare are not worldly but have divine power to destroy strongholds." The Spirit is the power of God in action.

Since the resurrection begins with Christ, and all who are in Christ shall be made alive, Paul describes his rising from the dead as " the first fruits " (I Cor. 15:23). In addressing the Romans he states that Christians " have the first fruits of the Spirit " (ch. 8:23). The Greek word is the same in both cases, *aparchē,* and the reason is clear. Both the resurrection and the Spirit are already felt and yet give promise of much more to come. That the fullness of the Spirit belongs to the age to come and is not to be expected before then is indicated by the twofold reference to the gift of the Spirit " as a guarantee " (cf. II Cor. 1:22; 5:5). Even though it may be true that in New Testament times the required down payment on a purchase was larger in proportion to the total price than is our own custom, the distinction between a part and the whole remains. That portion of the Spirit which is bestowed upon the faithful is truly the Spirit and not a facsimile or substitute. At the same time it must be admitted that we have now only a glimpse of what God will do. Using some words of Isaiah, Paul declares that what God has prepared for those who love him, he has revealed to us through the Spirit (cf. I Cor. 2:9). Yet these things remain unseen, unheard, and beyond our human comprehension. Moule suggests: "A vivid expectation of a future consummation is perfectly compatible with a doctrine of the Spirit on an even deeper level than the Johannine: that is proved by Romans 8." [23]

The Spirit is one of the major characteristics of the last age, and yet believers, who possess the Spirit, are no longer "in the flesh" (Rom. 8:9). H. Wheeler Robinson has discovered that out of 146 cases in Paul in which the term *pneuma* occurs it signifies in 116 places not a normal element in human nature but "supernatural influences." [24] As Paul understands it, the Spirit is the sign of the breaking in of the coming age upon the present. E. Schweizer has asserted: "Paul is a Hellenist in so far as he understands the Spirit as the power which releases men from 'this age' (I Cor. 2:6) and places them in the next." [25] Yet Paul does not maintain that Christians are living in the next age, and it is not just the Spirit but Christ who has delivered them from "this age." In its aspect of a gift already possessed, the Spirit conveys the new life, whereas in its aspect of the power of God to be fully manifested on the Last Day, it provides a goal and a true perspective. In the Spirit, the present anticipates the future, and the future alters the present. If it is the Spirit that turns the body of the individual disciple into a temple (cf. I Cor. 6:19), it is the same Spirit that makes of the entire community of Christians also a temple of God (cf. ch. 3:16). We can thus see the basis for the assertion of John Knox: "The whole ground of the Christian life lies in the fact that in the church the Kingdom of God is really, though partially, present, and that in the Spirit, which has already been given, we have a foretaste, an advance installment, of the whole eschatological order of the Spirit." [26]

In Judaism, the Spirit is always the Spirit of God, and this belief is the foundation and starting point for Paul's approach. Yet in some Old Testament prophecy and frequently in the intertestamental literature the Spirit is associated with the coming Messiah. Since Paul accepted Jesus as the Christ, he might be expected to look for the working together of Jesus and the Spirit. The thought of Paul in this matter is clearly a reflection upon his prior experience. The remark of Dodd is a true assessment of Paul's view: " The presence of the Spirit in the Church *is* the presence of the Lord." [27] The crucified and risen Christ has instituted a new creation in the Spirit, but the nonbelievers do not share in this renewal. To be in Christ is to be in the Spirit, and to be in the Spirit is to be in Christ (cf. Rom. 8:10 f.). The Christian knows the two to be inseparable, but the precise nature of the connection between the two constituted a serious problem for Paul and the early church. On the one hand, there are indications of a desire to preserve their separateness. E. F. Scott has declared: " Paul . . . distinguishes the Spirit and Christ, and probably it never occurred to him that they could be thought of as identical." [28] The two are separately mentioned in I Cor. 6:11, where Paul writes: " You were justified in the name of the Lord Jesus Christ and in the Spirit of our God." In the same epistle there is a reference to Spirit, Lord, and God, in that order, presumably progressing from immediate experience to that which lies behind it (cf. ch. 12:4-6). The different order of Lord, God, and Spirit is set forth in the familiar Pauline grace of II Cor. 13:14.

On the other hand, there are many passages which, on the surface at least, tend to confuse the Lord and the Spirit. In Rom. 8:9 the term " Spirit of Christ " is used as a synonym of " Spirit of God," which immediately precedes it. Power is said to come sometimes from the Spirit and sometimes from Christ. The problem comes to its sharpest focus in II Cor. 3:17 where Paul refers to "the Spirit of the Lord" and makes the unqualified statement that "the Lord is the Spirit" (cf. also v. 18). If taken by itself, this passage might indicate Paul's belief that the two were absolutely and essentially identical. However, both the context and Pauline usage elsewhere must be considered. Davies is justified in speaking of "the Christifying of the Spirit."[29] The redemptive work of God is completed in Christ but the application and extension of that salvation is the task of the risen Lord and of the Spirit. Their functions are at times so similar that they can be distinguished only with difficulty. C. A. A. Scott arrives at the conclusion: "It was St. Paul who brought the Spiritual Christ and the Spirit of God into the very closest relation, yet a relation not so much of identity as of equivalence."[30]

If Paul seems to equate the two and in this regard breaks new ground, it is only because the facts of his own religious life have led him to this interpretation. He has no interest in philosophical and metaphysical questions. He knows, however, that Christ dwells within him (Gal. 2:20) and that this is due to the power and love of God (cf. Rom. 5:8). He is also certain that this life in Christ is life in the Spirit (cf. Gal. 5:25). Through Christ and through the Spirit, God has taken hold of him and made him a new being. And he writes of his own experience only because it is a pattern for all the faithful. The reminder of Moule constitutes a true interpretation of the thought of Paul: "Christ and Spirit are sometimes interchangeable — or nearly so — within the Church, but never outside it."[31] The words of Paul are directed toward his fellow believers and presuppose the openness to God's initiative provided by faith.

The Meaning of the Present

Traditional Jewish eschatology revolved around just two ages: the present time and the time to come. The present world was to be brought to an end and the future world introduced by the coming of the Messiah and the Last Judgment. It was the Christian belief that the Messiah had appeared in Jesus, had died and been raised and that the last age was still to come. Obviously, then, these facts could not be fitted into the old scheme, and a new pattern was required. The attempt must be made to define the period between the resurrection of Christ and his Parousia and to relate it to the two ages of the old conception. Goguel observes: " For this system with two terms Paul substitutes a system with three terms, by interposing between the old world and the new world an intermediary period in which the two worlds co-exist." [32] What we could call " the present age with Christ " is first of all related to " the world without Christ " as fulfillment and completion. For the faithful, the old age is ended by the coming of Christ in humility and suffering and resurrection. He was henceforth regarded as the turning point of all history and the one way to discover its significance. Moule explains: " Upon Jesus converged the whole history of Israel in the past, and from him deployed the whole future of the people of God. It was the coherent organizing of all this into a single inclusive personality that made a completely new thing of Old Testament exegesis." [33] Whereas for the believers the present (evil) age has ended, the coming of Christ points to the approach and inevitability of its ending even for the nonbelievers. Paul proclaims: " The rulers of this age . . . are doomed to pass away." (I Cor. 2:6.)

This age with Christ is at the same time tied to the coming age. So Barrett interprets Paul's view: " With Jesus the last age, the age of the new creation, has dawned, though it has not been consummated." [34] The light is in the sky, and its warmth is felt. If the old has disappeared, it would seem that the new has arrived. The nature of the age to come begins to be seen as never before. Existence must be interpreted eschatologically. But the sun is not yet risen and can't be seen; Christ is yet to return in power and glory. The present must, then, be regarded as a strange anomaly — a state that is neither the old nor in reality the new. Some may be led to consider it only a meaningless point between. Dinkler reflects this mode of thought: "The present appears to be an existence in between the times, a period of waiting. . . . To be sure, there is a heightened quality of existence, but there is also a not yet."[35]

However, in the Pauline view the present, for the Christian, is a unique and meaningful period. It possesses its own special characteristics and has been given its own role. It is as definitely a part of God's plan as any other age. The point is well put by Cullmann: "The New Covenant throws this process of salvation in greater relief than the Old by introducing the present as an interim period with its own autonomous and essential significance between the decisive past event of the death and Resurrection of Christ on the one hand, and the final fulfillment of the return of Christ on the other."[36] The fact that the Christian present looks in both directions does not mean that it has no definable or purposeful existence. Rather, this "time between" is given its own responsibility and opportunity. Of this era Barrett writes: "It continued to be an essential element in Paul's thought that this period could be looked on as a unit of time rather than an indefinite duration."[37] The present age without Christ and the present age of the Lord are contemporary, but their separate and different natures are not lost by any process of intermingling. They are engaged in conflict though not in an ultimate compromsie or appeasement. Lindars has stated: "The effect of the apocalypticizing tendency on theology is to stress the interim between the redemption and the End."[38] It is not necessary to see apocalypticism as the only factor, however, since the same result may be produced by independent causes; but in any case it must be recognized that Paul does attach great importance to the interim. It is in this interim that the Christian life is to be carried on. The characteristics of this unique period have to be recognized for what they are and then utilized. It is a time of suffering and of joy. It has to do with the things that are above and also with things transient, whose reality, in this age, is no less than that of the things eternal. It waits expectantly for that which has not appeared, for " in this hope we were saved," but " hope that is seen is not hope " (Rom. 8:24). It is grounded in the realization that the faithful " have put on the new nature " (Col. 3:10).

The apparently illogical, contradictory character of the Christian present, which can only be described as " already — not yet," is beyond man's powers of comprehension. It may cause some to abandon the suggestion of three ages and to seek some other explanation. Yet, again, Paul is not concerned with mere human wisdom: " Has not God made foolish the wisdom of the world? . . . For the foolishness of God is wiser than men " (I Cor. 1:20, 25). Having accepted these conditions of the present as determined in " God's mystery " (Col. 2:2), Paul outlines the necessary course to be followed by the disciple. From the point of view of the outsider he may seem to be living in two worlds at once, but Paul has in mind the realities of the present age with Christ. Once Paul uses the compound conjunction *hōsei,* " as if," in an exhortation to the Romans to " yield yourselves to God as men who have been brought from death to life " (Rom. 6:13).

It is true that they who had been spiritually dead in their sin had been spiritually restored to life in Christ; but Paul's main point is that they are, in this present Christian age, to conduct themselves as if they had actually been brought by resurrection into the age to come. We can, in the light of this verse, understand why Paul, who frequently employs the simple conjunction " as," or " in the manner of," in at least twenty instances signifies by it " as if." A typical verse is I Cor. 4:7: "If then you received it, why do you boast as if it were not a gift?" In most of these cases Paul is referring to the necessary form of discipleship in this present time. His view is most clearly seen in II Cor. 6:8-10 (my own translation): "We are treated as if we were impostors, and yet we are true; as if we were unknown and yet we are well known; as if we were dying and behold we live; as if we were punished, and yet we are not killed; as if we were sorrowful, yet we are always rejoicing; as if we were poor, yet we are making many rich; as if we had nothing, and yet we possess everything." Nowhere is there a more vivid or more accurate portrayal of the peculiar nature of the interim in which Christians are to be faithful to the Lord who is already risen and still expected.

Paul at times becomes so aware of the impact of the future upon the present that he emphasizes the shortness of the time remaining. This apocalyptic interpretation is especially strong in I and II Thessalonians, and in I Cor., ch. 7, Paul does not foresee the possibility that there will be even a second generation of Christians. He advises the Corinthians not to alter the external conditions of their lives "in view of the impending distress" (I Cor. 7:26). In I Cor. 10:11 he refers to his fellow Christians as those "upon whom the end of the ages has come." In part, he is speaking apocalyptically. The end of one age is at hand and the next is about to be ushered in. The interval is a matter of months or a year or two. But Paul has an even deeper meaning. "The end" and "the ages" are eschatological terms found twelve and nineteen times respectively in Paul's epistles. Whether or not Paul's contemporaries form the last generation of mankind is a secondary consideration in view of his manifestly qualitative view of the age of Christ. Since Christ has brought life and light for the first time into the possible experience of man, all time before him is of an entirely different kind. The midpoint of history has arrived. The duration of this aeon with Christ is inconsequential because no matter what the length of time it may endure, nothing essential will be added to it. Cullmann is a faithful interpreter of Paul when he proclaims: "The present is itself an eschatological period, however long it is to last." [39]

Paul's assessment of the situation of the Christian on this earth is such that it is just as applicable to the believers of this century as it was for the members of the apostolic church. The words of C. H. Thompson may be used to describe the teaching of Paul: "The accent of kerygmatic theology is . . . 'the isness of the shall be.'" [40] Paul pays close attention to what is in the world because Christ lived, died, and rose again. This stress is most clearly demonstrated by the fact that Paul employs two words for "now," *arti* and *nun,* a total of fifty-eight times. In addition, he utilizes "today," *sēmeron,* in three cases; and "already," *ēdē,* is to be found eight times. The contrast between the earlier age and the present is expressed nine times by the phrase "until now" or "until today." A clear statement of Paul's emphasis is presented in II Cor. 6:2. After quoting a verse from Isaiah which has to do with the day of salvation, he announces: "Behold, now is the acceptable time; behold, now is the day of salvation." Thus, the present is a continuing time, until the Parousia; but it is also a condition in which opportunity demands response. Within this area the persistent "now" is timeless.

The presence of Christ in the believer in this age imparts to it something of the nature of the age to come. The blessings to be enjoyed now were not possible in the pre-Christian world. Life, freedom, and the Spirit have been graciously bestowed by God. And yet it must be admitted that the end is not yet. Barrett has noted: "Paul never goes so far as to say that the Age to Come has come." [41] Until the Parousia those on earth "walk by faith, not by sight" (II Cor. 5:7). Our perception is decidedly limited: "Now we see in a mirror dimly, but then face to face" (I Cor. 13:12). Discipleship in this world must always be at least partly aware of the fact that there is one more higher and finer age to come. C. A. A. Scott makes the observation: "Again and again in St. Paul . . . [there appears] the paradoxical assertion of an experience which is complete and yet in process, certain and yet conditioned, present and yet an object of aspiration and hope."[42]

If there is in the present an irresolution between realization and expectation, there is also an unsettled conflict between the old and the new. The plight of the individual believer is forcefully stated by Goguel: "If the justified Christian has become spiritual, he is not so totally. He continues to live in the flesh and to experience its force which pushes him to sin. He has not become incapable of sinning."[43] There is in the Christian awareness a fundamental contradiction. On the one hand, there is the force of "the upward call of God in Christ Jesus" (Phil. 3:14). But on the other, there is the inescapable environment of the present evil age. According to Grundmann: "The Christian is in a state of tension between two actualities. Fundamentally he is delivered from sin, redeemed, reconciled and sinless; as a matter of fact he is at war with sin, which is still threatening, aggressive and dangerous."[44] Paul is able to remind the Romans that those who are in Christ "know that our old self was crucified with him so that the sinful body might be destroyed" (ch. 6:6); yet in the following chapter he is forced to admit that there is in his physical body "another law at war with the law of my mind and making me captive to the law of sin which dwells in my members" (ch. 7:23). The faithful at Colossae, who have "put off the old nature with its practices and have put on the new nature" are nonetheless exhorted not to lie to one another (ch. 3:9 f.).

Believers are not exempt from feeling the power of the flesh which has been captured by sin and is in league with death, but they also have received a real portion of the lifegiving spirit. In order to encourage his bewildered converts Paul announces: "Though our outer nature is wasting away, our inner nature is being renewed every day" (II Cor. 4:16). Ellis interprets this verse as "a contrast between the Christian, i.e., the total self, as he is still related (in his mortality) to the old aeon and the Christian as he is now also related (in his ethic and *Weltanschauung*) to the new aeon through the indwelling Spirit."[45] Romans 12:2 points to the possibility that a believer may slip back and "be conformed to this world," and so Paul calls for a transformation. Since he is a realist, he acknowledges that the Christian is in one sense still in the flesh (cf. Phil. 1:24). Discipleship is not a foolish attempt to deny physical realities. And yet it is also true that discipleship does involve a dying to the flesh. Believers cannot hold to the standard of "this world" because they have begun to live the life of the coming age, but Christianity has not produced a magical change in human nature so that the new nature is suddenly substituted for the old.

The challenge given to the Christian is brilliantly formulated by William Baird: "The man of faith must continue to live in the age of Adam according to the principle of the age of Christ."[46] For Paul peace is one of the qualities of the Kingdom, and it is one of the blessings conveyed by Christ. It is integral to the Pauline figure of reconciliation. However, in this present age with Christ, peace does not mean absence of strife. Tension, contradiction, and contrast are most characteristic of this era. The Christian, and of course only the Christian, is caught in the middle of the play of the forces of the world's age and the coming time. The problems and the opportunities of the Christian life arise from this fact. It is union with Christ that introduces the disciple to a severe conflict that is impossible for the nonbeliever. Only the faithful can know the full truth that "the desires of the flesh are against the

Spirit, and the desires of the Spirit are against the flesh" (Gal. 5:17).

It is at least a possible interpretation, and probably the most convincing, of Rom., ch. 7, that the dramatic account of inner struggle is Paul's description of his own experience since his conversion rather than before it. He discloses the intensity of the contest within him so that his fellow Christians may understand better and be encouraged to remain faithful to their calling. Of this chapter Tasker writes: "Now that salvation had come to him in the mercy of God, he was conscious of a moral struggle such as he had never known before."[47] The present Christian era is not under the control of Satan, but neither is it the time when God will be everything to everyone. Therefore, the faithful are living in a special period which is also "the time between."[48] Life in Christ is a paradox of joy and suffering, victory and combat, realization and hope. Without the tension and the paradox it is not discipleship but something of a different order.

The interim between the resurrection and the Parousia is not, then, simply an awkward interval of waiting in which past and future are mixed in a meaningless jumble. This age of the Lord is in accordance with God's will and therefore has its proper place in the succession of the ages. By the cross the old era is proleptically destroyed and the new life is released. But the cross required suffering (cf. II Cor. 1:5). The fact that Jesus, whom the faithful recognized as Christ, was crucified was therefore "a stumbling block to Jews and folly to Gentiles" (I Cor. 1:23). However, Paul maintained that Christ was obedient unto death before God bestowed on him the name of the Lord (cf. Phil. 2:8 f.). Whitely sees a further result of the Pauline argument: "It would seem that the death of Christ, just because it is once-for-all, not in spite of the fact that it is once-for-all, has lasting effects. And these include a reflection in the church of His suffering."[49]

Union with Christ means a participation in his triumph as well as in the suffering that preceded it. Paul confesses that he has renounced all worldly advantages for Christ " that I may know him and the power of his resurrection, and may share his sufferings " (Phil. 3:10). In fact, in order to share with Christ in the glory of the Last Day it is necessary first of all to suffer together with him (cf. Rom. 8:17). In some manner believers reproduce within themselves the dying and the rising of Christ, and in so doing they manifest his life (cf. II Cor. 4:10). Leivestad makes the careful observation: " It is when dealing with suffering that he [Paul] contemplates most impressively the intimate connection between the Apostle and the Lord, between the Church and Christ." [50] When Paul must defend his apostleship, he reminds the Galatians: " I bear on my body the marks of Jesus " (Gal. 6:17). The tribulations that have scarred his flesh are detailed in II Cor. 11:23-28. Paul is no masochist and has no pathological desire for martyrdom, but his union with Christ enables him to cry: " We rejoice in our sufferings " (Rom. 5:3). The insufficiencies and imperfections of the physical body keep before him his dependence on God (cf. II Cor. 12:10). Moreover, the sufferings of this present time are only a " slight momentary affliction " when compared with the glory of the last age (cf. Rom. 8:18; II Cor. 4:17). The sufferings will sometimes be for fellow Christians (II Cor. 1:7), sometimes for the Kingdom (II Thess. 1:5), sometimes for Christ (Phil. 1:29), and sometimes for God. Rowley summarizes Paul's belief: " All who suffer persecution because of their loyalty to the will and way of God are doing something of vast significance." [51]

It is not easy to perceive Paul's meaning in Col. 1:24: " In my flesh I complete what is lacking in Christ's afflictions for the sake of his body, that is, the church." A preliminary study suggests that Paul may be claiming to fulfill by his own activity a deficiency in Christ's self-offering for the whole world. However, this interpretation is rejected by J. A. T. Robinson: " Paul is not saying that he is making up anything lacking in the sufferings of the head; rather, that, of the overflow of Christ's afflictions which is ever pouring into the Church, he is glad to absorb in his flesh what should be the share of his Colossian brethren and to fill up in *their* stead, *antanaplēroō,* the tax of suffering still outstanding to them." [52]

Pictures of the final sufferings of the world are prominent in apocalyptic writings. They are constructed upon the tenet that there is a fixed amount of tribulation to be endured before the end can come. It is possible that Paul under that apocalyptic influence thought of his own distress as a significant part of the adversity that must still be borne and that he saw himself as thus hastening the end and sparing the church additional hardship. However, he refers to his own afflictions primarily as an example of what all Christians are to accept for their Lord. At one point he makes mention of " the priestly service of the gospel of God " (Rom. 15:16), and he commends the Philippians for " the sacrificial offering of your faith " (Phil. 2:17). It is plain that Paul views all the sufferings of Christians undergone in the name of Christ as a continuation of the work of their Lord. In this way his vicarious passion is not added to but extended.

The life, death, and resurrection of Jesus are not to be repeated. They occurred once in the past and are the one sure foundation for salvation. Nevertheless, as long as there is an age without Christ, contemporaneous with the realm over which he reigns as Lord, there is work to be done. Part of that work is the bearing of suffering, and part is witnessing to the gospel by preaching and mission. Robinson acknowledges: " The circle of Christ's kingship must be filled in and filled out. And the agent of that filling is the Church." [53] Although the age of Christ is a state in which Christians of every century from his resurrection to the Last

Day are in tension and struggle against evil, it is also a segment of time marked by progression toward a goal. Paul's vocabulary, which includes a large number of words for such concepts as "beginning" and "end," "first" and "last," "old" and "new," "before" and "after," "now" and "then," "present" and "coming," "already" and "until," is objective evidence that he possessed a clear sense of chronological order. This principle of development is important to him as he considers that segment of time in which he was placed. Thus, he alerts the faithful in Rom. 13:11: "Salvation is nearer to us now than when we first believed." The reign of Christ is not static. This is basic to Paul's whole conception and is independent of the immediacy with which he expected the Parousia. Hunter has injected a proper note of caution: "Because Paul held that the Day of Christ was not far distant, we too easily forget that he believed the years of grace had a purpose and would last long enough for its fulfillment. That purpose was the evangelization of the world. . . . Clearly Paul does not share modern pessimism about the future of Christ's cause in history." [54]

Paul's attempt in Rom., chs. 9 to 11, to explain why the Jews had not accepted Christ up to that moment reveals one of his central eschatological assumptions. First, the Gentiles are to be converted, and only when that objective is reached, "the full number of the Gentiles" (Rom. 11:25), will salvation be extended to the Jews, "and so all Israel will be saved" (v. 26). When Jews and Gentiles have received the gospel, God's plan to redeem mankind will be accomplished. This end time is determined by God alone, and the earthly failures or successes of the church are not a judgment on the Word of God (cf. Rom. 9:6). Nevertheless, as Barrett has called to our attention: "There is . . . a good deal in the epistles to suggest that Paul viewed the preaching of the Gospel, and the building up of the churches founded under its influence, as a part of the process of eschatology." [55]

Paul speaks of apostles and missionaries as soldiers of Christ, and by this term he links himself to his fellow workers for the gospel (e.g., Phil. 2:25; Philemon 2, 23). They are asked not only to endure but also to attack. They are not fighting a worldly war, yet there are battles to be won in the army of the Lord (cf. II Cor. 10:3 f.). Paul, therefore, at times describes his own commission as one of the chosen leaders in the campaign (e.g., Rom. 15:18). F. C. Grant has noted this characteristic: " In his own self-estimation he was an emissary of the Risen and Glorified Christ, the Heavenly Lord, sent on a flying journey throughout the Gentile world to call all men to prepare for the coming Judgment." [56] In II Thess. 2:6 ff., Paul declares that a restrainer is temporarily preventing the appearance of the man of lawlessness whose absolute perversion will cause the end to come. The traditional interpretation of this reference is offered by Charles: " The power and person who restrain the Antichristian revolution are none other than the Roman empire and its imperial head." [57] In this view the law and order of Rome are making it possible for Christian missionaries to preach to Gentiles first and then to Jews before the final divine intervention. On the other hand, Munck, who regards the call of the apostle to the Gentiles as proceeding from the eschatological plan for evangelizing the whole world before the end of the age, proposes another interpretation: " It must be Paul . . . who is described as *ho katechōn."* [58] By his missionary activity Paul is himself delaying the end and helping to carry out the will of God. The apocalyptic details of this passage in II Thessalonians are unimportant, but in any case they point to the role of this time between. Moreover, Paul knows that he is only one of the apostles, and thus his responsibility is shared by all his brethren.

Although Paul thought only in terms of one generation, he would nevertheless agree with the position of Leivestad:

"The Kingdom of Christ is an expansive power that spreads throughout the world, making ever new territories and people subject to his reign, for salvation and for judgment." [59] The present function of the church is necessarily to be defined eschatologically. Paul's conviction of what the community of the faithful is to do now is manifested in his use of the term "body of Christ." He proclaims to his converts in Corinth: "You are the body of Christ and individually members of it" (I Cor. 12:27; cf. Rom. 12:5 and Col. 1:18). For Paul, "body" always implies function, and the task of the church is to spread the gospel until God gives the order to stop.

Paul does not, of course, hold any view of the progressive realization of the Kingdom on earth. It is not within the power of man to accelerate or retard the purposes of God. Leivestad very properly raises the question: "Are we then to imagine something like a steadily rising curve from the Resurrection to the Parousia, a continuous process in which the events of the Parousia only mean its ultimate perfection?" [60] Paul never forgets that this present time, even though it does include the expanding rule of Christ and other transforming blessings, is not the end. He knows that the age of God will be greater still and that it is not an evolution from this Christian era. Nevertheless, it is the peculiar nature of this age with Christ to contain within itself characteristics of what has taken place in the past and what will happen in the future. The "already" of our experience is a product of the clash between the "no longer" and the "not yet." It is this strange blending which gives significance to the here and now. Eschatology, which is concerned with all ages and times and not just the end, in the opinion of Minear, "elucidates the loyalties and purposes which determine the direction of human activity." [61] When the present Christian aeon is considered by itself for what it is apart from other eras, its qualitative character becomes all the more striking. It is then that, according to

E. F. Scott, " the apocalyptic outlook changes . . . from the category of time to that of place. It is concerned not with the two ages but with the two worlds." [62] Our existence is subject to " the things that are seen " and also to " the things that are unseen " (II Cor. 4:18) ; but our choice between them is real, and the effects are eternal. Eschatology is not a theory of some far-off future but a matter of present import.

Chapter VII — BEGINNING THE NEW LIFE

THE RESPONSIBILITY of the Christian is to be discharged right at this moment. Within the enigmatic age of Christ there is an eternal " now " that recognizes no distinction between the position of the disciples in the first century and that of the faithful in any other period. Without the mighty historic deeds of Christ there could be no salvation, but the only thing that can be done about them now is to accept them by faith or to reject them by unbelief. The last of the ages, the Kingdom of God, is also beyond man's control. Its coming is dependent upon nothing except the divine will. Yet this future, like the past, provides the perspective in which the present finds its meaning. Since the concern of Paul, the missionary, is never theoretical and abstract but always practical that he " might by all means save some " (I Cor. 9:22) , it is to this " time between " in which the faithful are " called to be saints " that he relates all of his eschatological doctrine. The past and the future are directly related to God's redemptive activity. The present, too, is an opportunity provided entirely by his love; but that provision demands a response from every man. The teaching of Jesus on this point is reflected in the frequent occurrence in the Synoptic Gospels of the words " repent " and " repentance." Because Paul is careful not to suggest that man can do anything that will earn salvation, he generally avoids the concept of repentance, with its Hebrew meaning of a deliberate change of direction. The verb is found only once, and the noun is used three times in the Pauline epistles. However, the positive response to the call of God which Jesus termed repentance is at the root of Paul's understanding of baptism. The kerygma had provided the connection as we learn from Peter's sermon on Pentecost: " Repent, and be baptized every one of you " (Acts 2:38). A surprisingly large number of both direct and indirect references to baptism are found in the Pauline writings.

Baptism

There are many reasons why we might expect to find little concern with baptism in Paul's theology. The sacraments were not taken over from normative Judaism but were generally peculiar to Christianity and subject to a large degree of development in the first generations of the church. Paul's writings are the earliest in the New Testament and are not far removed from the beginnings of the new religion. Moreover, an emphasis on the external side of the sacraments led easily and quickly in some quarters to a form of " works righteousness " which was contrary to the basic Pauline principle of justification by faith. The fact that Paul does regard baptism highly and has much to say about it becomes, therefore, all the more significant.

The immediate connection between the baptism of John in the wilderness of Judea and early Christian baptism forms a part of the gospel story. We may also allow for the possibility of influence from the baptismal practice of the Qumran community on the shores of the Dead Sea. It was not just a sacred ceremony that the Christians took over from John; it was also his theology. According to Albrecht Oepke: " The baptism of John is an initiatory rite for the gathering Messianic community." [1] For Paul, too, as well as for primitive Christianity as a whole, baptism presents, first of all, an eschatological perspective. For the Jew, circumcision was the necessary sign and seal of membership in the chosen people of Israel with whom God was working out his purposes. So for Paul entrance into the Christian community (through baptism) is " a circumcision made without hands " (Col. 2:11) . When God imparts his Spirit (in baptism) , he puts his seal upon us (cf. II Cor. 1:22) .

It is everywhere assumed that a Christian is one who has been baptized, no matter what else may be required. Thus, Paul reminds his readers: " By one Spirit we were all baptized into one body " (I Cor. 12:13) . To the Galatians he writes: " As many of you as were baptized into Christ have put on Christ " (ch. 3:27) . There is never a suggestion that one may become united with Christ in any other manner. Furthermore, it is clear that baptism is the ceremony of initiation into the church, which is in this age the body of Christ. As the community of the Spirit, the church is the agency for the furthering of the divine plan for this interim period. By baptism, then, we associate ourselves with the eschatological realities. G. P. Beasley-Murray sums up the argument: " Baptism witnesses a deliverance from the old aeon, an entry into the Kingdom of God's beloved Son, resurrection from the dead, and participation in the victory over all evil powers." [2] By baptism we are brought into the present reign of Christ, and through our union with Christ we are made children of God and so heirs of his coming Kingdom (cf. Rom. 8:16 f.) .[3] To be one with Christ is to share in his work and in his triumph.

The sacraments are symbols of a deeper truth toward which they point and also the effectual means whereby that truth is brought to bear upon this time and place. Paul regards baptism in this double light, and for both aspects the basis is the crucifixion and the resurrection which form two halves of one decisive event. Baptism is a fresh statement of several of the primary assertions of the kerygma and at the same time it is the means of recreating those past occurrences in the lives of the individual believers. Just as Jesus died and was raised once for all, so is baptism administered only once. It is the reception in one moment of a new status, but the stress is inevitably put upon commencement of a continuing life. The baptismal action, as Paul knew it, dramatized its meaning. The descent of the candidate into the water so that the whole body was covered as it is for a drowning person indicated the end of the former existence in the evil world. Paul speaks of the baptized Romans as " men who have been brought from death to life " (ch. 6:13). The believer dies with Christ: " We have been united with him in a death like his " (Rom. 6:5). Grundmann supplies the correct interpretation: " Surrender to Christ in baptism is the real death of the human ego, which is launched upon a new life in the obedience of faith, no longer pleasing itself and managing by itself, but belonging to Christ and under his direction." [4]

As Jesus entered fully into death and then was raised on the third day, so the baptismal candidate is separated by the water from the world and then is led up out of the water into his new existence in Christ. Paul's teaching is direct: " If we have died with Christ, we believe that we shall also live with him " (Rom. 6:8). The Colossians are reminded: " You were buried with him in baptism, in which you were also raised with him through faith in the working of God " (ch. 2:12). Even though the baptized must still undergo physical death, that is now seen as nothing more than a manifestation of the evil in this present world from which the Christian has been freed. It is surely true to say that the resurrection of the faithful begins at their baptism. W. F. Flemington comes to the firm conclusion: " That baptism in St. Paul must be understood eschatologically becomes yet more clear when we penetrate farther into the significance of the connection he traces between baptism and the death of Jesus, and the frequency with which he sees the new moral life of the Christian as a sharing of our Lord's Resurrection." [5]

Although the historic happenings on Calvary and at the tomb are not to be repeated, they are represented and re-created in the baptized so that he may receive the life released for all mankind by the passion of Christ. As in Biblical thinking sin always leads to death, so the righteousness of God in Christ is the source of life. Moule sees that Paul's views lead to still another result: "Those who have been buried by baptism with Christ are already beyond the judgment." [6] To express his convictions Paul utilizes the present indicative: "He who has died is freed from sin" (Rom. 6:7). Because of the fact of baptism in the past, there is a new present reality. And so the Colossians are told: "You have died, and your life is hid with Christ in God" (ch. 3:3). A momentous transformation has occurred, and the former life has been left far behind. Thus, Flemington has sound reason for concluding: "For St. Paul, as for those who were before him in the Gospel, baptism is a sacrament of realized eschatology. St. Paul looks back to baptism as that which marked for each Christian the inauguration of the New Age, the transition from the old life to the new." [7] Of Christians it can be said that God has made alive those who were dead, and because of this sacramental resurrection the new life is the mode of our being.

Baptism, however, cannot properly be a basis for complacency. It is the form of initiation by which we enter the present age with Christ, and by anticipation we are granted eternal gifts. Yet the new life which is thus commenced carries with it its own challenge. The baptized person has not lost the real freedom of his will. Rather, he must now make his decisions upon a higher level. Davies is well aware of this fact: "Paul's manner of referring . . . to baptism in order to enforce the ethical implications of dying and rising with Christ implies that it had ethical significance for the baptized, that the Christian at baptism had been made aware of the moral nature of the new life upon which he was entering." [8] Accordingly, Paul habitually uses imperatives to address the will of the baptized. He charges the Colossian believers: "If then you have been raised with Christ, seek the things that are above" (ch. 3:1). In this verse Paul significantly employs the present and not the aorist tense of the imperative. The obligation imposed by baptism cannot be discharged by a single act; it is a matter of constant and unrelaxed effort.[9] What God does for man in baptism by granting forgiveness and a new status has to be received affirmatively. The Christian is to recognize and act upon the true nature of the divine gift. Paul informs the believers at Rome of their responsibility: "So you also must consider yourselves dead to sin and alive to God in Christ Jesus" (ch. 6:11).

Cullmann has asserted: "In the Eucharist it is the constituted *community,* in Baptism the *individual* inside this community, to whom the death and resurrection are related." [10] It is indeed the individual who by baptism is enabled to become a new creation. It is his sins that are specifically forgiven. The descent into the water and the rising from it are the acts of one person. The free will that is appealed to in order that subsequent conduct may conform to the new life is of necessity the possession of the single man. Repentance requires the unconditioned decision of the individual, and so also must baptism unless it is to be only an external form. And yet this sacrament is for Paul fundamentally corporate. It is the mode of entrance into a community. It is initiation into the present body of Christ. The life that is thus imparted to the individual is the life of the Spirit shared by all the faithful. When the candidate is brought into union with Christ through baptism, he is thereby united with all others who are in Christ. The body of Christ is regarded by Paul as the fellowship in which he alone is the head and in which, therefore, all of the distinctions by which men are otherwise divided have been left behind. In all of his principal references to baptism which have been noted, Paul repeatedly describes the environment as " with Christ " or " in Christ." Baptism necessitates the conversion, decision, and effort of the individual; but its real significance arises from the community and fellowship to which it admits the faithful member. It is only in this corporate relationship that a man may be a part of this interim age.

In the midst of his relatively lengthy discussion of the resurrection in I Cor., ch. 15, Paul suddenly makes a brief reference to the practice of baptism on behalf of the dead (v. 29). There are no indications of such a custom elsewhere in the Pauline epistles or in other Christian literature of the early period. It is unlikely that it was very widespread, and it is by no means certain that Paul gave his approval to it. It is quite possible, on the other hand, that he is taking notice of the practice of just one group of Christians at one place solely to support his argument regarding the certainty, through Christ, of resurrection. In referring to this Pauline verse, Schoeps makes the comment: " In primitive Christianity the sacrament . . . was a miracle-working event." [11] There is a strong implication that by this use of baptism there could be some kind of effective influence over the dead who are otherwise beyond any human control. Whatever may have been the meaning of the custom of baptism for the dead for those who practiced it, it seems clear that Paul's understanding was something different. In his view baptism was surely not a piece of magic. It did not produce a miracle in the commonly accepted sense of the word. As has been already indicated, in I Cor., ch. 15, Paul's argument that the resurrection of Christ assures that of the believers rests squarely on the principle of solidarity, namely, of the identification of the disciples with their Lord, and vice versa. Since it is in the course of this argument that Paul introduces the reference to baptism for the dead, it is evident that what he sees in baptism is the same principle of solidarity. It is, moreover, one further example of Paul's connection of death and resurrection with the baptismal experience.

Since baptism is the door into the present life with Christ and since this interim period is characterized by the unmistakable activity of the Spirit who will be fully revealed in the end, a direct connection between baptism and the Spirit is a logical conclusion. Thus, Paul declares that baptism is " in the name of the Lord Jesus Christ and in the Spirit of our God " (I Cor. 6:11). All who become Christians, no matter what their earthly status, are " made to drink of one Spirit " (I Cor. 12:13). In one instance (II Cor. 1:22), seal, an accepted figure for baptism, and Spirit are mentioned in conjunction with one another. Such evidence is firm support for the statement of E. F. Scott: " For Paul . . . baptism marks the moment in which the Spirit is vouchsafed to the believer." [12] This connection is demonstrated also in Paul's references to the divine sonship which is ours in Christ. Thus, Paul believes: " In Christ Jesus you are all sons of God, through faith " (Gal. 3:26). In the verse following he makes it clear that those who are so reckoned because they are in union with the Lord have been first baptized. The circle is completed when he adds: " Because you are sons, God has sent the Spirit of his Son into our hearts " (ch. 4:6). Two of the three terms are joined together and the third is implied by the context when Paul reminds the faithful at Rome: " You have received [in baptism] the spirit of sonship " (ch. 8:15).

The beginning of the Christian life brings the gift of the empowering Spirit, and it is only in the Spirit that men can comprehend what it means to be sons of God. Against this background we must agree with the position taken by Lee: " It is clear . . . that the work of the Holy Spirit when brought into association with baptism should be placed in an eschatological setting." [13] The Spirit is granted to the individual at his baptism, yet it is given, not for selfish or personal ends, but in accordance with the plan of God for this age. This eschatological aspect is in Paul's mind when he discusses the relation between baptism and the resurrection. Those baptized into Christ have put off the old nature and put on the new man. They have entered a new existence and have already risen with Christ. The explanation for such a result is provided by Paul: "He who is united to the Lord becomes one spirit with him" (I Cor. 6:17). The life-giving Spirit is the source of the new being now, and the same Spirit will be present in the resurrection of the faithful at the last day.[14] Paul is silent about the possibility that the Spirit may come in any other way beside baptism, but that silence testifies to his belief that the Spirit is not a private possession but does the work of God and of Christ.

As Christ died once and cannot die again, so the Christian is baptized once and cannot again assume the position of the unbaptized. Yet unlike Christ, whose death and resurrection are single, decisive, historical acts, the disciple must continue day after day to mortify his body and to seek the heavenly things in order to preserve the identification with the passion of his Lord symbolized and begun in baptism. The sacramental act is not repeated, but the appropriation of its meaning is never finished. It is the required start of life with Christ, but that life is a road to be traveled and not a static point. From Paul's own day it has been all too evident that the Christian may not move along the path marked out at his baptism and may even stray in another direction entirely. As Paul set forth his high doctrine of baptism as the sacrament of initiation into discipleship, he was forced to come to terms with a major problem. The picture has been plainly drawn by E. F. Scott: "Paul is faced by the difficulty that after baptism the Christian remains, to all seeming, as he was before. The quality of his body is unaltered; he is still subject to earthly weakness and accident, and even to the inroads of sin." [15] The mere possibility of postbaptismal sin requires an initial definition of baptism that will not be denied by its occurrence. And yet Paul was certain that baptism meant a final and complete renunciation of all evil. He knows that there can be only one answer to his question: "How can we who died to sin still live in it?" (Rom. 6:2). The conviction of Paul has been rephrased by Flemington: "A Christian who lives an immoral life is utterly belying the meaning of his own baptism." [16] Baptism has produced an essential change, and so Paul asks again: "What has a [baptized] believer in common with an [unbaptized] unbeliever?" (II Cor. 6:15). It was on the basis of such a distinction that the early church began to exclude from its membership those who had made a practical denial of their baptism by openly immoral conduct. The church and the world outside were regarded as two irreconcilable realms. This view is the basis for the discipline proposed for the Corinthian offender in I Cor. 5:1-5.

Whatever baptism may have accomplished, it did not prevent further sin. Thus, Whitely comments: "St. Paul does not regard baptism as something which acts mechanically." [17] The Romans are reminded that whereas the Jews were temporarily rejected because of their unbelief, the Christians remain firm only through faith (and not because of baptism). (Cf. Rom. 11:20.) The Philippians are admonished to "work out your own salvation" (ch. 2:12), and once more the present imperative is used to indicate that it is a continuing responsibility. In I Cor. 10:1-22 Paul reviews the events of the exodus and then by a typological approach relates them to the Christian sacraments. The Jewish people under Moses were the objects of God's special care as manifested in the safe passage through the sea, the moving cloud, and the provision of manna and water in the wilderness. Such providence was a prefiguration of God's final gift of Christ.

Nevertheless, because the people forgot their deliverer and returned to idolatry, they were punished. Paul's conclusion is that the record of these events is a warning for all Christians. The sacraments are signs and channels of the divine power and love; but their operation is not magical, and they do not abrogate the principle of punishment for wrongdoing. They provide strength only for the believer who sees in them the hand of God and offers his own life in response. Paul's understanding of the nature of sacramental operation as applied to baptism is set forth by Barrett: " It admits not to a settled and final state of salvation, but to the dialectic of death and resurrection; not the age to come, but to the inter-penetration of this age and the age to come, which becomes actual for the man who dies and rises daily." [18] Baptism clearly belongs to this " time between " and partakes of its paradoxical nature. It cannot take place more than once for each individual because it does in fact effect a transfer from one age to another. On the other hand, since it is just a beginning and points out the way which may or may not be followed, it speaks also of the " not yet."

The Lord's Supper

Baptism is necessarily a single happening in the life of the disciple, but Paul assumed that the Lord's Supper would be repeated within the Christian community at frequent intervals as long as this age might last. Twenty years of experience and practice lay behind the Pauline accounts. Cullmann writes of the pattern inherited and transmitted by Paul: " The eschatological miracle of the Church is realized above all in the assemblies for worship, which find their crown in the Supper celebrations." [19] Just because the Supper occupied a central place in the tradition in which Paul himself was instructed after his conversion, he does not feel a need to give much special instruction of his own about it. Nevertheless, the earliest extant account of the institution of the Supper is found in I Cor. 11:23-26, even though, like many of the most notable Pauline sections, it is not presented for its own sake but as a support for Paul's injunction to dignified conduct at the celebrations of the Sacrament.

Peculiar to Paul and to the longer text of Luke (ch. 22:19 ff.) is the command of Jesus: "Do this in remembrance of me." The present imperative clearly implies that there is to be a repeated memorial. The celebration is to be continued until the Parousia, which is also the end of the age; and each occasion is a proclamation of the death of the Lord, which marks the beginning of this age and imparts to it its distinctive character. This is the foundation for the declaration of A. J. B. Higgins: "His tradition of the Last Supper preserved the eschatological thought enshrined in it." [20] It is to be noted that the same eschatological element appears in the accounts of each of the Synoptic writers. The Lord's Supper, then, also belongs to this present age with Christ. It is rooted in the start of the age, the crucifixion; and it will be brought to an end at the Parousia. It relates the present believer to the past and to the time to come.

Paul as a Jew recognizes that behind the Lord's Supper is to be seen the concept of the Messianic Feast. According to Schoeps, "This great banquet of the righteous . . . is not mentioned in Tannaitic sources, although it must be older than the latter, as allusions in apocryphal writings show." [21] In any case, the idea undoubtedly forms part of the background for the teaching of Jesus as presented in the Gospels, where a banquet is the setting for several parables, discourses, and a miracle. After an examination of the life and belief of the primitive church Dodd states: "The Eucharist was from the beginning an eschatological sacrament, an anticipation of that heavenly banquet which was the august and mysterious symbol of the perfection of life in the Age to Come." [22] These ideas Paul shared and provided with a sharper development. He alone, along with the longer version of Luke, reports the words of Jesus as declaring that his body was (given) in behalf of the disciples. Likewise, only in these two accounts is there specific reference to Jesus' blood as of the new covenant. In I Cor. 15:50, Paul mentions the traditional phrase " flesh and blood " as a synonym for physical body, but in the three remaining instances where the word " blood " is used it represents the eucharistic presence of Christ under the form of wine. Whitely feels justified in affirming: " The Eucharist is viewed partly as a proleptic participation in the Messianic Banquet, partly as a recalling and making effective of the death on Calvary, regarded as the new covenant." [23] One sure way by which the believer becomes a part of the age of Christ is the reception of the elements of bread and wine in the Lord's Supper.

The word " body," is used by Paul in a number of different senses. In a few cases it denotes the physical organism of Jesus which was put to death upon the cross (cf. Rom. 7:4). It can also stand for the identity and form of self-expression belonging to the risen Christ. Frequently it is a term for the fleshly aspect of our present existence and as such is sinful and perishable. Often, however, it refers to what should be an instrument for God's service and what is for the faithful a temple of the Holy Spirit. The same word defines the mode of being which will be given to those in Christ at the resurrection. In at least nine instances (and there are seven more in Ephesians) it signifies the fellowship of believers with their Lord, the church, by which he continues to extend his rule on earth. Finally, " body " is the reality that is symbolized and conveyed by the bread of the Lord's Supper. Deliberately Paul described the eucharistic presence of Christ by the word which he had already employed in these other ways. For Paul the Lord's Supper was built upon the vicarious self-offering of Christ, and without the resurrection it would be nothing but the memorial of a tragedy. The Lord's death, which is proclaimed in each celebration of the Supper, took place in order to redeem men from their sins and enable them to render acceptable service as sons of God. When sin is overcome, the way is open, through the church, for God to share with all the faithful the eternal life that belongs to his final age. Thus, all the meanings of " body " in Paul's letters are included in " the sacramental body of Christ "; and if we are to understand Paul's view of the Supper we must consider the totality of his thought regarding this word.

Every participant in the Supper must " eat of the bread and drink of the cup " (I Cor. 11:26). Yet Paul is not much interested in the purely material aspect of the Sacrament. Higgins concludes soundly: " In Paul we see the beginnings of a new emphasis on the eucharistic elements themselves. But they are a means of sharing the body and blood of Christ, and are not equated with them." [24] What Paul is trying to present is the meaning of the Supper, first for Jesus himself and then for the loyal participants. The body of the first man, Adam, was physical and was animated by the life of this created world; but the body which Christ now possesses is spiritual and is suited for the life of the Spirit (cf. I Cor. 15:44 ff.). The eucharistic body of Christ, which presupposes the death of his physical body upon the cross, is likewise spiritual. Paul recalls that his Jewish fathers in the time of Moses: " all ate the same supernatural food and all drank the same supernatural drink. For they drank from the supernatural Rock which followed them, and the Rock was Christ " (I Cor. 10:3 f.). It is plain that Paul regards the Lord's Supper as also providing supernatural food and drink. Johannes Behm, commenting on Paul's account in I Cor. 11:25 asserts: " According to the Eucharistic words of institution the blood of Christ is a guarantee of the actualization of the new divine order." [25]

The nature of this interim age allows the faithful to share in Christ's own existence with a concreteness and a reality no less than those of the physical elements of bread and wine. But as the physical body of the historical Jesus has given way to the spiritual body of his resurrection, so the bread and wine point beyond themselves to a divine fellowship. Higgins has suggested: "Union with Christ finds its expression in this societary way in membership of the body of Christ." [26] The unity of the church is demanded and advanced by the sacramental bread. Paul declares in a few words: "Because there is one loaf, we who are many are one body, for we all partake of the same loaf" (I Cor. 10:17). The Christian worshipers are bound to one another and to their Lord through a body, that of the church and that of the Lord's Supper. The concept of the body is essential to Paul's understanding of the nature of Christianity.

Paul does not speculate in the manner of a philosopher as to how the material bread and wine can transmit spiritual power, but he is absolutely convinced that Christ is present in the Eucharist as he is, through the Spirit, in the church. In speaking of the Pauline idea of the Supper, Cullmann declares: "Christ returns already to the assembled congregation, as he one day will come in a way visible to all." [27] And yet the coming of Christ in the Sacrament is not primarily for the comfort and strength that the individual seeks for himself. The Lord's Supper began on the eve of the crucifixion, and it will continue until the Parousia; but in the meantime at each repetition it is a proclamation of the death of the Lord to remind all men that Jesus would not have had to die if it had not been for man's sin. All evil deeds are, therefore, a rejection of Christ's own sacrifice on our behalf. One of the most serious of all offenses against God is sinful conduct at the occasion of the Lord's Supper. Paul feels he must review the narrative of the institution of the Sacrament because selfishness and overindulgence in food and drink mark the church assemblies in Corinth. He is aroused and finds it necessary to rebuke the wrongdoers: "Whoever, therefore, eats the bread or drinks the cup of the Lord in an unworthy manner will be guilty of profaning the body and blood of the Lord" (I Cor. 11:27). The Eucharist is thus not necessarily a blessing. It is the opinion of Higgins that "eating and drinking without discerning the body, which is the same as doing so in an unworthy manner, means conduct at the Lord's Supper which is due to failure to recognize the Church for what it is, the body of Christ, in which the living Lord is present."[28] The Lord is the agent of God's judgment both now and at the Parousia.

The Lord's Supper is inevitably a time of judgment. The only instruction that Paul gives for preparing for participation in the Eucharist is that first "a man examine himself" (I Cor. 11:28). Unless the worshiper fully understands the significance of the sacred meal and conducts himself accordingly, he will be in danger. Paul's warning is direct: "Any one who eats and drinks without discerning the body eats and drinks judgment upon himself" (I Cor. 11:29). The principle is explained by Moule: "To renounce one's Baptism and to display selfish greed at the Lord's Supper are both alike to incur judgment for outrage against the death of the Lord — his body and blood surrendered to death for us."[29] In the section that immediately follows the narrative of institution (I Cor. 11:27-34) Paul concludes his teaching on the necessity for righteous behavior at the gatherings for worship. In order to reinforce his warning he here uses in rapid succession a large number of words, some occurring several times, relating to judgment, which have been previously noted in Chapter IV. They are: unworthy, guilty, examine, judgment, judge, chasten, and condemn. All are connected with the Eucharist. After censuring the unworthy celebrations at Corinth, Paul concludes: " That is why many of you are weak and ill, and some have died " (I Cor. 11:30) . He certainly does not mean to suggest that there is some mysterious and dangerous power resident in the bread and wine which has produced a magical result, but he does proclaim that the principle of divine retribution is not abolished but expounded in the Lord's Supper because the work of Christ, in the crucifixion and in his present rule, is to conquer sin.

The Sacraments and the Ages

Paul's emphasis upon being " in Christ " as constituting for all believers the core of the Christian life has caused some scholars to conclude that he was no longer concerned with time or the passing of the ages. Thus, according to F. C. Grant, " *Paul was a mystic.* At the very heart of his religious life . . . glowed a union with the divine person which transcended language and even thought. . . . This is the topmost peak of the religious approach to God, where the next step is off into a realm beyond space and time and concrete thought." [30] Albert Schweitzer also stresses the mysticism which he believes was central in Pauline thought. However, he places it in a different perspective, and he maintains that an eschatological concern is manifested in the Sacraments. It is his conviction that " separated from the eschatology, the Pauline sacraments would become meaningless and ineffectual. . . . The sacramental conception of the Apostle is therefore derived from an entirely different world of thought from that of the Mystery-religions." [31] It is not mysticism but eschatology that accounts for Paul's view of Baptism and the Supper of the Lord.

It is undeniable that for Paul the Sacraments do lead to

the presence of the Lord in the believer, but their purpose is not a mystical communion. Their essential context is a corporate entity, and only within the body do they strengthen the individual. Schoeps points out: " In the understanding of the apostle, baptism and the Lord's Supper anticipate the saving gifts of the future, making them effective in the present; they are the link between the two aeons." [32] That which strictly speaking belongs only to the age to come is through the Sacraments partially experienced in this time. Dahl has written: " The resurrection hope looks forward to a mode of existence different from the present one, which is, nonetheless, already anticipated in the sacramental fellowship of the Church." [33] We have seen above how the Last Judgment is foreshadowed in both Baptism and the Eucharist. The revealed will of God which will be fully established in the last time is already at work in this age, and thus what is to come is not different in kind from what the Christian encounters in his sacramental worship. The statement of Dodd is solidly supported by the writings of Paul: " Past, present and future are indissolubly united in the sacrament." [34] The same thing is true also of Baptism. Both Sacraments are inexplicable without reference to all three tenses.

The claim that in the Pauline view the Sacraments are basically mystical experiences is weakened also by their foundation in historical events. Firmly embedded in the Gospel tradition is the statement that Jesus himself was baptized by John. Christian Baptism, which follows his example, includes in its meaning the redemption brought about by the passion of Jesus. Thus, Oepke maintains: " Standing in a definite and absolutely indispensable historical context, baptism derives its force from the reconciling action of God in Christ." [35] Paul's review of the events of the Last Supper is prefaced by his careful claim that he had received this information " from the Lord " and that he had in turn transmitted it to the Corinthians. These are solemn facts which were included in the common tradition long before Paul's conversion. The Supper is precisely dated as having occurred " on the night when he was betrayed " (I Cor. 11:23). The concern for historicity is of the same kind as was to be reflected in the creedal affirmation that Jesus was crucified under Pontius Pilate. Higgins makes the suggestion: " It is very probable . . . that what Paul did was to lay a renewed emphasis on the remembrance of the death of Christ which was already present, but which at Corinth was in danger of being forgotten." [36] Paul acknowledges that the present realization of future joys is a part of the sacramental life, but he insists that without the historic deeds of Jesus there would be no " time between " in which the believers are invited to share.

Although they draw upon the past and the future, the Sacraments are limited in their operation to the present. For each Christian, baptism is a past event, but its real significance lies in its continuing force. It has conveyed to us the very life in which we live. The Eucharist does far more than simply recall the past. Of course, it must be granted that in Paul's Corinthian correspondence we have a picture of Christianity at a relatively early stage. Eucharistic theology, with its attempt to define the mode of Christ's presence, has not yet been developed. Nevertheless, Paul describes the Lord's Supper as a participation in the body and blood of Christ (cf. I Cor. 10:16). It is only in this service that these two aspects of the physical life of Jesus surrendered in death are found together, and they appear in this context, not as reference to history, but as the basis of a living fellowship between the faithful and Christ. The primary reality is a vertical communion with the Lord, but because the participation is by all believers together, there is also a horizontal sharing that creates a new bond of union.

It is in the Eucharist that Christians have their first true knowledge of the nature of the coming fulfillment and consummation. Neville Clark shows how this Christian experience grows out of the old covenant: " As the Jewish passover stood between the Exodus-Sinai deliverance and the messianic age, so the eucharist stands between the passion-resurrection and the parousia." [37] Paul acknowledges with regard to the revelation granted to all disciples: " We have this treasure in earthen vessels " (II Cor. 4:7). Christians must still live on earth and not in heaven; they have received grace but not yet glory. They know only in part and only later will understand fully; they have been redeemed but still are sinful. For these reasons the Eucharist is needed in this age. The repeated command, " Do this in remembrance of me " (I Cor. 11:24 f.) does provide that the celebration of the Supper shall be in memory of Jesus' acts; but the word translated " remembrance," *anamnēsis,* includes the idea of receiving Christ in a realized, corporate experience. This interpretation is supported by Behm, who declares: " Christians are to enact (*poieō*) the whole action of the Lord's Supper . . . in recollection of Jesus, and this not merely in such sort that they simply remember, but rather, in accordance with the active sense of *anamnēsis* . . . in such a way that they actively fulfill the *anamnēsis.*" [38] When the death of Christ is viewed clearly and when it is accepted as the sure basis of salvation, then there is such union with him that he is truly at hand.

Baptism and the Lord's Supper fulfill their divinely determined role in this present age, yet a portion of their task is to point beyond themselves to the time of the end. The new life that is begun in Baptism can never be brought to perfection in this world. It is Baptism that gives the promise of sharing in the glory belonging to the sovereign God. According to Clark, " The rite remains a sacrament of inaugurated eschatology." [39] The end does not belong to the " time between." Moreover, Paul proclaims that all those in Christ shall be resurrected at the last day (cf. I Cor. 15:22). Inasmuch as the Sacraments enable the believers to be and to continue to be in Christ, they are guarantees of that resurrection. The Sacraments are gifts of the Lord, but Paul preaches that the Lord has come already and also that he will come again at the end. More than any single practice of the Christian life the Sacraments provide the answer to the problem of time. In the fullness of their meaning they are inseparable from the past and the future, and they speak to our present. They are the fruit of the work of Christ, and only in him can we see that all the ages are in the hand of God.

Chapter VIII | GROWING UP TO GOD

THE PRESENT AGE with Christ begins with his cross and empty tomb, and will persist until his task of reconciling the world to God is finished. It is one of the succession of ages which together constitute the plan of God, and it follows the time before Christ had come and precedes the era of God's absolute rule in which every enemy will have been destroyed. Yet within this age considerations of chronological order give way to an emphasis upon the unique quality of a particular moment. The nature of the " now " is such that it makes no distinctions among Christians of one or another generation. The date of the expected Parousia is far less important than the sense of urgency that it conveys. The Sacraments point to the " existence " that is peculiar to the Christian aeon. There is a tendency to regard the past and the future as of largely theoretical interest because they lie beyond the control of the disciple and to lay hold of the possibilities that lie at hand. It is only the present to which the believer can respond. At first glance eschatology may seem to have been left along the way in a more " practical " concern.

Moreover, it is as we view the present in this manner that we are led to assess the problem of the relationship between the individual and the group. All existentialism deals with the actual and potential meaning of each single life. It speaks of the utilization and interpretation of experiences as they happen to human beings one by one. In these terms Paul is something of an existentialist. On the other hand, eschatology supposedly has to do with large groups of races and nations. As it portrays the goal toward which all things are being led, it describes movements and powers and the larger framework in which alone the individual finds a place. In this approach Paul is an eschatologist. It would seem that Paul is logically inconsistent in presenting at the same time two irreconcilable poles of thinking. According to Goguel, the insistence upon the responsibility of the individual and the vision of God's purposes for society and nature " are not two phases in Paul's eschatology, but two currents which run side by side without commingling. One comes from Judaism and is a collective eschatology. The other, which is an eschatology for the individual, springs from Paul's experience as a Christian." [1] We have discovered that in spite of the fact that a faithful disciple is already in Christ, salvation in Paul's view is basically a future concept because only at the consummation is reconciliation complete for all creation. Yet Paul teaches that the believer is resurrected immediately at physical death without having to wait for the end, and judgment is taking place now even though there will be a universal tribunal on the last day. Accordingly, some scholars have maintained that an overall view of Paul's thought must lead to the conclusion that even in his eschatology he provides a much larger place for the individual than for the group. Grundmann's opinion is representative: " The temporal-apocalyptic expressions are helpful introductions which serve as illustrations; not they but the personal-communicative expressions are determinative for the eschatological thought of Paul." [2]

It must be granted that there is much in the Pauline writings that rises above limitations of time and place in dealing with that which is eternal and that which is not seen. This material is expressive of the fact that the individual is the final center for Christian experience. However, Paul's eschatology would seem to rest solidly upon the twin foundations of the individual and the corporate and upon the timeless and the temporal; and it is more likely that it is the corporate and the succession of time which give meaning to the qualitative experience of the single believer. The truth can be found only by a thorough study of the place of the individual in Paul's teaching.

The Basic Decision

Paul presents the entire range of the Christian life in terms of a fellowship or sharing. The body of Christ is a corporate reality in which believers are joined to their Lord and to one another. The gifts of the Holy Spirit are depicted only in terms of the church. Baptism is initiation into its fellowship, and the Lord's Supper is the feast of the body. Nevertheless, Paul's limited sympathy for idealism and the theoretical causes him to give attention to the actualizing of the fundamental principle of communion in the response of the individual. Ellis has made the clear observation: " It is not without significance, therefore, that virtually every reference to the Christian's crucified and resurrected status is coupled with an ethical command." [3] The faithful at Rome, like all baptized persons, have died to sin and are alive to God. Yet Paul is compelled to order them, through their individual wills: " Let not sin therefore reign in your mortal bodies " (ch. 6:12). For the Christian there still remains a free choice, and each alternative has its foreseeable results: " If you live according to the flesh you will die, but if by the Spirit you put to death the deeds of the body you will live " (Rom. 8:13). Those who have already received baptism are told: " Put on the Lord Jesus Christ, and make [present imperative] no provision for the flesh " (ch. 13:14). The new life that is bestowed in Baptism can be retained only by the constant obedience of the human will which has no meaning unless it is subject to personal decision. In his discussion of marriage in I Cor., ch. 7, which shows knowledge of the teaching of Jesus on the same subject, Paul recognizes the power of the influence of husband and wife upon each other so that an unbelieving partner may receive consecration from the faith of the other (vs. 14 f.). Yet the individuals continue to be known by the basic distinctions of believer and unbeliever. Again, social forces and obligations do not alter or obscure the assigned place of choice and decision.

The genuineness of the freedom of the disciple to act is demonstrated negatively by the all too evident evil found even in Christian circles. This is one further aspect of the "time between" that is incomprehensible to the human mind. All of the Pauline references furnish support for Oepke's conclusion: "An immediate and almost magical transformation of human nature, in which sin is eradicated, is no more a part of Paul's logic than an immediate destruction of sin and death."[4] For Paul, the gift of the Spirit, even in the form of a guarantee, a down payment of the initial products of the coming crop, is the proof of God's saving love and the source of strength for the disciple. It is the Spirit that enables us to call Jesus Lord and to obtain and cherish our status as sons of God. It is in the Spirit that we are to walk day by day. Yet the power of the Spirit does not overcome us and compel us to do that to which we have not consented. A believer is baptized only once, but he may fall from grace and in practice deny his baptismal status. Justification is offered to all in Christ, but sin is a human act that is still common in this age. Moule has made an observation as true of the time of Paul as of our day: "Individual Christians and the corporate Church alike are continually failing to live by the absolutes into which baptism is declared to have brought them."[5] Paul is very sure that a disciple who becomes unfaithful may in the end be rejected if he persists in his disobedience. Previous status provides no exemption from the law that the unrighteous will not inherit the Kingdom (cf. I Cor. 6:9).

Paul is deeply distressed wherever he encounters wrongdoing among Christians. In his eyes it is an intolerable situation because the church and the world represent two separate realms. He is intensely angered by the failure of the community at Corinth to drive out from their midst the member who had committed unspeakable immorality (cf. I Cor. 5:1-13). He instructs the church to exercise the extreme discipline of delivering " this man to Satan for the destruction of the flesh, that his spirit may be saved in the day of the Lord Jesus " (v. 5). Since Paul is dealing here with a disciple, he is admitting the possibility that salvation can be accepted and then lost again, and so he calls for urgent measures. On the other hand, he is unwilling to declare that even a grievous offender against God and the church is beyond the possibility of salvation.

Paul concludes his most extended account of his hardships and undertakings in behalf of Christ with a reference to " the daily pressure upon me of my anxiety for all the churches " (II Cor. 11:28). Surely that anxiety consisted in large measure of concern for the conduct of his converts. We find a reflection of this apprehension in I Thess. 3:5: " I sent that I might know your faith, for fear that somehow the tempter had tempted you and that our labor would be in vain." A similar concern is shared with the Galatians, Corinthians, Philippians, and Colossians. The possibility of refusing by disobedient actions the salvation offered by the love of God was so strong in Paul's understanding that we discover in his letters a surprisingly large number of allusions, thirteen in all, to his own struggle with the threat of failure. In his more exuberant moments in which he reviews his accomplishments Paul can say: " His grace toward me was not in vain " (I Cor. 15:10). In fact, no work done in Christ is pointless (cf. ch. 15:58).

But in discouraging situations, as when the Galatians are apparently turning to the legalists, Paul cries out: "I am afraid I have labored over you in vain" (ch. 4:11). His unending care, therefore, is that the gospel may be so preached and so followed that his converts and he may not fall short of the opportunity before them.

If the Christian is thus free to disobey even though the principle of retribution remains unchanged, he is equally free to obey the demands of God. In fact, it is precisely because man has been given freedom that he is also entrusted with responsibility; and since Christian freedom is the highest form of liberty possible in this age, the divine imperative meets the believers most directly. We have to do not with an ethical philosophy that advocates the systematic elimination of vices and the cultivation of virtues but with the requirement for radical obedience. Moreover, at no point does Paul ever insist that moral character must precede or in any way contribute toward salvation. It is essential in Paul's thinking to see that the love of God is free and unconditioned and that man is incapable, even by the positive exercise of his free will, of coming to his own aid. Yet an immoral life is incommensurate with Christian discipleship, and moral conduct is the fruit of the Spirit reigning within. Filson has summarized: "The demands of God are not withdrawn, but they are now [for the Christian] possible of fulfillment." [6] The righteousness of God becomes a resident force providing a new dimension to man's existence.

The sole standard that is relevant for the activities of the faithful is the holiness in which they have been called. Paul advises his converts that, provided their faith is unfaltering, the Lord Jesus Christ "will sustain you to the end, guiltless" (I Cor. 1:8). If we respond in love, Christ will establish our hearts "unblamable in holiness" at the last day (cf. I Thess. 3:13). The expectations are absolute and contain no allowances for adjustments or compromise. The believers, who in this life are permitted to enter the body of Christ, are assigned their special duties. They are both individually and corporately a temple of the Holy Spirit, but a temple where sin is always at the door and often makes a forcible and violent entry. All of the baptized are " called to be saints " (cf. Rom. 1:7; I Cor. 1:2). They have received a new life in which they are to be free from bondage to things of this world. However, this world is still very much at hand and remains a strong challenger for man's allegiance. The resulting anomaly is well described by Donald J. Selby: " Paul's admonitions are therefore ' to become what you are ' in Christ. . . . [They] are addressed to the paradoxical situation in which the believer finds himself." [7] The disciple both is and is not yet because the age of which he forms a part also is and is not yet.

The reality of the freedom to choose which belongs to the disciple is also demonstrated by the nature of the unshakable responsibility placed upon him. For Paul, as for Jesus, what a man does is the external expression of what he is. Faith and conduct cannot be separated. Likewise, the deeds that a Christian does perform must be ascribed ultimately to God's Spirit when they are good, but cannot be blamed on any power other than our own consent when they are evil. Filson examines the literature and reaches the conclusion: " In addition to the plain references to judgment scattered through his letters, the constant use of the imperative mood implies that man is responsible for the use of his abilities and opportunities." [8] God is just in not requiring more than he has made possible through the gift of the Spirit, and the man in Christ does share his life. Therefore, the Christian is held accountable for his potential as God knows it.

At this juncture, however, we must take note of the Pauline emphasis upon the sovereignty of God. In the course of his argument regarding the divine purpose for Israel according to the flesh, Paul makes perhaps his strongest statement regarding predestination: " So then he has mercy upon whomever he wills, and he hardens the heart of whomever he wills " (Rom. 9:18). By itself, this verse along with several others allows no room for human free will and so for human responsibility. However, in the context of Rom., chs. 9 to 11, Paul passes quickly from the argument from divine ordering to a second argument from the disobedience of Israel and then to a third based on a judgment from final results. It is true that Paul holds fast to the belief in the supremacy of God's will, yet he does not thereby abandon his conviction that the Christian is free and accountable. After careful study Sanday admits: " There is an . . . inconsistency in St. Paul's language regarding divine sovereignty and human responsibility." [9] The two principles are made a part of one statement addressed to the Philippians: " Work out your own salvation with fear and trembling; for God is at work in you " (ch. 2:12 f.). The interpretation of Filson is consistent with all the facts: " Paul held the two lines of thought together at the same time and without any feeling of inconsistency." [10] Paul was certainly not aware that he was contradicting himself, but he was convinced that the truth in this matter was twofold. In commenting on the Pauline view A. B. D. Alexander has suggested: " The work of God requires also the activity and co-operation of man, and therefore this progressive sanctification is frequently presented by the apostle as a *human* act." [11]

God himself has chosen to respect the free will that he granted to man in creation as a share in his own sovereignty. Even salvation is therefore not forced upon man. That is why Paul affirms that justification, the effective offering of redemption by God, is by faith, the channel of man's positive response. The presence of God's power in man's good deeds does not destroy his individuality; it fulfills it. The usually unexpressed assumptions of Paul are succinctly set forth by Beardslee: " Paul's deepest understanding of man's work is that God, in His great task of saving men, has chosen to act through the work of men." [12] Men do not, of course, bring the work of God to completion. That is reserved for the final triumph with which God's age will begin. However, in this intermediate age the faithful are correctly described as " fellow workers for God " (I Cor. 3:9). It is in the acceptance and discharge of this commission that the disciple is enabled to realize his individuality. God has need for the services of each believer in the working out of his plan. Every Christian is to be regarded as " the brother for whom Christ died " (I Cor. 8:11). Accordingly, each man in Christ may find the fulfillment of his own life by such a perfect obedience to God's command that outward circumstances will no longer matter and also by making whatever particular contribution his special gift from God is intended to add to the advancement of the divine plan (cf. I Cor. 12:4 ff.).

Reinhold Niebuhr has shown how this Pauline emphasis has affected our present understanding: " Each individual has a direct relation to eternity; for he seeks for the completion of the meaning of his life beyond the fragmentary realizations of the meaning which can be discerned at any point in the process where an individual may happen to live and die. . . . But each individual also has an indirect relation to eternity. Insofar as he takes historical responsibilities seriously, he must view the problem of fulfillment from the standpoint of the ultimate and final 'end.' " [13] The redemptive work of God is personal. It is sustained by groups but made effective in the intimate relationship of faith.

Since Christian discipleship can fairly be termed the lifelong discharge of the obligation imposed upon the individual in his baptism, it requires his maximum effort. In this matter one's own responsibility cannot be taken over by another or by a group. With the help of the Spirit, Christians are to work for attainable goals, which are those of this age of Christ. From his own experience Paul knows that discipleship involves toil, suffering, and hardship. He has seen the exertions of an entirely different sort offered by athletes and soldiers in their own causes, and he turns to them for graphic illustrations of the required dedicated effort. Thus, the Christian life may be looked at as a race to be won by the swiftest and best controlled runner (cf. I Cor. 9:24). The Christian, like the winning trackman, refuses to dissipate his energy by looking behind him but concentrates on the goal by straining forward (cf. Phil. 3:13 f.). Present effort is directly related to future results. The believer may also be said to be participating in a boxing match in which every blow is to count and none can be wasted, and therefore the preliminary training is as important as the actual engagement (cf. I Cor. 9:26 f.). But there are military metaphors, too. We are all involved in a decisive conflict (cf. Phil. 1:30). The Christian is to put on the armor of light, the breastplate of faith and love, and the hope of salvation for a helmet (cf. Rom. 13:12; I Thess. 5:8). He is a soldier, under orders and charged to defeat the enemy; and in the struggle the stronger contender will prevail.

In the full sense of the word, salvation lies beyond this intermediate age of Christ. Its time draws nearer but cannot come until the end (cf. Rom. 13:11). The culmination of discipleship is to be "with Christ"; but that, too, belongs to the last time, and in this age the faithful are "in Christ" (cf. Phil. 1:23). The resurrection of the believers forms part of the beginning of God's age even though the resurrection of Christ ushered in the interim period. However, it must also be made clear that in Christ the disciples may experience in the present time something of the affairs of eternity. Cullmann observes in this regard: "A hope that is directed entirely to the future paralyses action in the present." [14] Thus, a futuristic eschatology is usually judged to be irrelevant for contemporary needs. However, according to Bicknell, " In St. Paul, eschatology does not weaken but strengthen the call to present sanctification." [15] It is striking that most of Paul's appeals to the free will of the Christian to decide for moral behavior are put in an eschatological setting. Life in Christ and life in the Spirit are constant reminders of the passing from the old to the new. They stand closer to the coming age than to the past. In spite of the fact that salvation belongs essentially to God's coming age, twice Paul refers to us " who are being saved," as a description of our existence now (cf. I Cor. 1:18; II Cor. 2:15) . In its root form, salvation is a personal relationship of the individual.

The word for " temptation " is an apocalyptic term which, in the Lord's Prayer and elsewhere in the Gospels, refers to the severe afflictions that were expected to mark the end of this evil age. However, the usage is different in the Pauline letters. Lindars declares in this regard: " Paul . . . shows a tendency to treat the expected time of testing in a virtually timeless way, applied to temptation in the spiritual life." [16] We read in I Cor. 10:13: " God is faithful, and he will not let you be tempted beyond your strength." The strength in question is the Spirit of God released for work by a personal surrender. Paul has no doubts about the reality of this internal sustenance, but he acknowledges that it cannot be observed by the physical senses. Beardslee has made a further comment on this aspect of the apostle's thought: " Paul does not interpret the struggle of God and the powers of darkness in an objective, speculative way, as often in the apocalyptic literature. Rather he transfers the metaphors of struggle into the life of the believer and of himself." [17] In Col. 3:3, Paul asserts that the faithful have died and that their life " is hid with Christ in God." They are also said (ch. 3:1) to have been " raised with Christ." That which is above is one with that which is within. Baptism involves an identification with the passion of the Lord (cf. Rom. 6:4 ff.; Col. 2:12) . So that we may be glorified with him, it is necessary and possible that we suffer with him (cf. Rom. 8:17). Paul confesses that because he has been crucified with Christ, Christ lives in him (cf. Gal. 2:20).

Throughout the epistles the historic salvation events are brought into the closest connection with the innermost experiences of the individual Christian. Paul's "Christ mysticism" has seemingly produced a reinterpretation of eschatology. Schweitzer has pointed out the effects of this emphasis: "Paul's conception is, that believers in mysterious fashion share the dying and rising again of Christ, and in this way are swept away out of their ordinary mode of existence, and form a special category of humanity."[18] Dying with Christ means the reenactment of the love, dedication, and obedience of his death, whereas rising with him means the renunciation of the things of this world and sole reliance on the power of God's Spirit. Such discipleship is the life of the present age of Christ. Its home is the Christian community, but its field of operation is the commitment of the individual believer.

Salvation Continues

Paul resisted firmly any suggestion that the deeds of God in Christ were not sufficient to achieve the salvation of all mankind. He reacted violently to all forms of Gnosticism with their implication of adding something essential to Christian truth. On the other hand, he believed that the historic Christ events had produced the present intermediate time in which Christians are to follow their Lord. Referring to the past deeds that constitute the vital core of our belief, Caird observes: "Man's appropriation and understanding of that revelation is a slow and lengthy process."[19] It is important to remember that in Paul's thinking the age without Christ and the age of Christ are contemporary in the same world. The age of Christ is, therefore, placed within the framework of human history; and its course is to be understood at least partially in terms of growth and development. This is especially true of the lives of the individual Christians. For them the meaning of salvation requires the use of the concept of continuing process. Moule makes the helpful observation: "The Christian's hope is not to be measured primarily in terms of lapse of time but in terms of the continuous working out to its completion of a *datum* already given — namely the incarnation." [20]

The quantitative fact of the passage of time has in itself very little significance either for society or for the individual in Paul's eyes. The work of God is advanced not by time but by the use of time. Nevertheless, discipleship demands perseverance and endless effort. Paul's task was to convert and to sustain, because baptism is a beginning and a continuation. Davies states: "Paul the *kērux* had to become *didaskalos,* the father of his converts in life as well as in faith, their trainer in 'the race' or 'boxing contest' of the Christian discipline." [21] Paul is concerned to show how the initial step of baptism is followed by a relentless struggle to remain faithful to what has been begun and to reject its opposite. The end of the way is the glory of God, and there are innumerable signs along the road. Paul sees the Spirit, received in Baptism, as effecting a gradual but ultimately complete transformation if it is not hindered. Thus, he proclaims: "We all . . . are being changed into his likeness from one degree of glory to another; for this comes from the Lord who is the Spirit." (II Cor. 3:18.)

Paul's most extensive treatment of the final events of history is contained in I Cor., ch. 15. Yet even here he moves rapidly from the entrance of sin into the world in Adam to the death and resurrection of Jesus, and then from the destruction of all God's enemies, including death itself, to the coming of Christ and the resurrection of the faithful. The end is God's perfect rule. Robinson makes a powerful protest: " The habit of treating I Cor. 15 in isolation from the rest of Paul's writing has tended to obscure its connection with the very much larger number of passages which depict this gradual transformation and glorification of the body from baptism onwards." [22]

Perhaps the majority of scholars understand sanctification to be one of a number of figures for salvation in Paul's highly colorful language. On the other hand, there are those who claim that sanctification is a Pauline designation for the advance in holiness that must characterize healthy discipleship. Goguel, who is a representative of the latter group, has explained this interpretation briefly: " Sanctification is at the same time an effort demanded of man on which depends the achievement of his salvation . . . and also a work of the Holy Spirit." [23] Sanctification means, first of all, the release of the Spirit to provide needed strength and direction in daily discipleship, but secondly, it means depth and perseverance in personal response. Justification recalls a single act and point in which the faithful are given a new status, but sanctification reminds us that the course of salvation requires effort and time. Paul instructs the Christians at Rome: " So now yield your members to righteousness for sanctification " (ch. 6:19). Firmness in our loyalty to the revelation of God in Christ will result in the extension of Christ's control.

Salvation has many of the aspects of a process, and discipleship is a constant and developing course; but the Christian life is not without termination or goal. As long as this present age endures, there is time; but the time is always short, and there is an urgency about our decisions (cf. Rom. 13:11 f.). What we seek, therefore, is a clue regarding the meaning of the time that is available now. Paul accepted the view that the age of creation preceded the historical age before Christ. He also believed that this present interim time would be followed by the age to come. Of this scheme Dodd writes: " History, as a process of redemption and revelation, has a beginning and an end, both in God. The beginning is not an event in time; the end is not an event in time. The beginning is God's purpose; the end is the fulfillment of His purpose." [24] In this interpretation, time, too, is a creature and thus an instrument of God. It is important only as it relates to the divine plan embracing all the ages.

Bultmann is a true interpreter of Paul when he declares: " The time between the Resurrection of Christ and his expected Parousia has not only chronological but also essential meaning. It is this meaning which gives to the Christian life its character as Christian." [25] In Rom. 10:4, Paul proclaims that " Christ is the end of the law." He describes how the whole legalistic system symbolized by Moses has been done away with by the one who has provided a new and effective salvation. The Law is finished, and its day is now over. But the word " end " has a second denotation: it indicates the purpose or goal that is there from the beginning and becomes a part of the course being run. Thus, Paul is also saying that Christ is the goal of the Law. The Law is given by God and is included in his plan; but its function is dependent, and its time is strictly limited. The Law must always look beyond itself to Christ. It becomes apparent, then, that in Paul's thinking eschatology is not just a question of the end of things but of the relationship of present experience to that which permeates all things. Niebuhr again relates the Pauline view to our understanding: " This double connotation of end as both *finis* and *telos* expresses, in a sense, the whole character of human history and reveals the fundamental problem of human existence." [26] Through Christ we who have our discipleship in this " time between " are joined to the beginning and the end of all history.

Redemption springs solely from the love and power of God. His goodness is prior even to our need, and our love is a reflection of his. The ground of our hope is the fact that God is faithful. Nevertheless, God has assigned a necessary role to man. Filson summarizes Paul's teaching: " Ultimately all credit goes to God. . . . But the human will is responsible for complete obedience and devotion to the purposes of God." [27] Paul asserts that in the gospel " the righteousness of God is revealed through faith for faith " (Rom. 1:17) . The form of the Greek *ek pisteōs eis pistin* indicates that by his own decision man accepts God's offer and that his will is strengthened to make more and more such decisions until his only aim is the service of God. We are asked to surrender all our selfish interests, but the resulting discipleship is not our achievement. We have created nothing. It is, rather, our response to God's initiative.

Paul's most frequent and characteristic description of discipleship is life " in Christ." It should also be noted that what seems most desirable to him about the coming age is that the faithful will be " with Christ." He confesses: " For to me to live is Christ " (Phil. 1:21) . Christ is at the center of his theology of salvation and of his hope for the future. Beare presents a sound interpretation of the Pauline evidence: " As risen with Christ from death to a new and heavenly life, the Christian is to focus all his thoughts and desires upon heaven, the sphere of his risen and exalted Master." [28] And yet this is not escapism from an evil world. The sphere of Christ's rule is not some unknown place above the earth, but where he has been accepted on earth. The moral life of the disciple is not something that he deliberately fashions in accordance with a recognized standard. It is the inevitable expression of the acceptance of Christ as Lord. Since Jesus demonstrated a unique character, it is to be expected that the qualities of his life will be reflected in the lives of his followers.

The much discussed christological passage dealing with the " self-emptying " of Christ is introduced with the injunction: " Have this mind among yourselves, which you have in Christ Jesus" (Phil. 2:5). What follows is theology, but the occasion for its inclusion in the epistle is the need to stress the importance of humility in the Christian life; and humility, like all the virtues, is found supremely in Jesus. Because he was "born of woman, born under the law," he is also "the first-born among many brethren." He is a pioneer and a guide, and the disciple follows his lead. Paul's deep sense of responsibility for all that happens to his converts is exhibited on every hand, but his task is to win them to God through Christ and not to himself. As a father in the faith he urges, without presumption: "Be imitators of me, as I am of Christ" (I Cor. 11:1). Christ is the example and pattern for all the believers, the Corinthians and Paul himself. Thus, Davies declares unequivocally: "The imitation of Christ is part and parcel of Paul's ethic." [29] That imitation cannot be understood as consisting of a mechanical or literal reproduction. It is an awareness of the presence of Christ, the yielding to his Spirit, and a voluntary association with his unfinished work. We can discover the basis for the conclusion of Beardslee: "Imitation of Christ, in Paul's thought, thus does not lead toward any conception of an independent repetition, in the believer, of what God has done in Christ." [30] For Paul, Christ and his atonement must always remain unique, but the wonder is that we have been called to enter into a union with him. One further truth has been noted by Alexander: "Christ is example, but He is more, He is also *Power*." [31] He is not simply up ahead of us; he is alongside of us and in us. He shows us the goal and he is himself the way.

The Kingdom, as the establishment of God's will, is not built by any human progress. Furthermore, growth and development in this interim period are always relative and can never be absolute. Perfection is to be found only in the coming age. Yet growth is clearly a constituent element of this present time, and as such it demands further treatment. Barrett reminds us that "Paul is always cautious of expressions which might suggest that the Christian has already reached his goal." [32] Paul is himself no exception since he admits: "Not that I have already obtained this or am already perfect" (Phil. 3:12). On the other hand, he is very far from leaving all striving to the future. The Pauline viewpoint is presented by Hamilton: "Because the new age has made itself felt, the Christian experiences spiritual growth, ethical victory, a sloughing off of sins, and exercising of gifts to the strengthening of the Church, and obedience to God." [33]

As a way between the "no longer" and the "not yet" the Christian life cannot be truly understood in terms which do not include the concept of growth. The relativities of this age always stand in sharp contrast against the absolutes of the last day, and one of these present limitations is the inevitability of an end to time, usually dramatized by some form of apocalyptic speculation. Yet Weiss offers a sober judgment of what is revealed in the epistles: "Paul still counts upon a considerably protracted continuance of present conditions." [34] In Gal. 5:19, 22, Paul draws a sharp distinction between "the works of the flesh" and "the fruit of the Spirit." Even though Paul was a city dweller, he has deliberately chosen an agricultural term with the full understanding that before fruit can mature there must be time and effort for cultivation. Alexander furnishes a careful observation: "It is in the Epistle to the Romans that we find the conception of growth most clearly indicated. This is all the more remarkable, as it is in this same epistle that the idea of the Christian life as a finished product is also most prominent." [35]

It is evident that Paul freely acknowledged that a mature relationship with Christ presupposes development. His anger is never greater than when he writes to the Galatians to rebuke them for heeding the legalist teachers because instead of retrogression he expects progress among his converts. But walking in the Spirit is not guaranteed by baptism (cf. Gal. 5:25). In fact, sin may resume command at any moment. First Thessalonians 4:1 contains one of Paul's clearest references to the necessity for sustained growth: "Finally, brethren, we beseech and exhort you in the Lord Jesus, that as you learned from us how you ought to live and to please God, just as you are doing, you do so more and more." Bicknell's commentary on this verse reads: "As always, he insists that growth is a law of life, and that progress in goodness is the surest safeguard against falling away into sin."[36] Paul confidently works for development in the Christian community as well as in the individual believer. Beardslee, who recognizes that Paul does not share the modern interest in self-realization and a progress curve, nevertheless calls attention to the surprisingly large number of instances in which the concept of growth is emphasized by him.[37] In reviewing the history of the church at Corinth, Paul calls attention to his own contribution and that of Apollos as a work of planting and watering, and adds: "But God gave the growth" (I Cor. 3:6). To the same community he writes at a later time: "Our hope is that as your faith increases, our field among you may be greatly enlarged" (II Cor. 10:15; cf. also Col. 1:10).

What is important for Paul is not the product or even the rate of the growth, but the spiritual state from which alone the growth may proceed.[38] The new nature, too, undergoes change. Even the new man grows from more to more. Robinson declares: "Because of our incorporation into Christ the new solidarity is continually being built up within us."[39] We are daily buried and raised with him. Perseverance in well doing is both the sign and cause of growth, and what is development in this life has something of the quality of the age to come. So Paul addresses himself to earnest disciples: "The return you get is sanctification and its end, eternal life" (Rom. 6:22).

Baptism, the beginning of the Christian life, is usually described by Paul in glowing, idealistic terms. It is called a death with Christ to the evil world and a rising with him into a new and superior form of existence. The baptized person has become a new man. And yet most of the old man is not far below the surface. According to Alexander, " A prolonged experience of human nature taught the apostle to cherish moderate expectations in reference to beginners." [40] The deficiency is not in Baptism but in the baptized. Those who have not yet progressed far from their point of departure are both young and undeveloped in their faith and are closer to the flesh than to the spirit. Paul describes the recently converted and baptized Corinthians as " babes in Christ " who had to be fed with milk and not solid food (cf. I Cor. 3:1 f.). In fact, the continuance of jealousy and strife among them is an indication that they have remained stationary. They are still of the flesh and merely men even though they have been called to sanctification (cf. vs. 3-4). Christians are to be " babes in evil " but not in righteousness (cf. I Cor. 14:20). Yet over against ignorance there is wisdom, against the flesh there is the spirit, and against evil there is good. Just as the Christian life does have its lowest levels, which are close to the old life theoretically left behind, so it has its highest levels, which are close to the life of the age to come.

Discipleship is a course that runs from religious infancy to religious maturity. Paul is referring more to his spiritual state than to his social adjustment when he confesses: " When I became a man, I gave up childish ways " (I Cor. 13:11). In Paul's usage, at the opposite end of the scale from the infant is the mature person. This adjective occurs seven times in Paul's letters, and its precise meaning is not always easy to determine. In one or two instances Paul is apparently referring to " the perfect " as distinguished from " the imperfect " (cf. I Cor. 13:10; Rom. 12:2). But in the remaining cases he is not considering perfection but that maturity which stands at the end of a long line of development. He conceives of his own responsibility as to "present every man mature in Christ" (Col. 1:28). Beardslee makes the observation: "Sometimes the *teleios* ('perfect') is contrasted with the child, suggesting that perfection may be considered the result of a process of growth and that the term is best translated 'mature.'"[41] Paul cannot feed meat to babes, but he does teach true wisdom to those who are mature (cf. I Cor. 2:6). Only such are ready for the highest ventures (cf. Phil. 3:15).

The concept of maturity inevitably presupposes the process of growth, yet Paul is not speaking of perfection because that pertains only to God and to his own age to come. Furthermore, man can grow, but he cannot attain unto perfection. The maturity that is the goal of discipleship is always "in Christ," because he who was sent as God's Son is also with regard to us "the first-born." His own maturity is thus the link between our upward growth and God's perfection.

The Individual and Society

The idea of progress has frequently been understood in ways that make a truly Christian philosophy of history impossible. It has sometimes been held to describe an automatic or inevitable process of growth, and often it has been used as a support for an overemphasis upon the powers of man as an individual to produce through his own effort an improvement in our order of existence. For Paul the concept of development is carefully safeguarded, however. He shared with Jesus and with Judaism generally the conviction that the individual and his group are ultimately inseparable. He never applies the adjective "holy" to just a single believer. A Christian is called to be a "saint" as a member of the holy community and not for his own benefit. One of Paul's most constant assumptions in all his thought is the concept of human solidarity. On the basis of this reality the plan of God is carried out. Barrett explains: "The work of the new Adam is . . . to produce a new unit of existence, which is as truly one in Christ as the human race as a whole is one in Adam." [42]

The purposes of God must be described with reference to this corporate dimension. The progress of the individual is always conditioned by the state of his society. Moreover, it is never man who wins the triumphs in this age. Caird forces us to reflect: "Paul repeatedly and indignantly rejects the idea that by our own obedience to God's commands we may achieve a victory over the powers of evil." [43] Paul is certain that this is the time of Christ's rule and that "he must reign until he has put all his enemies under his feet" (I Cor. 15:25). He knows that the Christian life from beginning to end is the result of God's grace. The statement of Beardslee is of prime importance: "What is lacking in Paul's comments about growth is any conviction that the results which are to be expected will be in any significant way permanently cumulative in this world." [44] This is a necessary blow to our pride. In Paul's view all our efforts are offered to Christ that he may do with them what he will. The human categories of size and amount are meaningless when applied to Christian discipleship. Spiritual growth has other measurements even though it occurs within the material world. Our progress is movement toward the maturity of Christ, and of this age he is the Lord.

Chapter IX | PAUL'S MESSAGE TODAY

THE APOSTLE TO THE GENTILES has been the most influential and the most faithful theological interpreter of the fact of Christ in all history. All his thoughts are reflections on the action of God in Jesus of Nazareth. The significance of that revelation is for him necessarily set forth by means of Hebrew and Greek concepts and language. Yet in the end his writings are his own; and although he is conditioned by his environment and influenced by the past, he describes Christ in a manner previously unknown and never since precisely paralleled. The Pauline view is the product of many factors of which one of the most important is Paul himself.

Yet just as the Pauline epistles set forth a powerful explanation of the effect of Jesus on one man, so the content of these letters has itself been subject to unending interpretation. It has been exceedingly difficult to arrive at any agreement as to what Paul intended to say or did in fact say to the recipients of his correspondence. Each successive generation of readers has been carried farther away from the immediate circumstances of Paul's day and place. Moreover, the complexities and profundities of the mind of the apostle have presented a formidable challenge to all Biblical scholars. Every historical and critical resource is needed to recover his original meaning and thus his import for later times. In this central area of Pauline study each age is called upon to investigate the problems afresh with only a limited reliance upon what has been done in the past, and it must bring its own questions, which in turn will suggest the answers to be found. It is impossible to avoid the conclusion that the interpretation of Paul is never finished, although there is no reason to be discouraged. Tremendous progress has been made. In our continuing search, however, the caution of Filson is to be heeded: " There is a danger of estimating what is vital in Paul by modern conceptions of what is true." [1]

Thus, our modern approach to eschatology is not that of Paul; but his view is not thereby rendered irrelevant or antiquated. He must be allowed to speak for himself. Any possible relevance of his eschatological thinking for our day will be rooted in what he believed. His ideas are necessarily different from ours, but the Pauline assumptions and statements may contain truth which is no longer perceived. Moreover, Paul's own meaning has been obscured frequently by later prejudices and approaches that he would not have shared and may not even have understood. As far as is possible, then, Paul's words are to be examined objectively and without presupposition if we are to have any hope of determining his own intentions.

Paul was a first-century Jew who, though trained as a Pharisee, knew Greek as his first language and spent most of his life in the Gentile world. By the time of his conversion to Christianity he had already persecuted those who were in Christ before him. He bridged the two worlds of Judaism and Christianity and was clearly indebted to both. The elements of Christian doctrine in which he had been instructed and the facts of his own experience alike had to be interpreted so that others, and especially the Gentiles, might believe too; and to that end he drew upon his Jewish background, in which eschatology played a major role. Yet Jewish doctrines were not sufficient to explain all that had happened in Jesus Christ. For Paul there was in

Christ an element of newness and uniqueness that demanded fresh interpretations and that corresponded closely with Paul's own relationship with Christ. From one point of view Paul was only one of innumerable interpreters of the fact of Christ, but he was, nevertheless, one of the first and the most effective of this vast company. Because no one had yet done what he felt called upon to do, he was forced to break new ground and to become a pioneer.

It is in the area of eschatology that we can observe with special clarity his unique contribution. The point is well made by Schoeps: "The eschatological approach . . . is able to clarify the Jewish faith-presuppositions from which the apostle of Jesus Christ, placed in a new and unforeseeable situation, namely, the post-messianic, developed something original and really new: that is, Christian theology." [2] Jewish thinking regarding the Messiah was purely futuristic and could not consider the possibility that he might have come already. For Paul, however, the Messiah had in fact come in Jesus, who had also been crucified and raised from the dead. Paul believed that he was living in an age that must be described in Jewish terms as post-Messianic but that in Christian terms was a very important part of God's purpose. The life of Jesus is both the fulfillment of Old Testament prophecy and also the beginning of a new order. His significance, therefore, can be seen only in an eschatological framework.

Our problem of understanding Paul is obviously complicated by the fact that the apostle wrote his letters in Greek. The difficulty of transmitting thought by means of written language is intensified when that language must be translated into another. Much of Paul's thinking must have been done by means of Hebrew concepts and words. Moreover, his Greek usage is not always consistent. He does not stop to define his terms, nor does he always employ them in the same way. At this point Barr asks a searching question: "If there is such a thing as a 'New Testament view of time,' can it be maintained that its outlines are wholly obscured for the reader of the Latin or the English Bible because these languages do not reproduce the supposed structure of the Greek *kairos* and *chronos*? "[3] In order to study Paul's eschatology we do need some knowledge of Hebrew and of Greek, but this kind of word study has its decided limitations. It is also essential to arrive at some comprehension of Paul's general position and purpose as these can be discovered from reference to the whole body of his writings. A study of Paul's use of the Greek language cannot be an end in itself but only a means to looking into his mind.

As we have seen, Paul's writings contain a large amount of eschatological, and some purely apocalyptic, material. It is impossible to eliminate such references by suggesting that they are in any way secondary. Paul's thought as a whole is inextricably bound up with his eschatology, and therefore the way in which we accept the latter will directly affect our attitude toward the former. For better or for worse some of Paul's most basic teachings are expounded through vivid pictures of the succession of the ages and the end of earthly time. The coming judgment by God through Christ is sometimes described as a day of wrath. The wicked and the righteous will receive their proper reward. The last day will involve the coming of Christ and the presence of a cloud, angels, and fire; and trumpets will sound. Satan and the demons will be overcome in a divine victory against all evil forces. The faithful will reign with Christ in glory as he delivers the Kingdom to his Father. Obviously, such concepts are far removed from much contemporary Christian thinking and from almost all secular reflections. Bultmann holds that this "expectation of the end of the world as occurring in time" belongs to mythology and therefore cannot form a part of the core of Christianity.[4] Yet the Pauline letters do reflect throughout such an expectation. The modern reader is given two alternatives. If he follows Bultmann, he must demythologize Paul by removing the mythical elements through a process of subjective judgment so that what remains is acceptable to his thinking. Or he may admit the totality of the Pauline text and approach the undeniably mythical sections by an interpretation which is similar to that present in Paul's own mind as he wrote.

The difficulty is presented most sharply in the apocalyptic passages, of which the clearest examples are found in the Thessalonian correspondence. Regarding I Thess. 4:13-18, Bicknell has concluded: " The picture of the advent of Christ given in these verses is one that our modern minds cannot take literally." [5] Here Paul is deliberately utilizing traditional word pictures as one way of expressing his own underlying convictions. But it is not thereby to be assumed that Paul regards these pictures as literally true. In fact, it is most unlikely that he ever did so. Caird has pointed out that " Biblical eschatology is a characteristic product of the Semitic mind, which only Gentiles or pedants would dream of taking literally." [6] There can be no doubt but that Paul felt all of these literary borrowings to be inadequate vehicles for the expression of his ideas, but they were employed nevertheless so as to put general concepts in a dramatic and unforgettable form in somewhat the same way that Jesus taught in parables.

Ultimate truths and events of spiritual significance always transcend the words and ideas by which they are symbolically described. Even though the tentativeness and inaccuracy of the myth or symbol is readily granted, there is respect and sometimes awe in the face of the attempt to describe the indescribable. According to E. F. Scott, " Nothing is more remarkable than the hold they [the apocalyptic forms] have always maintained on the Christian mind." [7] Too often these forms have been maintained as exact predictions of the future, but for Paul they were a means of appealing to and directing the imagination. He asserts on many occasions that these aspects of the end belong to the mystery of God's eternal purposes. There has been very significant revelation; and even though it is sufficient for our salvation, it remains partial and incomplete and beyond human understanding. Petry has summed up the situation: " Certainly one need not commit himself to every vagary of symbolism in the process of seeing some worth represented by otherwise untenable pictures of the universe." [8]

If Paul's eschatological pictures are not intended by him to be blueprints of the future, it is necessary to seek for the truths toward which they point. Only in this manner can the applicability of Paul's eschatology for our day be recognized.[9] Paul's writings contain word pictures, myth, symbols, and direct statement; and all flow from one mind. In spite of some human inconsistencies, Paul does not write at cross purposes, and he reflects one carefully considered set of convictions. Subsequent reinterpretation of Paul cannot safely disregard the forms found in the epistles because in and through them the content has been given. Dahl states very frankly: " The only way in which such eschatological realities can be described is in the language of myth and parable. . . . The language and thought-forms of the Bible are of this nature and their insights cannot be separated from the mythology through which they are mediated." [10]

Systematization and rationalization are always subject to the limitations of the human mind and are therefore only partially satisfactory approaches to divine truth. It is unlikely that by our own reasoning we may produce categories which are more adequate vehicles for the content of revelation than those which the Bible employs. The frequent images used to express Paul's eschatology are not to be confused with the truths that the apostle is presenting through them. In many instances these figures appear to be misleading and irrelevant, but for Paul they were essential. Their presence in the Pauline writings calls not for demythologization but for a remythologizing in which every attempt is made to understand the background of his symbolism so that by it his meaning is not obscured but, rather, clarified. Paul's eschatological concepts are inextricably tied to mythological language, but his beliefs are not thereby either outmoded or incomprehensible. They cannot, however, be understood without the most careful study; and to that end contemporary thought has significant contributions to make.

The Relevant Truths of Paul's Eschatology

For the greater part of history Paul has not been influential among those who have developed Christian eschatology.[11] His thought has been judged not sufficiently imaginative on the one hand or not sufficiently materialistic on the other. He is positively rejected or tacitly ignored by many modern seekers because his answers do not seem to fit with any precision the questions raised by contemporary life. This situation is described by Kennedy: "Some of those eschatological problems which press most heavily upon us did not appeal to the apostle at all. Others, on which we care for nothing but a definite decision, St. Paul is content to leave on a borderland of mystery."[12] It will have to be granted that some of our eschatological concerns are not reflected in the extant letters of Paul and also that some of his doctrines in this area are of little or no interest to us.

What we now possess as the Pauline corpus is the result of a selective process, first of all by Paul himself as he wrote only of things that seemed of first importance to him, and secondly, by the life of the early church, which preserved some of his letters and allowed others to be lost. It is not of great significance that there are parts of Paul's eschatological thought that are unacceptable to us. There are other sources of eschatological doctrines than Paul, and no single generation can be expected to appropriate the totality of Christian theology. Paul's eschatological statements are admittedly incomplete and are entwined with a mythology that belongs to Paul's own time and place and that therefore raises serious problems for the contemporary mind.

Yet behind the specific formulations is the conviction of Paul, the Christian thinker. In his eschatology there is a significance which is not affected by changing generations and thought patterns. Cave has argued: " Because he [Paul] thought that he was at the end of time, his words have a timelessness which otherwise they would have lacked." [13] As has been noted throughout, Paul's eschatology permeates a large section of his thought and includes a vast variety of topics. Not all of these are of permanent value or of present relevance. However, his eschatology as a whole, just because it is an integral part of the body of his doctrine, constitutes a normative expression which speaks to Christians of this century as forcefully as to those of any other. Emerging from the mythological images and the figurative language and spanning the gaps between widely scattered references we can discover at least four major affirmations that are clearly central for Paul and that therefore mediate his eschatology to the modern world. In these ideas Paul's thought is raised above the peculiar conditions of his own time and place and it becomes largely independent of narrow traditional categories. In fact, these underlying assertions provide a clear perspective by which any single portion of his eschatological thought may be judged. These are the reasons for his borrowings from the Jewish past and the Greek present, and these are the direct representations of his own reflections and conclusions. It is here that we are able to penetrate behind convention and form and discover the apostle's essential interpretation of Christian truth.

First of all, Paul is absolutely certain that history is a primary medium of God's activity and revelation. Without an eschatology history must find its meaning within itself and is thus judged by its own inconsistencies and frustrations. It is almost impossible to see in it more than a meaningless succession of unconnected events or else a series of happenings causally connected but without any indication of reason or purpose. Paul, however, is constantly pointing to the end, which will surely come because it has been fixed by God. Although Paul is very careful not to lay undue stress upon any progress being made by man in this present age with Christ lest it be judged a work advancing the cause of salvation, he postulates at every turn a progression of ages. The present age with Christ will completely supplant the present (evil) age without Christ when the Lord's work is done, but the age of Christ will in turn be followed by God's (final) age.

This succession of the ages is at the heart of Paul's thinking because he knows that nothing has occurred in the past or is happening in the present or will take place in the future apart from God's knowledge and ultimate control. The hand of God is seen directly in creation, in the history of Israel, and above all in the life, death, and resurrection of Jesus. God's plans for all mankind have thus been set forth in unmistakable form. The past, the present, and the future are for Paul all aspects of one history; and the coming age of God is not qualitatively different from those which have preceded it. That which is fulfilled in the last age has been partially present in all the others because of the continuing activity of God. Accordingly, the eternal significance of that period which man generally describes as historical must be underlined. Paul, in the words of Purdy, "has lifted the eschaton out of the 'dimension of cosmic into the realm of historic occurrence.'"[14] All events have the same ultimate reality in God, and the time to come can throw important light back upon our present existence. Moule's comments apply to Paul at this point: "The future (in detail) was never the primary concern; it was the past leading to the present that occupied the attention of Christians when they were really Christian." [15]

The ground of Paul's confidence that God is involved in the present is his certainty that God has acted in the past and that he will accomplish his purpose in the future. All time is meaningful to God and so also to man. It takes on a real importance because God has chosen to reveal himself in it. Dahl has commented: "The realistic biblical conception of time precludes the idea of a radical dichotomy between time and eternity. Eternity is not the absence or opposite of time, but its fulfillment." [16] Therefore, as we have seen, for Paul as for John eternal life begins for the disciple now in the midst of this present age even though by definition it belongs essentially to the next world. The one thing that holds the different ages together is the activity and self-revelation of God in all of them. An analysis of Paul's writings causes Hunter to conclude: "We should think of the coming of Christ not as an event in history but as . . . the point at which our time — that is human history with all its values acceptable to him — will be taken up into God's eternity." [17]

History is not thereby swallowed up by the thought of eternity, but rather, eternity is given immediate relevance and concreteness in historic realities. Our present history is not all there is, but neither is it futile and doomed to destruction. Because he conceives the birth of Jesus as bringing something new and final into this world, Paul can conclude that henceforth time and eternity, the present and the future, are indissolubly connected. For him the meaning of history cannot be found in reference to man and human history alone but, rather, in reference to what God has begun in Christ and therefore to that which he must complete. It is at this point that Paul introduces the concept of the Parousia. The divine plan is already in full operation and must be brought to a successful conclusion. The work of God, now openly declared, cannot be halted or overthrown; and the return of Christ will mark the close of this age and the beginning of God's own age. Therefore whether the Parousia comes quickly or whether in the sight of men it be long delayed is of no real significance for Paul. His eschatology is not tied to time as man reckons it by duration alone, but it is rooted in an understanding of time as transformed by eternity in the work of Christ. For him, then, time when properly understood is the very medium in which God acts.

In the second instance Paul asserts that by the possession of hope and the continuous operation of the principle of judgment Christians are directly related to the future as well as to the past. Hope occupies a very important place in Paul's thinking, and it is therefore essential to recognize that for him the term is not at all an expression of unreality or desperation but on the other hand intimately related to the assurance of faith. Hope springs out of what God has already done. It also points to what surely lies ahead as the divine plan is realized, but it is most of all a characteristic of discipleship in this age. Paul did not claim to have been given special information as to particulars of the events of the last age. He knows only primary theological truths, and his descriptions of the end are based on those truths but elaborated in borrowed literary figures and in products of a dedicated imagination. For Paul the future can be predicted in terms of what can now be known of God.

According to Cullmann, the eschatology of Paul as of that of the other New Testament writers " is not hope in some kind of reality which is always available to us in the world beyond. It is not hope in a ' beyond ' as opposed to a ' below,' but hope in a ' then ' as opposed to a ' now.' " [18] Because God has entered this world in Jesus Christ, many of the blessings of the last age, God's own time, are currently available for the believer. For the Christian the present is given an entirely new dimension and quality. Quantitatively the end will be very different from this age. The fulfillment of God's purpose must follow the Parousia, but the Christian present and the future are for Paul linked in God's will. The outlook of Paul is set forth by Fison: "An eschatology totally divorced from either the present experience of the individual or the present character of society cannot claim to represent adequately the Christian future hope, which springs straight out of present faith and love and cannot for one moment be separated from them." [19]

Likewise, for Paul, judgment will be fully carried out at the end of this age and at the beginning of the last time. Thus it is frequently referred to with a future tense of the verb. The judicial activity of Christ will be one of his final acts before he turns the Kingdom over to his Father. The inequalities of this life are so great that they cannot be rectified under any conditions that man can foresee in himself. Justice, like mercy, belongs to God alone, and therefore is carried out only by his power and will. Yet Paul knows that the God who will judge the world is also the one who has created it and redeemed it in Christ. He has never abandoned his creation but from the beginning has deliberately out of love involved himself in it. His dealings with his creatures are understood as righteousness or justification, grace and compassion, yet God cannot deny himself. He is "faithful," that is, he can be trusted and relied upon because he does not change. His mercy does not contradict his justice, and his love is not in opposition to his wrath. He has met sin not by avoiding it as if it didn't really matter but by defeating it in open confrontation. As God's Son, Christ suffered on behalf of all men in their wrongdoing and so he became both sin and a curse for us. God must always resist evil wherever it appears just because he is holy. Since creation comes from him, it must possess within itself a moral principle in which right reflects God while evil opposes him. This principle, which is proclaimed in varying degrees throughout the Old Testament, is wholly revealed in Jesus Christ. He is the supreme demonstration of God's fight against sin and of his victory over it. Evil has been beaten but still struggles on in ignorance and futility. The bases on which the final judgment will be made are already laid down. Nothing essentially new will be added in the future age, but then all resistance to God's will will be ended. The judgment to come is also at hand now that Christ is Lord.

Paul's third conviction is that the Christian life on earth is marked by paradox and apparent logical inconsistency. The present age with Christ has some things in common with the present evil age, although it shares other conditions with the coming age of God. Those living within it experience a pull in the two directions at once and as a result are characterized by uncertainties and ceaseless striving. Existence in Christ in this time is something of an anomaly and is not easily classified. Cullmann has admitted: " Only an understanding of this tension in which the Church lives can prevent the Gospel from looking like a tissue of contradictions." [20] Christian discipleship cannot be described by human reason because it is entirely dependent upon the divine calling. It is of this fact that Barrett is speaking when he writes: " The basic terms in which Christian existence must be understood are eschatological." [21] The follower of Christ continues to live within this world, and the external conditions have not been altered. In fact, his calling includes a mission to those who still refuse to surrender themselves in faith, and any withdrawal from society is a denial of his Lord. On the other hand, it is not involvement in the present life which in itself gives meaning to discipleship. Christian activity of any kind is significant, not for what it may accomplish according to human standards, but for its conformity to the plans of God and for its relation to the divine last things. Thus, tension is the inevitable condition for life in Christ, and it must then be characterized by the three elements of the divine calling, the mission to the present world, and the experiencing of varying pressures from both poles.

It is difficult for Paul to view this present age with Christ in isolation, not because it follows the age before Christ and precedes the last time, but because it necessarily is connected with both past and future. Yet there is also in the apostle's view a succession of ages in which before the future can come the present must come to an end. Paul's eschatology agrees that the Kingdom of God cannot be produced by human effort as the end of a long process of growth and development. In its fullness the Kingdom belongs to God's own age and will be ushered in by his power alone. Likewise, the grace of God is unconditioned and beyond man's control. Salvation is God's gift and can never be earned in the Pauline view. On the other hand, salvation is not automatic and can be rejected or accepted by faith. And for Paul, faith, if it is real, will bring about visible results. Self-surrender to God is not self-annihilation but the end of resistance to his will so that our lives become vehicles for his Spirit. The behavior and activity of the Christian must be different from that of the nonbeliever. Yet just as that which is revealed in the life of the disciple is not his own power or goodness but the strength of God at work in him, so the coming of the Kingdom is determined by nothing but the divine will. The response of faith does not hasten the end but provides a partial indication of what will be fully declared in the last age.

The present time is not the last of the ages. Paul was careful to declare that the Parousia has not yet occurred. Something greater than what exists now lies ahead. Even though God created it, matter has been corrupted; and the physical world is subject to evil, suffering, and death. Dodd has noted: "Apocalyptic eschatology implies a radical devaluation of the present world-order in all its aspects."[22] At times Paul appears to share this attitude of apocalypticism, and he constantly assumes the superiority of the spiritual and the heavenly to what is of the earth. However, the Pauline dualism is essentially moral and not philosophical or ultimate. When God created matter it was good, and for Paul as for all eschatologists the end must be as the beginning. Evil is opposition to God and therefore can have no existence apart from reference to him. God forever opposes sin, but the battle is not equal; and he has triumphed already and will completely conquer. The life of the disciple on earth is carried on in the flesh but is to be a demonstration of faith and love and power. The redemptive work of Christ extends to all things in heaven and on earth. Nothing that God has made can be lost. What the flesh is when controlled by sin is not what it was at creation or what it will be when redeemed in fact. The necessity for a continuing struggle against evil in this age does not condemn the physical world to permanent enslavement. God's victory has been won and will be fully applied when the end comes.

The life, death, and resurrection of Jesus form the real dividing point between the reign of evil and the reign of God. The First Coming tells us all that we need to know of the Second Coming. What happened when Christ came into the world provides absolute assurance of what will take place at the end. Paul is certain that the accomplishments of the life of Jesus are final for all time and for all people and things. Jesus Christ has, however, in turn been sent by God to secure his purpose of salvation. Paul always discovers the significance of Jesus in the love of God. The experience of the disciple is therefore an anticipation of that which properly belongs to the age of God. Barrett has stated explicitly: "It is of the essence of Paul's thought that the eschatology is partly, but only partly, realized — the futurist eschatology is not to be dismissed as an unfortunate hang-over from the primitive Church — and it remains for Christians to work out their new existence, under the guidance of the Holy Spirit, in a strange interim period, 'between the times.'" [23] The relationships among future, present, and past tenses force a consideration of the meaning of time itself. Marsh points out: "The problem of eschatology was not to find reasons for delay, but to find the theological significance of a time which chronologically succeeded the end of time." [24]

The apparent postponement of the Parousia was not a problem for Paul just because he saw in Christ as the Lord the meaning of all time and existence. The goal of history is thus to be found in all of the ages considered individually and in their succession, for God is concerned in every aeon. Accordingly Paul thinks first of God and then of the particular qualities of each division of time. Petry concludes: "What Jesus so unflinchingly demands and Paul so faithfully reports is just the quality of attachment to the eternal kingdom which alone can provide any real redemptive power in the present society." [25] The eternal kingdom is what Paul understands as the purposes of God begun at creation and most surely to be brought to perfection in the coming age. Since Christ is God's unique and all-sufficient provision for salvation, his followers may participate in eternal life now; but the end is not yet.

Even though this world is corrupt and weak, the life of the Christian in the flesh is, in Paul's mind, of lasting significance. The coming age will be infinitely finer than anything that has gone before it, and Paul admits that "to depart and be with Christ" (Phil. 1:23) is the most that he can desire. He does believe that the things that are above and unseen speak more directly of God than does the physical in its present state. However, at the center of his gospel is the proclamation that God has decisively revealed himself within the conditions of this world. Thus, Cadbury has stated: "It would be unfair to think of him [Paul] as one whose eye is fixed mainly on the future, living in this world only for the next. His Christianity is not primarily other-worldly." [26] The events of this present time are for Paul just as important in God's sight as those of any other aeon. The plan of God is directed to every age, and the end is the fulfillment of the whole succession of ages and not just of this present epoch.

Beardslee, aware of the distance between Paul and our day, comments: "The interpreter must relate Paul's eschatological vision to the contemporary situation of man and the Church. The simplest form of adaptation is to affirm that during the 'time of the Church' the eschatological process has stopped temporarily, to be resumed at the final end." [27] Although such adaptation has been proposed many times, it is not at all the position of Paul. Rather, he finds it necessary to describe this age in eschatological terms if it is to have any real significance. Nevertheless, Paul holds that each period of time has its own special characteristics; and our life with Christ on earth is a constant struggle that cannot end until the coming age has begun. Until then discipleship means fidelity to Christ in an imperfect world. Stewart has pictured the case in a few words: "The thrust of the demonic has to be met with the fire of the divine." [28] Paul has shown that Jesus fought, suffered, and died, and so he has stressed that the followers of Christ must also fight, suffer, and die. There is no victory without the overcoming of opposition. There is no atonement or reconciliation without sacrifice. As Paul conceives it, the reign of Christ as Lord is the putting down of all rebellion against God until he is everywhere acknowledged. Those who are in Christ share with him this task of resisting evil on every hand.

Finally, Paul proclaims that God's supreme gift to all men is life. He alone is the life giver, and his unconditioned love is first expressed in the creation. On the other hand, the life that God has given includes the exercise of free will; and when Adam disobeyed God, sin entered what had been hitherto a perfect world. Along with sin, as an intruder into God's good handiwork, came death. Sin has been in the world ever since, kept alive by the disobedience of all men. Thus, death too has been a part of existence on the earth; and death is a strong enemy of God and foreign to his purpose. Paul criticizes the Law most severely because by pursuing it men have been brought to death and not to life. In Jesus, Paul sees a new creation because the life of God flows full in him. However, because Jesus identified himself completely with the lot of mankind, he too had to die. The cross would have been a tragedy and not a triumph without the resurrection, and Paul understandably always speaks of these two events together. The latter is the determining defeat of death because by God's power the life of Christ, which had been interrupted by three days in the grave, now continues forever and is made available for all his followers. In God's age there will be no death; but in this age death persists and is, in accordance with Paul's outlook, an evil. It is the last of all the enemies of God to be destroyed before the end. Christians must undergo physical death even though this was not a part of God's plan and purpose. Thus, Paul is a realist and faces facts openly.

However, God is far stronger than death, and the life he gave at creation is inextinguishable in Christ. The faith, hope, and love of Christian discipleship enable us to see death in a true perspective. It does exist now in opposition to God, but it has been essentially and proleptically overcome by the far mightier force of the divine life. Again, those in Christ share his being. They have by their baptism died to the world, but even on earth they have been spiritually raised with Christ and made partakers with him of the new and transformed life. Insofar as Paul looks to the future to complete the truth known in the present, he envisages a fellowship of disciples with their Lord in which life will not be hampered by sinful flesh or threatened with inevitable physical death. Yet Paul's greater concern is with the quality of our present existence. He knows that because God, the life giver, has entered our age in Christ, sin and death have been defeated. They will not be a part of the coming age, and therefore they can be opposed in the present with reliance upon the victorious power of God.

◈ ◈ ◈ | NOTES

INTRODUCTION

1. Cf. R. C. Petry, *Christian Eschatology and Social Thought,* p. 13: "Today . . . eschatology is a term virtually unknown. Its connotations of final things and world's end are still a part of our Hebrew Christian ideology. But they are decreasingly effective as conditioning forces in our everyday social reactions."

2. J. A. T. Robinson, *In the End, God,* p. 10.

3. Note the comment of A. N. Wilder, *Otherworldliness and the New Testament,* p. 7: "The one great and telling charge made against the Christian religion in the modern period is that it is otherworldly, escapist and irrelevant to the problems of this life."

4. This has been observed by A. M. Hunter, "The Hope of Glory," *Interpretation,* 1954, p. 132: "To minds taught to think in terms of progress and evolution . . . St. Paul's apocalyptic pictures of the ultimate destiny of man and the cosmos are strange and scandalous." "Apocalyptic" is a term used to indicate that form of eschatology which flourished from ca. 200 B.C. to A.D. 100 and which was marked by transcendentalism and highly imaginative, vivid pictures of future events.

5. Cf. C. C. McCown, *The Promise of His Coming,* p. 225.

6. J. E. Fison, *The Christian Hope,* p. 33.

7. Reinhold Niebuhr, *The Nature and Destiny of Man,* Vol. II, *Human Destiny,* p. 288.

8. Robinson, *op. cit.,* p. 18.

9. Cf. H. H. Rowley, *The Relevance of Apocalyptic,* p. 8.

10. M. E. Dahl, *The Resurrection of the Body,* p. 92.

11. Robinson, *op. cit.,* p. 9.

12. Hunter, *op. cit.,* p. 131.

13. Cf. James Kallas, *The Significance of the Synoptic Miracles,* p. vii: " Much of modern ' Bible study ' is not really exegesis or explication of the text, but rather a search for a synthesis between ' outmoded ' Biblical world views and the concepts of the twentieth century."

14. Amos Wilder, " Eschatological Imagery and Earthly Circumstance," *New Testament Studies,* 1958–1959, p. 229.

15. F. C. Grant, *Ancient Judaism and the New Testament,* p. 93, supports Bultmann at this point when he says: " If anything in the New Testament needs to be ' demythologized,' it is surely the apocalyptic hope with its traditional imagery, its strange concepts, figures, symbols, presuppositions, its idea of history and even its conception of God."

16. Rudolf Bultmann, *History and Eschatology,* p. 37.

17. *Ibid.,* pp. 151 f.

18. *Ibid.,* p. 40.

19. Wilder, " Eschatological Imagery," p. 240, n. 6.

20. Cf. C. H. Dodd, *The Apostolic Preaching and Its Developments,* p. 64.

21. *Ibid.,* p. 80.

22. *Ibid.,* p. 82.

23. Cf. C. H. Dodd, *The Parables of the Kingdom,* pp. 31 f.

24. *Ibid.,* p. 159.

25. Cf. Dodd, *Apostolic Preaching,* p. 88.

26. Cf. the judgment on Dodd's position by Kallas, *op. cit.,* p. 105: " The final conclusion is that the kingdom is not a future in time when the world itself shall be redeemed and recreated but rather the kingdom is a timeless entity, purely spiritual, which transcends time and space."

27. C. K. Barrett, " New Testament Eschatology," *Scottish Journal of Theology,* 1953, p. 239.

28. Cf. D. J. Selby, " Changing Ideas in New Testament Eschatology," *Harvard Theological Review,* 1957, p. 21: " The message of the primitive church was an eschatological message and any account of it must deal with the problem of eschatology." Cf. further A. M. Hunter, *Interpreting Paul's Gospel,*

p. 123: " The New Testament Gospel is radically eschatological."

29. W. Grundmann, " Sin," *Bible Key Words,* p. 87.
30. Robinson, *op. cit.,* p. 33.
31. G. V. Jones, *Christology and Myth in the New Testament,* p. 272.
32. Cf. G. B. Caird, *Principalities and Powers,* p. x: " It is the nature of religious symbolism and myth that it can convey truths which defy the precision of analytical thought."
33. G. V. Jones, *op. cit.,* p. 270. Cf. also F. W. Dillistone, *Christianity and Symbolism,* p. 104.
34. J. A. T. Robinson, *op. cit.,* p. 67.
35. Wilder, " Eschatological Imagery," p. 231.
36. Hunter, *Interpreting Paul's Gospel,* p. 124.
37. Cf. Dillistone, *op. cit.,* p. 89.
38. Rudolf Bultmann, " History and Eschatology in the New Testament," *New Testament Studies,* 1954, p. 16.
39. Maurice Goguel, *The Birth of Christianity,* p. 283.
40. James Muilenburg, " The Biblical View of Time," *Harvard Theological Review,* 1961, p. 225.
41. Dahl, *op. cit.,* p. 65.
42. James Barr, *Biblical Words for Time,* p. 25.
43. Niebuhr, *op. cit.,* p. 299.
44. C. F. D. Moule, *The Birth of the New Testament,* p. 102.
45. Oscar Cullmann, *Christ and Time,* p. 96.
46. J. E. Fison, *op. cit.,* p. 29. Cf. also the comment of T. W. Manson, " Some Reflexions on Apocalyptic," *Aux Sources de la Tradition Chrétienne,* p. 139: " The meeting-point of ethics and eschatology is the contrast between what is and what ought to be."
47. John Marsh, *The Fulness of Time,* p. 143.
48. Paul Minear, " The Time of Hope in the New Testament," *Scottish Journal of Theology,* 1953, p. 337.
49. Rowley, *op. cit.,* p. 170.
50. W. A. Beardslee, *Human Achievement and Divine Vocation in the Message of Paul,* p. 16.
51. Moule, *op. cit.,* p. 98.
52. Niebuhr, *op. cit.,* p. 289.
53. Cf. E. Dinkler, " Earliest Christianity," *The Idea of His-*

tory in the Ancient Near East, ed. by R. C. Dentan, p. 210: "One cannot derive a philosophy of history from the New Testament. One cannot extract a Christian methodology of history or any indication for a Christian periodization of history."

54. E. G. Bicknell, *The First and Second Epistles to the Thessalonians,* p. 49.

55. N. Q. Hamilton, *The Holy Spirit and Eschatology in Paul,* p. 90. Cf. also A. M. Hunter, "The Hope of Glory," p. 132: "It is growing clear that the time is ripe for a fresh approach to the whole subject of Christian eschatology."

56. Cf. E. C. Dewick, *Primitive Christian Eschatology,* p. 289: "It would be hard to name any man in the history of the Christian church who has done so much as St. Paul to influence the development of the Christian Doctrine of the Last Things."

57. The author accepts as genuine Pauline writings the following epistles: Romans, I and II Corinthians, Galatians, Philippians, Colossians, I and II Thessalonians, and Philemon. Ephesians is regarded as doubtful, and its evidence is parenthetically noted. Even though questions may be raised regarding the authorship of Colossians and II Thessalonians, it will be seen that for the most part they provide only supplementary material and are not primary sources for the study of Paul's eschatology.

58. The individual books are eschatological to the following extent: II Thessalonians, 55 percent; Colossians, 47 percent; Romans, 36 percent; I Thessalonians, 33 percent; I Corinthians and Galatians, each 30 percent; Philippians, 28 percent; II Corinthians, 21½ percent; and Philemon, 12 percent. In Ephesians, 18½ percent of the 155 verses may be classed as eschatological.

59. Cf. F. C. Porter, "The Place of Apocalyptical Conceptions in the Thought of Paul," *Contemporary Thinking About Paul,* compiled by T. S. Kepler, p. 292: "The eschatology of Paul is of such a nature, so vital, so alive with the force of his personality . . . that it is impossible to approach toward an understanding of it except by the use of his own words."

60. Barr, *op. cit.,* p. 147.

61. Cf. Albert Schweitzer, *Paul and His Interpreters,* p. 240:

"It must be somehow possible, by the discovery of its inner logic, to reconstruct it [Pauline eschatology] from the scattered statements in the documents."

Chapter I

1. F. V. Filson, *St. Paul's Conception of Recompense,* p. 128.
2. Cf. E. Earle Ellis, *Paul and His Recent Interpreters,* p. 32: "Whether Paul's eschatology is rooted in Jewish or Greek concepts is a matter of continuing debate."
3. W. D. Davies, *Christian Origins and Judaism,* p. 145.
4. Cf. F. C. Grant, *Roman Hellenism and the New Testament,* p. 136: "Not only in his attitude toward the Law . . . but in his allegiance to the great religious affirmations of the early Pharisees . . . Paul remained a Pharisee to his dying day."
5. H. J. Schoeps, *Paul,* p. 43.
6. E.g., W. D. Davies, *Paul and Rabbinic Judaism,* p. 287; Beardslee, *op. cit.,* p. 16; Dewick, *op. cit.,* p. 261; F. V. Filson, *op. cit.,* p. 117; A. M. Hunter, *Paul and His Predecessors,* p. 98.
7. Cf. W. Barclay, *The Mind of St. Paul,* p. 223. So also C. H. Dodd, *New Testament Studies,* p. 121: "His [Paul's] picture of the end in II Thessalonians is painted in colors from the crudest palette of Jewish eschatology."
8. Cf. W. D. Davies, *Christian Origins,* p. 29.
9. Cf. Ragnar Leivestad, *Christ the Conqueror,* p. 4.
10. Thus, E. J. Pratt, *Studies in Pauline Eschatology,* p. 193: "It seems clear that Paul's treatment of the special concepts coming under our review shows many affinities with, and considerable divergences from, antecedent and contemporary Jewish tradition."
11. Rowley, *op. cit.,* p. 115. Cf. also Schoeps, *op. cit.,* p. 99: "If we are to understand the eschatology of Paul aright . . . we must make its apocalyptic presuppositions more central in his thought than is usually done."
12. Cf. Dodd, *New Testament Studies,* p. 109: "It seems clear that Paul started with eschatological beliefs of the type best represented by such Jewish writings as the Book of Enoch,

the Apocalypse of Baruch, and the Apocalypse of Ezra."

13. Cf. McCown, *op. cit.*, p. 170: "His description of his hope in I Thess. is the most apocalyptic of all the New Testament outside the Book of Revelation." See further, I. F. Wood, "Paul's Eschatology," *Biblical World*, 1911, p. 86: "II Thess. 2:1-12 is the most concise presentation of apocalyptic ideas in the New Testament."

14. B. Lindars, *New Testament Apologetic*, p. 222.

15. Schoeps, *op. cit.*, p. 95, n. 1.

16. Cf. C. K. Barrett, *op. cit.*, p. 138: "It is characteristic of prophetic eschatology that the significant last term in the series is continuous with the series itself and identical in kind with the preceding events. . . . In Apocalyptic eschatology the last term is different from and discontinuous with the bulk of the series which it concludes."

17. Johannes Weiss, *The History of Primitive Christianity*, Vol. II, p. 545.

18. Sydney Cave, *The Gospel of St. Paul*, p. 237.

19. Cf. J. Weiss, *op. cit.*, p. 543: "The further *details of the apocalyptic drama* of the day of judgment are of little interest to us in this connection since they are taken from the apocalyptic tradition as more or less conventional decorative features and are to be considered more as evidence for the latter than for the religion of Paul."

20. Cf. A. C. Purdy, "Paul the Apostle," *The Interpreter's Dictionary of the Bible*, Vol. III, p. 703.

21. Davies, *Paul and Rabbinic Judaism*, p. 320.

22. W. D. Stacey, *The Pauline View of Man*, p. 38.

23. Barr, *op. cit.*, pp. 159 f.

24. Leivestad, *op. cit.*, p. 307.

25. Cf. T. Francis Glasson, *Greek Influence in Jewish Eschatology*, p. 76.

26. Caird, *op. cit.*, p. 72.

27. Millar Burrows, *More Light on the Dead Sea Scrolls*, p. 342. Cf. F. M. Cross, Jr., *The Ancient Library of Qumran*, p. 203: "The Essene literature enables us to discover the concrete Jewish setting in which an apocalyptic understanding of history was living and integral to communal existence."

28. Cf. Lucetta Mowry, *The Dead Sea Scrolls and the Early Church*, p. 129.

29. Matthew Black, *The Scrolls and Christian Origins,* p. 136.

30. Cross, *op. cit.,* p. 200.

31. Cf. Burrows, *op. cit.,* p. 119; and S. E. Johnson, " Paul and the Manual of Discipline," *Harvard Theological Review,* 1955, p. 157.

32. Cf. Schoeps, *op. cit.,* p. 200.

33. Cross, *op. cit.,* p. 234.

34. W. D. Davies, *Christian Origins,* p. 177.

35. Albert Schweitzer, *The Mysticism of Paul the Apostle,* p. 113. Cf. also Schweitzer, *The Quest of the Historical Jesus,* p. 365: " In seeking clues to the eschatology of Jesus, scholars have passed over the eschatology which lies nearest to it, that of Paul."

36. Mowry, *op. cit.,* p. 144.

37. A. M. Hunter, *Paul and His Predecessors,* pp. 105 f.

38. Cf. Leivestad, *op. cit.,* p. 86.

39. Cf. Schoeps, *op. cit.,* p. 109.

40. F. C. Porter, *op. cit.,* p. 288: " The very fact that Paul's religion is embodied in his personality distinguishes him from all the writers of apocalypses and puts him rather in the class of the great prophets."

41. Schweitzer, *The Mysticism of Paul,* p. 76.

42. Cf. Hunter, *Paul and His Predecessors,* p. 104: " We can never again regard Paul's conception of the Last Things as simply Jewish Messianism réchauffé."

43. Cf. Goguel, *op. cit.,* p. 202: " While in the case of the apostle Paul a direct connection between experience and doctrine can be established, it must not be supposed that his theology is essentially subjective in character and is nothing more than speculation on his own personal experience. On the contrary, he considers it to be the expression of an objective redemptive drama the reality of which does not depend in any way upon the experience of believers or on the benefits they can gain from it."

44. Cf. I. F. Wood, *op. cit.,* p. 162: " The student of Paul must never forget the tremendous influence wielded in his life by his conviction that he had seen with his own eyes the glorified Christ, not in vision, but in reality."

45. Cf. W. D. Stacey, *op. cit.,* p. 240: " It is evident that no

language would sum up adequately a life and experience that had never been known before, so Paul had to attach to all his terms, Greek and Hebrew, a meaning of his own."

46. Cf. F. W. Beare, " New Testament Christianity and the Hellenistic World," in *The Communication of the Gospel in New Testament Times,* by A. Farrer, C. F. Evans, *et al.,* p. 72: " The swift and bold movements of thought which are reflected in the New Testament documents, the freedom with which New Testament Christianity adopted its Gospel, sprung from the soil of the Old Testament and later Jewish eschatological hopes and apocalyptic visions, to forms of expression and frames of thought which enabled it to challenge effectively the Hellenistic world – this reflects the essentially dynamic character of Christianity itself."

47. Filson, *op. cit.,* p. 114.

48. E.g., M. Goguel, " Le caractère, à la fois actuel et futur, du salut dans la théologie paulinienne," in *The Background of the New Testament and Its Eschatology,* ed. by W. D. Davies and D. Daube, p. 336.

49. Cf. J. Lowe, " An Examination of Attempts to Detect Developments in St. Paul's Theology," *Journal of Theological Studies,* 1941, p. 133: " The basic eschatological outlook, the conviction that the coming of Christ meant the beginning of the end, the belief that the crisis is at hand, the consequent sense of tremendous urgency, the ardent looking forward to the final consummation – all this runs, so far as I can see, the whole way through."

50. Dahl, *op. cit.,* p. 85. Cf. also R. H. Charles, *Eschatology: Hebrew, Jewish and Christian,* p. 368: " That some ideas morally irreconcilable should exist in the same writer is easily conceivable."

51. Cf. McCown, *op. cit.,* p. 208: " Consistency of language and thinking is the mark of small souls."

52. The words of Albert Schweitzer, *Paul and His Interpreters,* p. 241, are to be noted here: " We have no right to assume that for Paul there existed in his expectation manifest obscurities, much less that he had overlooked contradictions in it."

53. Cf. Weiss, *op. cit.,* p. 545: " His [Paul's] only concern is

with the aid of these apocalyptic ideas, to set in motion ethical and religious forces, to suppress morbid unrest, to waken dull indifference, to spur on missionary zeal, to keep alive the hope of the conversion of the whole of mankind."

54. Cf. Leivestad, *op. cit.*, p. 92.

55. H. A. Guy, *The New Testament Doctrine of the Last Things*, p. 124.

56. Paul E. Davies, "The Relevance of Apocalyptic for Ancient and Modern Situations," *The Study of the Bible Today and Tomorrow*, ed. by H. R. Willoughby, p. 286. It is difficult at this point to follow H. J. Cadbury, "Concurrent Phases of Paul's Religion," *Studies in Early Christianity*, ed. by S. J. Case, p. 370, when he declares: "The events were real events, not pictorial symbols. . . . We may safely suppose that the whole current program was held by the Apostle and not merely the parts of it which he has occasion to express in the surviving letters."

57. J. S. Stewart, *A Man in Christ*, p. 261.

58. Goguel, *The Birth of Christianity*, p. 196.

59. Cf. Stewart, *op. cit.*, p. 261.

60. This is the basis for Schweitzer's view, *Paul and His Interpreters*, p. 244: "The Apostle's doctrine is integrally, simply and exclusively eschatological." See also Schweitzer's, *The Mysticism of Paul*, p. 140: "All his [Paul's] conceptions and thoughts are rooted in eschatology."

61. Dodd, *Apostolic Preaching*, p. 65.

62. Cf. Schoeps, *op. cit.*, p. 46: "The eschatological approach . . . is able to clarify the Jewish faith-presuppositions from which the apostle of Jesus Christ, placed in a new and unforeseeable situation, namely, the post-messianic, developed something original and really new: that is, Christian theology."

63. S. Sandmel, *The Genius of Paul*, p. 94, has defined his terms too narrowly when he states: "Apart from the letters to the Thessalonians, eschatology enters into Paul's epistles only tangentially. Paul's expectation of the end was vivid; but there was in his mind an interval of time still to be lived through between the now and the coming event."

64. A. M. Hunter, *Interpreting Paul's Gospel*, p. 121.

65. J. A. T. Robinson, *Jesus and His Coming,* p. 160, n.

66. Cf. McCown, *op. cit.,* p. 175, n. 2: "I can find no evidence of development in Paul's eschatology."

67. A further difficulty arises from the fact that there is no certain chronological order for Paul's writings, and all attempts at dating must be tentative.

68. Cf. Hunter, *Paul and His Predecessors,* p. 98: "Paul's thinking on the Last Things changed, developed, deepened. He grew in eschatological insight as in grace." Cf. also Dewick, *op. cit.,* p. 206: "It is difficult to avoid the impression that Paul's thought underwent important modifications, especially in eschatology, as the years passed and as his spirit deepened. There was at least a change in emphasis."

69. Charles, *op. cit.,* pp. 437–461.

70. Dodd, *New Testament Studies,* pp. 108–126.

71. Stewart, *op. cit.,* p. 270.

72. W. L. Knox, *St. Paul and the Church of the Gentiles,* p. 128.

73. Beare, "Exegesis of the Epistle to the Colossians," *The Interpreter's Bible,* Vol. 11, p. 197.

74. *Ibid.,* p. 211.

75. Cf. Hamilton, *op. cit.,* p. 61: "There is a strong presumption against any considerable change in Paul's thought."

76. Cf. J. E. Frame, *A Critical and Exegetical Commentary on the Epistles of St. Paul to the Thessalonians* (International Critical Commentary), p. 177.

77. Cf. Mowry, *op. cit.,* p. 137: "Perhaps . . . he came to feel that the expectation of Christ's return on the clouds was less meaningful than the experience of present union with Christ."

78. Cf. O. Cullmann, *op. cit.,* p. 46. An opposite view is expressed by Dahl, *op. cit.,* p. 89: "For men like St. Paul there can be different *kinds* of time, since time is made up of events to which quality belongs."

79. This may be in the mind of J. A. T. Robinson when he declares, *In the End, God,* p. 70: "St. Paul, as presumably Jesus, undoubtedly thought of the Fall and the Last Judgment as literal events."

80. There is a seventh occurrence in the doubtful passage, Rom. 16:25-27.

81. According to Sanday and Headlam, *A Critical and Exegetical Commentary on the Epistle to the Romans,* p. 378, *kairos* is " used of a definite, measured, or determined time, and so almost technically of the period before the second coming of Christ."

82. Cf. Barr, *op. cit.,* p. 22: " If there is a difference between *chronos* and *kairos* in New Testament usage, it is clear that it cannot correspond to the distinction between ' chronological ' and ' realistic ' time as expounded by Marsh and Robinson."

83. Cf. Sanday and Headlam, *op. cit.,* pp. 353 f.

84. Cf. Barr, *op. cit.,* p. 77: " The cases of *aiōnios* refer fairly uniformly to the being of God or to plans and realities, which, once established by him, are perpetual or unchanging." Cf. also F. V. Filson, " Exegesis of the Second Epistle to the Corinthians," *The Interpreter's Bible,* Vol. 10, p. 326: " The word ' eternal ' does not say that these realities [II Cor. 4:18 – " the things which are not seen "] belong to a timeless sphere, but that they will continue everlastingly."

85. A fourth word for time, *hōra,* " a short period, a moment," appears seven times in the Pauline epistles; and once more we notice Paul's awareness of the necessity to act in the present because time is moving on.

86. W. F. Arndt and F. W. Gingrich, *A Greek-English Lexicon of the New Testament,* p. 532, col. a.

87. Dahl, *op. cit.,* p. 120.

88. Cf. Hamilton, *op. cit.,* p. 70: " These futuristic elements in Paul's writings show that the Platonic conception of time does not fit the apostle's thought."

89. C. K. Barrett, *From First Adam to Last,* p. 82.

90. Cf. Kallas, *op. cit.,* p. 57: " Eschatology was not born in a vacuum. It was created by the earlier conviction that this world had become infected. It was created by the earlier belief in cosmic strife, in demonology, in a world alienated from God."

91. Some of these contrasts are made all the more striking by Paul's use of an alpha privative or other prefix to form a word of opposite meaning while retaining the same root. Some examples are: *kaluptō, apokaluptō; phthartos, aphthartos; thanatos, athanasia.*

92. Cf. Dahl, *op. cit.*, p. 116: "Life, in the Biblical sense, is always a matter of relationship with God."

93. *Ibid.*, p. 117.

94. Cf. Hamilton, *op. cit.*, p. 89: "Biblical eschatology makes possible a striving against evil which does not hesitate at failure because the ultimate victory is God's and is assured."

95. Cf. the definition of *apollumi* given by Dahl, *op. cit.*, p. 108: "To be destroyed without hope of restoration."

96. But for another view cf. Dinkler, *op. cit.*, p. 190: "In Paul two conceptions of eschatology are in tension *and* in balance, two ways of knowing time and temporal occurrences. We have *on the one hand* a conception related to Jewish apocalyptic in its variations of a divine plan of salvation, of an *oikonomia*. . . . Here we have the eschatological perspective on time. *On the other hand* we have an existentialist conception of eschatology and time in which the past and the future are drawn together in the present, in the *kairos*, in which there is a radical conversion into the present of that which eschatologically has taken place."

97. Cf. Wood, *op. cit.*, p. 167: "Important as the Messiah was in Paul's thought, still God was supreme, and Christ existed not for his own sake, but to bring men to God."

98. Cullmann, *op. cit.*, p. 63.

99. The verb used, *hypotassō* is defined by Dahl, *op. cit.*, p. 126, as "the placing of a totality in its rightful place in the eschatological scheme."

100. Cullmann, *op. cit.*, p. 79, has commented on this verse: "God . . . as Lord over time can 'compress' it inasmuch as he determines the duration of the different periods of time, the 'ages.'"

101. Barrett, *op. cit.*, p. 4.

102. Cf. E. Kenneth Lee, *A Study in Romans*, p. 139: "The foundation of Paul's life was his belief in God as the ultimate cause and final purpose of all things."

Chapter II

1. "The Hope of Glory," p. 131.
2. Cullmann, *op. cit.*, p. 66.
3. Filson, *St. Paul's Conception of Recompense*, p. 101.

4. Goguel, *Birth of Christianity,* p. 240.

5. H. L. Goudge, "The Theology of St. Paul," *A New Commentary on Holy Scripture,* ed. by Charles Gore, Part III, p. 435.

6. Goguel, *op. cit.,* p. 277, holds that Paul "interpolates between the reign of Satan and the reign of God an interim period when the two worlds coexist." There is some similarity in the words of Barrett, *From First Adam,* p. 117: "The paradox of time means that in this world, upon the bank and shoal of time, we are the inhabitants of two ages at the same time."

7. Note here the view of Goguel, "Salut dans la théologie, paulinienne," p. 328: "Paulinism is an eschatology not only because the two Epistles to the Thessalonians and the First Epistle to the Corinthians contain some apocalyptic pictures but especially because of its object, that is, an action which God pursues in view of a certain end which will be fully realized only in a beyond." On this point Dodd, *Apostolic Preaching,* p. 79, is in agreement: "This revelation will not be given until the last term in the historical series has come into view – the Day of the Lord."

8. C. H. Dodd, *The Interpretation of the Fourth Gospel,* p. 144, points to the fact that "the word *olam,* with *aiōn* as its equivalent, denotes properly a period of time of which the beginning or the end are both out of sight."

9. J. A. T. Robinson, *In the End, God,* p. 59, sums up this idea as follows: "The function of the imagery of the 'last day' is to indicate in unmistakable idiom the *finality* of the processes of life and death, salvation and judgment, already set in motion by the events of the Incarnation."

10. "*Basileia,*" *Theological Dictionary of the New Testament,* ed. by Gerhard Kittel, tr. by Geoffrey W. Bromiley, Vol. 1, p. 589.

11. See the view of E. F. Scott, *The Kingdom of God in the New Testament,* p. 165: "Where Jesus speaks of the nearness of the Kingdom, Paul thinks of the Spirit working in our hearts."

12. Guy, *op. cit.,* p. 117.

13. Frame, *op. cit.,* p. 105.

14. Schmidt, *op. cit.,* p. 584.

15. R. T. Stamm, "Exegesis of the Epistle to the Galatians," *The Interpreter's Bible,* Vol. 10, p. 565, observes: "Whether in heaven above or on the earth beneath, whether in this present evil age or hereafter in an earthly or heavenly society cleaned of all that defiles, the essentials of this kingdom were the same."

16. Cf. the words of W. D. Davies, *Paul and Rabbinic Judaism,* p. 100: "It is now generally accepted that the idea of a Messiah in apocalyptic did involve the idea of a community of the Messiah." Charles, *op. cit.,* p. 457, has also commented: "According to the doctrine of the kingdom the individual member cannot reach his consummation apart from the consummation of the blessedness of all."

17. See the words of J. A. T. Robinson, *The Body,* p. 80: "The completion of this transformation must wait upon the day of the Parousia."

18. Rudolf Bultmann, *Theology of the New Testament,* Vol. 1, p. 346.

19. F. C. Porter, *op. cit.,* p. 290.

20. J. A. T. Robinson, *Jesus and His Coming,* p. 117.

21. Cf. H. A. Guy, *op. cit.,* p. 111.

22. Noteworthy in this regard is the opinion of H. A. A. Kennedy, *St. Paul's Conceptions of the Last Things,* p. 190: "In marked contrast with the prophetic descriptions of the Day of the Lord, the apostle scarcely ever paints a picture of the Parousia. The only real instance occurs in the earliest of his letters, I Thess. 4:16-18." John Bright, *The Kingdom of God,* p. 238, provides a pertinent reminder: "This eager expectation of the infant church for the return of the Lord ought not to be exaggerated, as if the early Christians spent their time in futile gazing into the clouds and in morbid speculation."

23. Weiss, *op. cit.,* p. 526.

24. Note the perceptive comment of Johannes Munck, *Paul and the Salvation of Mankind,* p. 304: "All eschatological points of time are uncertain, and it is difficult for anyone living and taking part in the last days to know exactly at what eschatological point of time he is."

25. Such is the belief of Albert Schweitzer, *The Mysticism of Paul,* p. 92.

26. The judgment of C. K. Barrett, " New Testament Eschatology," p. 236, is good: " If the [Christian] faith was to survive in a recognizable form it was necessary to restate it in such a way that the eschatological tension, which belief in an imminent Parousia induced, should be retained without the conviction that the Parousia was necessarily imminent."

27. Cf. J. A. T. Robinson, *op. cit.,* pp. 51 f.

28. Niebuhr, *op. cit.,* pp. 289, 291.

29. Cf. Cullmann, *op. cit.,* p. 90: " Only where the Christ who died and rose forms the center do we have Christian apocalyptic."

30. Schoeps, *op. cit.,* p. 99.

31. Schweitzer, *The Mysticism of Paul,* p. 66.

32. Cf. R. H. Charles, *op. cit.,* p. 447: " The apostle did not expect the intervention of a temporary Messianic or millennial period between the Parousia and final judgment."

33. *Ibid.,* p. 463.

34. *From First Adam to Last,* p. 104. See further O. Cullmann, *The Early Church,* p. 147: " It is still possible for the forces and powers that have already been vanquished to manifest themselves within certain limits. Sin and death have not yet destroyed."

35. Leivestad, *op. cit.,* p. 122.

36. *Ibid.,* pp. 99 f.

37. This point is discussed by G. H. C. Macgregor, " Principalities and Powers," *New Testament Sidelights,* ed. by H. K. McArthur, p. 100: " In the first place the scientific mind, preoccupied as it is with the observed sequences of physical cause and effect, rejects spiritualistic causality in every shape and form, and finds Paul's conception of ' principalities and powers ' controlling the destiny of men utterly alien and fantastic. Secondly the theologian has difficulty in discovering adequate content for the conception of ' cosmic ' over against ' personal ' redemption."

38. Dahl, *op. cit.,* p. 50.

39. E. Earle Ellis, " II Corinthians 5:1-10 in Pauline Eschatology," *New Testament Studies,* VI (1959–1960), pp. 223 f.

40. Cf. Kennedy, *op. cit.,* p. 341: " It would be useless to speculate on the *manner* in which St. Paul conceived this great

consummation to be fulfilled. . . . For his mind, its interest and importance are wholly religious."

41. Joseph Klausner, *From Jesus to Paul,* p. 545, objects: "In Pauline Christianity God retains almost no function at all."

42. The observation of N. Q. Hamilton, *op. cit.,* p. 51, is sound: "In the last analysis, Paul's eschatology and pneumatology are determined by his Christology." It should be added, however, that Paul's christology is also a part of his theology.

43. The punctuation and consequent interpretation of Rom. 9:5 are still debated. Phillips and the RSV footnote agree that Paul is here calling Christ God. Most other authorities hold that Paul is only employing a doxology to express his praise of God who has sent Christ into the world.

44. D. E. H. Whitely, *The Theology of St. Paul,* p. 108.

45. C. A. A. Scott, *Christianity According to St. Paul,* p. 277.

46. C. K. Barrett, *op. cit.,* p. 101.

47. Goguel, *Birth of Christianity,* p. 225.

48. See C. K. Barrett, *op. cit.,* p. 93: "The work of Jesus, though complete in itself, required extension and completion in space."

Chapter III

1. So Kennedy, *op. cit.,* p. 89: "The Resurrection of Jesus Christ may be described as the foundation of all that is most vital, all that is most central in the apostle's view of the Last Things."

2. Whitely, *op. cit.,* p. 197.

3. Davies, *Paul and Rabbinic Judaism,* p. 297.

4. Schweitzer, *The Mysticism of Paul,* p. 97, observes: "The simple antithesis between Then and Now is no longer sufficient, because the Resurrection of Jesus, if strictly considered, was not a pre-Messianic but a Messianic event." C. K. Barrett, *A Commentary on the Epistle to the Romans,* p. 127, has also noted: "The death and Resurrection of Jesus were eschatological events, affecting the transition from this age to the age to come."

5. Charles, *op. cit.,* p. 448.

6. Cullmann, *The Early Church,* p. 148.

7. Stewart, *op. cit.,* p. 267. See also the words of Charles, *op. cit.,* p. 449: " The ground of man's resurrection hope was based on his living fellowship with Christ."

8. The remarks of Whitely, *op. cit.,* p. 252, are helpful: " St. Paul's thought includes both the eschatological transformation of the body and the soteriological transformation of the whole personality; and both these changes are made possible by the work of Jesus Christ."

9. Cf. Charles M. Laymon, *Christ in the New Testament,* p. 105: " Redemption in Christ, as Paul views it, is complete when the Christian reaches the state in which he is always to be with his Lord."

10. Cf. E. Earle Ellis, " II Corinthians 5:1-10," p. 224: " Paul's hope here, as throughout his epistles, is not in the abiding individual but in the abiding Christ."

11. F. W. Beare, " Exegesis of the Epistle to the Colossians," p. 170.

12. Cf. C. A. A. Scott, *op. cit.,* p. 263: " Until the Resurrection of Christ the highest thing that could be said of man was that he was ' a living soul,' and even that was qualified by the fact that he was ' of the earth, earthy.' " (Cf. I Cor. 15:45, 47.)

13. W. L. Knox, *St. Paul and the Church of the Gentiles,* p. 140.

14. Cf. Ellis, *op. cit.,* p. 223.

15. On this point see J. Weiss, *op. cit.,* p. 530: " It is characteristic of Paul that the hope set up for the individual is more often and more strongly expressed than the expectation of the great world-catastrophe."

16. Charles, *op. cit.,* p. 444, n. 1. Cf. also I. F. Wood, *op. cit.,* p. 164.

17. *Ibid.,* p. 449. Charles adds: " That the righteous only are raised we shall be forced to conclude also from the apostle's teaching on the origin of the resurrection body in [I Cor.] 15:35-49."

18. Schweitzer, *The Mysticism of Paul,* p. 67.

19. Weiss, *op. cit.,* p. 532.

20. Filson, *St. Paul's Conception of Recompense,* p. 67.

21. " Some Remarks on the *gymnos* in II Corinthians 5:3," *Studia Paulina,* ed. by J. N. Sevenster and W. C. van Unnik, p. 207.

22. Dahl, *op. cit.,* p. 76, n. 3. He continues, somewhat illogically: " The resurrection will mean the lifting of the whole totality of human nature into a new level of existence and this totality embraces all men."

23. Whitely, *op. cit.,* p. 272.

24. Davies, *Paul and Rabbinic Judaism,* p. 311. According to Weiss, *op. cit.,* p. 539, Paul reflects the view that the dead lie in the grave until the day of resurrection and also the view that the dead are already with God.

25. T. F. Glasson, *Greek Influence in Jewish Eschatology,* p. 41.

26. Cf. Bicknell, *op. cit.,* p. 43, commenting on I Thess. 4:13-18: " As yet there was no Christian doctrine of an intermediate state."

27. Note the comment of Sevenster, *op. cit.,* p. 212: " Not the individual dying has his [Paul's] interest primarily, but the eschatological sequence of salvation."

28. Schweitzer, *The Mysticism of Paul,* p. 113.

29. Cullmann, *The Early Church,* p. 149. See also Filson, *op. cit.,* p. 121.

30. R. F. Hetlinger, " II Corinthians 5:1-10," *Scottish Journal of Theology,* X (1957), p. 193.

31. So Cullmann, *Christ and Time,* p. 237: " The New Testament knows nothing of an immediate resurrection of the body that will occur for each one immediately after his death."

32. The modern viewpoint is stated by Hetlinger, *op. cit.,* p. 192: " The fact that for nineteen centuries the Parousia has not come and Christians in their millions have died has inevitably made the question of the ' intermediate state ' of much greater interest for us than it was for the church of the first century."

33. Cullmann, *The Early Church,* p. 148. Cf. Also his *Christ and Time,* pp. 240 f.

34. Hetlinger, *op. cit.,* p. 194.

35. Cf. Robinson, *In the End, God,* p. 94: " The idea of two kingdoms and two resurrections . . . is best viewed as an at-

tempt to harmonize, under the form of successive events, the two elements of the myth stressed by the Prophets and Apocalyptists respectively, namely, that the meaning of history must be vindicated *within* history and yet that the complete purpose of God must *transcend* history." Cf. also Schoeps, *op. cit.*, p. 107.

36. Albrecht Oepke, "*gymnos*," Kittel's *Theological Dictionary*, I, p. 774.

37. Ellis, *op. cit.*, p. 224.

38. Cf. Wood, *op. cit.*, pp. 165 f., where he suggests that Paul overlooks entirely the time of the intermediate state: "That is not the subject he is discussing in either of these passages. . . . We can only say that the problem seems to have no particular religious importance in his mind."

39. Sevenster, *op. cit.*, p. 209. Cf. also Hetlinger, *op. cit.*, p. 179: "There are insurmountable objections to understanding *gymnos* as a reference to the condition of dead Christians."

40. Davies, *op. cit.*, p. 318.

41. Cf. Hunter, *Interpreting Paul's Gospel*, p. 55: "In II Cor. 5:1 ff., he apparently holds that it is at death that the new body is assumed."

42. Charles, *op. cit.*, p. 453, answers the question "When does the resurrection of the body take place?" by stating: "Unless, our interpretation of this doctrine is wholly wrong, its entire trend points not to a period externally determined and at some possibly remote age, but to the hour of departure of the individual believer."

43. J. A. T. Robinson, *The Body*, p. 9.

44. *Ibid.*, p. 28. Cf. Hunter, *op. cit.*, p. 54: "For Paul, the 'body' is the organic principle of identity which persists through the years and all changes of substance."

45. W. D. Davies, *Paul and Rabbinic Judaism*, p. 303.

46. Stacey, *op. cit.*, p. 181.

47. So Weiss, *op. cit.*, p. 537: "Paul in his doctrine of the resurrection took a middle position between the crude physical belief of popular Judaism and the more spiritual hope common to Hellenistic thought."

48. *In the End, God*, p. 89. However, in a later writing, *The Body*, p. 78, he overstates the case and draws unwarranted

conclusions: "It is a mistake to approach Paul's writings with the modern idea that the resurrection of the body has to do with the moment of death, and that it is the guarantee of our survival as distinct individual selves. . . . The implication of 'the body' for Hebrew, as opposed to Greek and later Western, thinking is one of solidarity, not of individuation." We shall point out later how Paul's view of the Christian fellowship both defines and preserves individuality.

49. See Stacey, *op. cit.,* pp. 222 f.: "The use of *psychē, pneuma, sōma, sarx,* and *kardia* to describe man as a unity under various aspects is conclusive evidence of the Semitic cast of Paul's mind. . . . No word in Paul's anthropology is so precise that it does not somewhere overlap another." Dahl, *op. cit.,* p. 126, defines *psychē* as "the 'life' of a totality in its most elementary sense, namely as called out of the Void and, therefore, liable to 'slip back' into it."

50. Charles, *op. cit.,* p. 468.

51. Robinson, *The Body,* p. 31.

52. See Hetlinger, *op. cit.,* p. 187: "The traditional Jewish doctrine of resurrection was specifically associated with the end of the age for the very good reason that resurrection of the body was understood to involve the same material elements as had formed the natural body—and which, therefore, could not constitute the new resurrection body until the whole physical world of nature was transformed."

53. Robinson, *The Body,* p. 79.

54. The influence of this type of thought upon Judaism is recognized by W. D. Davies, *Paul and Rabbinic Judaism,* p. 308: "There would be many Pharisees prepared to argue, as Paul does, for a transformed resurrection body."

55. Knox, *op. cit.,* p. 127, n. 1.

56. Stacey, *op. cit.,* p. 127.

57. Cf. Sevenster, *op. cit.,* p. 210, and also Dahl, *op. cit.,* p. 25.

58. Charles, *op. cit.,* p. 469.

59. Leivestad, *op. cit.,* p. 117, n.

60. *Ibid.,* p. 140.

61. The comment of Cullmann, *The Early Church,* p. 166, is to be noted: "The Holy Spirit, while unable to change our carnal bodies into spiritual bodies before the Parousia, by an-

ticipation extends its activity here and now into the sphere of the *sōma*."

62. Charles, *op. cit.,* p. 473.

63. Niebuhr, *op. cit.,* p. 297.

64. Cf. Wood, *op. cit.,* p. 163: " The figure of the seed sown does not point to the body laid in the grave as the seed from which the resurrection body is formed."

65. Stewart, *op. cit.,* p. 267. Cf. also Dahl, *op. cit.,* p. 94.

66. Dahl, *op. cit.,* p. 94.

67. It is difficult to accept the opinion of Robinson, *The Body,* p. 72: " The depression from which even Paul himself suffers derives from the fact that we cannot be *sure* that this very fragile house of flesh will in fact last us until the Parousia, and that we shall not be required to face a temporary disembodiment." The words of Paul in II Cor. 5: 2-4 do not support such an interpretation, and we have already shown that Paul did not expect a period of waiting after death and before the Parousia.

68. See W. L. Knox, *op. cit.,* p. 137: " Paul was too good a Jew and too poor a Hellenist to describe the soul as being delivered from the clothing of the body so that it might ascend to heaven naked."

69. " Brèves remarques sur la notion de *sōma pneumatikon,*" *Background of the New Testament and Its Eschatology,* p. 361.

70. Cf. D. J. Selby, *Toward the Understanding of St. Paul,* p. 333: " The spiritual body . . . is unquestionably an indirect description of Jesus as in his conversion appearance Paul had seen him."

71. Note the interesting suggestion of Whitely, *op. cit.,* p. 260: " It may well be that if St. Paul had been questioned on this matter, he would have said that, when Christ comes again, all bodies will be transformed, both the ' physical ' bodies of the survivors and the building which God is to provide for the deceased."

72. See Dahl, *op. cit.,* p. 81: " [Man's] ultimate destiny is to be a totality . . . taken up into the life of the Spirit himself, so that the whole totality is so controlled and possessed by the Spirit that it shares his life-giving powers."

73. *Ibid.,* p. 75.

74. Cf. Cullmann, *Christ and Time,* p. 48, n. 21: " Since

eternity [*aiōnios,* 'agelong'] comes into consideration only as an attribute of God, the adjective *aiōnios* has the tendency to lose its time sense and is used in the qualitative sense of divine-immortal."

75. See Robinson, *op. cit.,* p. 32, n. 1: "It is indeed only in the light of the Resurrection and of the glorious destiny of the body revealed in Christ, the first fruits, that Paul, the Hebrew, comes to see a distinction between *sarx* and *sōma* as essential."

Chapter IV

1. Filson, *St. Paul's Conception of Recompense,* p. 28.
2. Barrett, *Commentary on Romans,* p. 33.
3. R. V. G. Tasker, *The Biblical Doctrine of the Wrath of God,* p. 40.
4. Caird, *op. cit.,* p. 40.
5. Tasker, *op. cit.,* p. 11.
6. Bicknell, *op. cit.,* p. 9.
7. Whitely, *op. cit.,* p. 72.
8. There is no need to discuss here the etymological connection between the verb "to justify," *dikaioō,* and the noun "righteousness," *dikaiosynē.* It is sufficient to indicate that man's justification comes either through his acceptance as if he were righteous by a righteous God or (preferably) by his gift from a righteous God of some of the divine quality. In any case, justification is due solely to the initiative and might of God.
9. Niebuhr, *op. cit.,* p. 292.
10. Filson, *op. cit.,* p. 55.
11. Kennedy, *op. cit.,* p. 198.
12. Tasker, *op. cit.,* p. v.
13. Ellis, "II Corinthians 5:1-10," p. 220.
14. Filson, *op. cit.,* p. 51.
15. Stewart, *op. cit.,* p. 269. Cf. also the statement of Rowley, *op. cit.,* p. 174: "The apocalyptists all look forward to a great Assize at the end of history, when men and nations shall be judged at the bar of God. All must one day render account of their actions and receive the due recompense of their deeds from the hand of God."

16. Kennedy, *op. cit.,* p. 202.
17. Niebuhr, *op. cit.,* p. 293.
18. Cf. Filson, *op. cit.,* p. 46: " The great conclusive expression of God's hatred of sin is yet to come and is regarded as a fearful event from which Christians may hope to escape safely but which holds out terror for defenseless sinners."
19. *Ho theos* as the subject of the verb *synergei,* " works together," is found in the early and important MSS P46, A and B, and has at least a good claim to be original. In any case, however, it is quite proper to assign the unexpressed " he " (referring to *ho theos* as the nearest antecedent) as the subject of the third person singular verb and to treat *panta* as its direct object or as an adverbial accusative.
20. Barrett, *op. cit.,* p. 45.
21. Filson, *op cit.,* p. 106. Cf. I Cor. 3:8.
22. Whitely, *op. cit.,* p. 163.
23. *Ibid.,* p. 156.
24. Tasker, *op. cit.,* p. 38.
25. Guy, *op. cit.,* p. 113.
26. Wood, *op. cit.,* p. 168.
27. Filson, *op. cit.,* p. 15.
28. *Ibid.,* p. 34: " Paul does not theorize about the fate of individuals whom he cannot possibly reach with the Gospel message."
29. Dodd, *New Testament Studies,* p. 123.
30. Charles, *op. cit.,* p. 455.
31. Cf. Dahl, *op. cit.,* p. 108.
32. Charles, *op. cit.,* p. 443. Charles proceeds (p. 444): " There is no reference to a resurrection of the wicked in these two epistles [I and II Thess.]."
33. Filson, *op. cit.,* p. 69.
34. Hunter, *Interpreting Paul's Gospel,* p. 138.
35. Barrett, *From First Adam,* p. 96.
36. Minear, *Eyes of Faith,* p. 229.
37. Dodd, *New Testament Studies,* p. 125.
38. Hunter, *Interpreting Paul's Gospel,* p. 139. Cf. W. L. Knox, *op. cit.,* p. 141: " He [Paul] was not prepared to abandon the eternal responsibility of man for his deeds."
39. Tasker, *op. cit.,* p. 39. Cf. Frame, *op. cit.,* p. 239: " Paul,

while practically certain that all believers will be acquitted at *bēma Christou* because of the presence in them of Christ or the Spirit as the power into righteousness, reckons with the possibility that believers may fall out of the realm of grace and disregard the promptings of the Spirit."

40. Caird, *op. cit.,* p. 95.

Chapter V

1. Barrett, *From First Adam,* p. 5.
2. Manson, *Teaching of Jesus,* p. 247, n. 2.
3. Mowry, *op. cit.,* p. 151.
4. Goguel, *Birth of Christianity,* p. 236.
5. Of course, Adam is the Hebrew word for man or a human being. Cf. Gen. 1:26 f.; 2:7.
6. Cf. the definition of Grundmann, *op. cit.,* p. 76: " Sin . . . is active hatred towards God . . . on the part of man in his determination to live for himself and manage by himself."
7. Cf. J. Jeremias, " *Adam," Theological Dictionary of the New Testament,* ed. by G. Kittel, I, p. 142.
8. Dahl, *op. cit.,* p. 69.
9. Barrett, *From First Adam,* p. 9. Cf. also his *Commentary on Romans,* p. 74, in a discussion of the statement in Rom. 2:23: " All fall short of the glory of God." " The present tense is used, and presumably means that man now lacks what he might now have had, that is, the glory with which Adam was created and which he (and all mankind with him) lost through sin."
10. Davies, *Paul and Rabbinic Judaism,* p. 44.
11. *Ibid.,* p. 34.
12. Scott, *op. cit.,* p. 47.
13. Wilder, " Eschatological Imagery," p. 244.
14. Barr, *op. cit.,* p. 28.
15. Bultmann, " History and Eschatology in the New Testament," p. 11.
16. Barrett, *From First Adam,* p. 36.
17. *Ibid.* p. 60.
18. *Ibid.,* p. 62.
19. Cf. Barrett, *From First Adam,* p. 52: " Moses remains a

figure of glory, but instead of exalting his glory, as Philo and the Rabbis do, Paul minimizes it."

20. W. D. Davies, *Paul and Rabbinic Judaism,* p. 105. Cf. also Bright, *op. cit.,* p. 204: "The comparison of the work of Christ with that of Moses is very much to the fore in the thought of Paul."

21. Elias Andrews, *The Meaning of Christ for Paul,* p. 76.

22. Porter, *op. cit.,* p. 287.

23. Whitely, *op. cit.,* p. 25.

24. Dinkler, *op. cit.,* p. 183. Cf. W. Gutbrod, "Law," *Bible Key Words,* p. 114: "Apart from the death of Christ and from death in Christ, man is still *en kosmō* and hence handed over to the law."

25. Leivestad, *op. cit.,* p. 124.

26. Ellis, *Paul and His Recent Interpreters,* p. 34.

27. W. B. Davies, *Paul and Rabbinic Judaism,* p. 19.

28. Stacey, *op. cit.,* p. 229.

29. Barrett, *Commentary on Romans,* p. 127.

30. Cullmann, *Christ and Time,* p. 193.

31. Cadbury, *op. cit.,* p. 381.

32. Caird, *op. cit.,* p. 51.

33. Whitely, *op. cit.,* p. 27.

34. Leivestad, *op. cit.,* p. 94.

35. Cf. Kallas, *op. cit.,* p. 53: "The literature of the intertestamental period abounds with accounts of the fall of the angels."

36. Grundmann, *op. cit.,* p. 80.

Chapter VI

1. Dodd, *Apostolic Preaching,* p. 65.

2. Cf. Porter, *op. cit.,* p. 287: "The Christian . . . has already been delivered out of it [the present world]. He is experiencing its end."

3. Schoeps, *op. cit.,* p. 98.

4. Cullmann, *Christ and Time,* p. 92.

5. Goguel, *Birth of Christianity,* p. 224.

6. Barrett, *From First Adam,* p. 69.

7. Jeremias, *op. cit.,* p. 142.

8. Robinson, *In the End, God,* p. 57, n.

9. Dinkler, *op. cit.*, p. 182. Cf. Goguel, *The Birth of Christianity*, p. 282: "[For Paul] the celestial realm and salvation ceased to be objects of hope and became objects of present experience."

10. Schweitzer, *The Mysticism of Paul*, p. 75.

11. Barrett, *Commentary on Romans*, p. 28.

12. Schweitzer, *The Mysticism of Paul*, p. 69. Cf. Schoeps, *op. cit.*, p. 171: "The abolition of the law is a Messianological doctrine in Pauline theology."

13. Gutbrod, *op. cit.*, p. 106.

14. *Ibid.*, p. 115.

15. Lindars, *op. cit.*, p. 56.

16. Robinson, *The Body*, p. 82. Cf. II Cor. 5:17 and Gal. 6:15.

17. Charles, *op. cit.*, p. 469. Cf. Hamilton, *op. cit.*, p. 6: "The Spirit is the agent on earth which communicates the benefits of the new covenant."

18. John Knox, "Exegesis of the Epistle to the Romans," *The Interpreter's Bible*, Vol. 9, p. 406. Cf. Schweitzer, *The Mysticism of Paul*, p. 99: "Resurrection powers, that is to say powers of the supernatural world, were already at work within the created world."

19. Cullmann, *Early Church*, p. 155.

20. Robinson, *Jesus and His Coming*, p. 34. Cf. Cullmann, *Christ and Time*, p. 151: "Christ rules over all things in heaven and on earth. The spatial center of this Lordship is the Church, which constitutes his Body upon earth."

21. Col. 1:13 f. Cf. Davies, *Paul and Rabbinic Judaism*, p. 296.

22. Goguel, *The Birth of Christianity*, p. 237.

23. Moule, *op. cit.*, p. 98.

24. Cf. H. Wheeler Robinson, *The Christian Doctrine of Man*, pp. 109 f.

25. E. Schweizer, "Spirit of God," *Bible Key Words*, p. 68.

26. John Knox, *Chapters in a Life of Paul*, p. 135.

27. Dodd, *The Apostolic Preaching*, p. 62.

28. E. F. Scott, *The Spirit in the New Testament*, p. 183.

29. Davies, *Christian Origins and Judaism*, p. 175.

30. C. A. A. Scott, *op. cit.*, p. 258.

31. Moule, *op. cit.,* p. 167.

32. " Salut dans la théologie paulinienne," p. 329. Cf. also Schoeps, *op. cit.,* p. 99: " This mingling of the two ages constitutes the distinctive eschatological standpoint of Pauline theology."

33. Moule, *op. cit.,* pp. 69 f.

34. Barrett, *Commentary on Romans,* p. 118.

35. Dinkler, *op. cit.,* p. 184.

36. Cullmann, *Early Church,* p. 144.

37. Barrett, " New Testament Eschatology," p. 235. Paul Minear, *Eyes of Faith,* p. 273, considers this question from a more philosophical point of view: " One result of the Messiah's coming is therefore a new apprehension of the nature and structure of time itself. Since the end has come before the end, something has happened to measurements of duration, to the relationship of the tenses. This event demonstrates the incommensurability of the world's time and God's."

38. Lindars, *op. cit.,* p. 257.

39. Cullmann, *Early Church,* p. 23.

40. C. H. Thompson, *Theology of the Kerygma,* p. 157.

41. Barrett, *Commentary on Romans,* p. 232.

42. C. A. A. Scott, *op. cit.,* p. 147. Cf. W. Manson, " Eschatology in the New Testament," *Eschatology,* by W. Manson, G. W. L. Lampe, T. F. Torrance, W. A. Whitehouse (Scottish Journal of Theology Occasional Papers, No. 2), p. 7.

43. Goguel, " Le caractère," p. 327.

44. Grundmann *op. cit.,* p. 83. Cf. on this point the position of Porter, *op. cit.,* p. 283: " Paul found himself a new being in a new world; and yet all things outwardly remained as they were. The other world must therefore be within and not beyond. A spiritualizing of the apocalyptical hope would be necessarily involved in the conviction that the new age was in a real sense present." Although Porter's analysis of the situation is basically correct, he seems to seek a reconciliation of the tension by a dualistic view of the " within " and the " beyond " which does not correspond to Paul's concept of the uniqueness of the interim period.

45. Ellis, *Paul and His Recent Interpreters,* p. 39.

46. Baird, *Paul's Message and Mission,* p. 155.

47. Tasker, *op. cit.*, p. 42.
48. Cf. Cullmann, *Christ and Time,* p. 72: "The time between the resurrection and the return of Christ cannot be regarded as a mere 'escape from embarrassment,' intended only to cover up the disillusionment that resulted from the delay of the Parousia."
49. Whitely, *op. cit.*, pp. 148 f.
50. Leivestad, *op. cit.*, p. 140.
51. Rowley, *op. cit.*, p. 158.
52. Robinson, *The Body,* p. 70.
53. *Ibid.*, p. 71.
54. Hunter, "Hope of Glory," p. 138.
55. Barrett, *From First Adam,* p. 99. Cf. A. C. Purdy, "Paul the Apostle," p. 700: "The Church is not so much an agency for promoting desirable causes; it is itself an invasion of the eschaton into time."
56. Grant, *Roman Hellenism,* p. 132.
57. Charles, *op. cit.*, p. 440.
58. Munck, *op. cit.*, p. 38.
59. Leivestad, *op. cit.*, p. 148.
60. *Ibid.*, p. 284.
61. Minear, *op. cit.*, p. 257.
62. E. F. Scott, *Kingdom of God in the New Testament,* p. 141.

Chapter VII

1. Oepke, "*baptō,*" Kittel's *Theological Dictionary,* I, p. 537.
2. *Baptism in the New Testament,* p. 162.
3. Cf. Barrett, *Commentary on Romans,* p. 127: "The sacrament of baptism does not in this life effect its own full meaning."
4. Grundmann, *op. cit.*, p. 76.
5. W. F. Flemington, *The New Testament Doctrine of Baptism,* p. 71.
6. Moule, "The Judgment Theme in the Sacraments," *Background of the New Testament and Its Eschatology,* p. 467.
7. Flemington, *op. cit.*, p. 59.
8. Davies, *Paul and Rabbinic Judaism,* p. 122.

9. Cf. F. Blas and A. Debrunner, *A Greek Grammar of the New Testament,* tr., ed., and rev. by R. W. Funk, p. 172: " The present imperative is durative or iterative; the aorist imperative punctiliar."

10. Cullmann, *Baptism in the New Testament,* p. 29.

11. Schoeps, *op. cit.,* p. 113.

12. E. F. Scott, *Spirit in the New Testament,* p. 154.

13. Lee, *op. cit.,* p. 135.

14. Cf. Cullmann, *Christ and Time,* p. 236.

15. E. F. Scott, *op. cit.,* p. 140.

16. Flemington *op. cit.,* p. 56.

17. Whitely, *op. cit.,* p. 172.

18. Barrett, *From First Adam,* p. 108.

19. Cullmann, *Christ and Time,* p. 155.

20. A. J. B. Higgins, *The Lord's Supper in the New Testament,* p. 37.

21. Schoeps, *op. cit.,* p. 116. Suggested references are Enoch 60:7 f.; IV Ezra 6:49-52; Syr. Baruch 29:4; Test. Isaac 8:11, 20.

22. Dodd, *Apostolic Preaching,* p. 93. Cf. Schoeps, *op. cit.,* p. 116: " After the resurrection the Eucharist has become for the disciples an anticipation and a present realization of the Messianic feast of the blessed."

23. Whitely *op. cit.,* p. 141.

24. Higgins, *op. cit.,* p. 70.

25. Johannes Behm, " *haima,*" Kittel's *Theological Dictionary,* I, p. 174.

26. Higgins, *op. cit.,* p. 69.

27. Cullmann, *Christ and Time,* p. 155.

28. Higgins, *op. cit.,* p. 72.

29. Moule, *op. cit.,* p. 471.

30. Grant, *Roman Hellenism,* p. 145.

31. Schweitzer, *Paul and His Interpreters,* p. 217.

32. Schoeps, *op. cit.,* p. 111.

33. Dahl, *op. cit.,* p. 95.

34. Dodd, *The Apostolic Preaching,* p. 94.

35. Oepke, *op. cit.,* p. 540.

36. Higgins, *op. cit.,* p. 63.

37. Neville Clark, *An Approach to the Theology of the Sacraments,* p. 70.

38. Behm, "*anamnēsis,*" Kittel's *Theological Dictionary,* I, p. 349. Cf. also Whitely, *op. cit.,* p. 178: "'Remember' suggests not only subjectively recalling the dead past which no longer exists, but, in the active sense, objectively *recalling* the past so that it is again present and living."

39. Clark, *op. cit.,* p. 26.

CHAPTER VIII

1. Goguel, *Birth of Christianity,* p. 227.

2. Grundmann, "Uberlieferung und Eigenaussage im Eschatologischen Denken des Apostels Paulus," *New Testament Studies,* 8 (1961), p. 17. Cf. further, Cullmann, *Christ and Time,* p. 217: "The redemptive history has as its goal the individual."

3. Ellis, *Paul and His Recent Interpreters,* p. 38.

4. Oepke, *op. cit.,* p. 542.

5. Moule, "The Judgment Theme in the Sacraments," p. 469.

6. Filson, *St. Paul's Conception of Recompense,* p. 36.

7. Donald J. Selby, *Toward the Understanding of St. Paul,* p. 327. Cf. the similar comment by Purdy, *op. cit.,* p. 702: "The Christian, Paul insists, lives a new life; he is a new creation; yet he must be exhorted and admonished to *be* what he *is,* to act in accordance with his new nature."

8. Filson, *op. cit.,* p. 88.

9. Sanday, *op. cit.,* p. 348.

10. Filson, *op. cit.,* p. 129.

11. A. B. D. Alexander, *The Ethics of St. Paul,* p. 206.

12. Beardslee, *op. cit.,* p. 65.

13. Niebuhr, *op. cit.,* p. 308.

14. Cullmann, *Early Church,* p. 158.

15. Bicknell, *op. cit.,* p. 51.

16. Lindars, *op. cit.,* p. 247.

17. Beardslee, *op. cit.,* p. 69.

18. Schweitzer, *Mysticism of Paul,* p. 96. However, Schweitzer still finds the eschatological hope strong. Cf. *ibid.,* p. 36: "It is clearly apparent from the actual substance of his [Paul's] teaching that his mysticism of the Dying and Rising again with

Christ is centered in an ardent eschatological expectation."

19. Caird, *op. cit.,* p. 87.
20. Moule, *The Birth of the New Testament,* p. 101.
21. Davies, *Paul and Rabbinic Judaism,* p. 112.
22. Robinson, *The Body,* p. 81.
23. Goguel, " Le caractère du salut," p. 335.
24. C. H. Dodd, *History and the Gospel,* p. 171.
25. Bultmann, " History and Eschatology in the New Testament," p. 14.
26. Niebuhr, *op. cit.,* p. 287.
27. Filson, *op. cit.,* p. 134. Cf. Beardslee, *op. cit.,* p. 41: " Paul places work in an eschatological setting, seeing it as a response to God's call and command, in relation to God's purpose."
28. Beare, " Exegesis of the Epistle to the Colossians," p. 209. Cf. Col. 3:1.
29. W. D. Davies, *Paul and Rabbinic Judaism,* p. 147.
30. Beardslee, *op. cit.,* p. 130.
31. Alexander, *op. cit.,* p. 107.
32. Barrett, *Commentary on Romans,* p. 124.
33. Hamilton, *op. cit.,* p. 87.
34. Weiss, *op. cit.,* p. 544.
35. Alexander, *op. cit.,* p. 204.
36. Bicknell, *op. cit.,* p. 37.
37. Beardslee, *op. cit.,* p. 70.
38. The Pauline vocabulary is rich in words expressing progress and development.
39. Robinson, *The Body,* p. 80.
40. Alexander, *op. cit.,* p. 200.
41. Beardslee, *op. cit.,* p. 72.
42. Barrett, *From First Adam,* p. 110.
43. Caird, *op. cit.,* p. 99.
44. Beardslee, *op. cit.,* p. 77.

Chapter IX

1. Filson, *St. Paul's Conception of Recompense,* p. 128.
2. Schoeps, *op. cit.,* p. 46.
3. Barr, *op. cit.,* p. 127.

4. Rudolf Bultmann, *Jesus and the Word,* p. 56.
5. Bicknell, *op. cit.,* p. 47.
6. Caird, " On Deciphering the Book of Revelation," III, *The Expository Times,* LXXIV, No. 3, Dec. 1962, p. 83.
7. Scott, *The Kingdom of God in the New Testament,* p. 116. Reinhold Niebuhr has reminded us (*op. cit.,* p. 294) : " It is unwise for Christians to claim any knowledge of either the furniture of heaven or the temperature of hell; or to be too certain about any details of the Kingdom of God in which history is consummated."
8. Petry, *op. cit.,* p. 30.
9. Cf. A. M. Hunter, *Interpreting Paul's Gospel,* p. 124: " Our task is to discover the basic truth embodied in Paul's myth or symbol . . . and to translate it into contemporary terms."
10. Dahl, *op. cit.,* p. 95.
11. Cf. J. F. Wood, " Paul's Eschatology," p. 168.
12. Kennedy, *op. cit.,* p. 27.
13. Cave, *op. cit.,* p. 242.
14. Purdy, *op. cit.,* p. 703.
15. Moule, *The Birth of the New Testament,* p. 103.
16. Dahl, *op. cit.,* p. 91.
17. Hunter, *Interpreting Paul's Gospel,* p. 130.
18. Cullmann, *The Early Church,* p. 144.
19. Fison, *op. cit.,* p. 242.
20. Cullmann, *The Early Church,* p. 156.
21. Barrett, *From First Adam to Last,* p. 105.
22. Dodd, *New Testament Studies,* p. 113.
23. Barrett, *From First Adam,* p. 89.
24. Marsh, *op. cit.,* p. 178.
25. Petry, *op. cit.,* p. 20.
26. Cadbury, *op. cit.,* p. 372.
27. Beardslee, *op. cit.,* p. 16.
28. Stewart, " On a Neglected Emphasis in New Testament Theology," *Scottish Journal of Theology,* Vol. IV, 1951, p. 301. Cf. also Tasker, *op. cit.,* p. v: " The severity of Biblical Christianity has largely been lost sight of, with far-reaching and disastrous results in many spheres of life."

◈ ◈ ◈ BIBLIOGRAPHY

Alexander, A. B. D., *The Ethics of St. Paul.* Glasgow: Maclehose, 1910.

Andrews, Elias, *The Meaning of Christ for Paul.* Abingdon-Cokesbury Press, 1949.

Arndt, W. F., and Gingrich, F. W., *A Greek Lexicon of the New Testament.* Cambridge: Cambridge University Press, 1957.

Bailey, J. W., " Exegesis of the First and Second Epistles to the Thessalonians," *The Interpreter's Bible,* Vol. 11. Abingdon Press, 1955.

Baird, William, *Paul's Message and Mission.* Abingdon Press, 1960.

Barclay, William, *The Mind of St. Paul.* Harper & Row, Publishers, Inc., 1958.

Barr, James, *Biblical Words for Time* (Studies in Biblical Theology, No. 33). London: SCM Press, Ltd., 1962.

Barrett, C. K., *A Commentary on the Epistle to the Romans.* London: Adam and Charles Black, Ltd., 1957.

——— *From First Adam to Last.* London: Adam and Charles Black, Ltd., 1962.

——— " New Testament Eschatology," *Scottish Journal of Theology,* Vol. VI, 1953, pp. 136–155, 225–243.

Beardslee, W. A., *Human Achievement and Divine Vocation in the Message of Paul* (Studies in Biblical Theology, No. 31). Alec R. Allenson, Inc., 1961.

Beare, F. W., " Exegesis of the Epistle to the Ephesians," *The Interpreter's Bible,* Vol. 10. Abingdon-Cokesbury Press, 1953.

Beare, F. W., " Exegesis of the Epistle to the Colossians," *The Interpreter's Bible,* Vol. 11, 1955.

——— " New Testament Christianity and the Hellenistic World," *The Communication of the Gospel in New Testament Times,* by A. Farrer, C. F. Evans, *et al.* London: S.P.C.K., 1961.

Beasley-Murray, G. P., *Baptism in the New Testament.* London: Macmillan & Co., Ltd., 1962.

Behm, Johannes, " *haima,*" and " *anamnēsis,*" *Theological Dictionary of the New Testament,* Vol. I ed. by G. Kittel, tr. by G. W. Bromiley. Wm. B. Eerdmans Publishing Company, 1961.

Bicknell, E. G., *The First and Second Epistles to the Thessalonians* (Westminster Commentaries). London: Methuen & Co., Ltd., 1932.

Black, M., *The Scrolls and Christian Origins.* London: Thomas Nelson & Sons, 1961.

Blass, F., and Debrunner, A., *A Greek Grammar of the New Testament,* tr., ed., and rev. by R. W. Funk. The University of Chicago Press, 1961.

Bright, John, *The Kingdom of God.* Abingdon-Cokesbury Press, 1953.

Bultmann, Rudolf, *History and Eschatology.* Edinburgh: Edinburgh University Press, 1957.

——— " History and Eschatology in the New Testament," *New Testament Studies,* Vol. I, 1954.

——— *Jesus and the Word,* rev. ed., tr. by Louise P. Smith and Erminie H. Lantero. Charles Scribner's Sons, 1958.

——— *Theology of the New Testament,* tr. by K. Grobel, Vol. I. Charles Scribner's Sons, 1951.

Burrows, M., *The Dead Sea Scrolls.* The Viking Press, Inc., 1956.

——— *More Light on the Dead Sea Scrolls.* London: Martin Secker & Warburg, Ltd., 1958.

Burton, E. W., *A Critical and Exegetical Commentary on the Epistle to the Galatians* (International Critical Commentary). Edinburgh: T. and T. Clark, 1921.

Cadbury, H. J., " Concurrent Phases of Paul's Religion," *Studies in Early Christianity,* ed. by S. J. Case. Century House Americana, 1928.

Caird, G. B., " Paul's Theology," *Dictionary of the Bible,* rev. ed., ed. by J. Hastings. Charles Scribner's Sons, 1963.

——— *Principalities and Powers.* Oxford: Oxford University Press, 1956.

Cave, Sydney, *The Gospel of St. Paul.* London: Hodder & Stoughton, Ltd., 1928.

Charles, R. H., *Eschatology: The Doctrine of a Future Life,* 2d ed. London: Adam and Charles Black, Ltd., 1913.

Clark, Neville, *An Approach to the Theology of the Sacraments* (Studies in Biblical Theology, No. 17). London: SCM Press, Ltd., 1956.

Clavier, H., " Brèves remarques sur la notion de *sōma pneumatikon,*" *Background of the New Testament and Its Eschatology,* ed. by W. D. Davies and D. Daube. Cambridge: Cambridge University Press, 1956.

Craig, C. T., " Exegesis of the First Epistle to the Corinthians," *The Interpreter's Bible,* Vol. 10. Abingdon-Cokesbury Press, 1953.

Cross, F. M., Jr., *The Ancient Library of Qumrân,* rev. ed. London: Gerald Duckworth & Co., Ltd., 1961.

Cullmann, Oscar, *Baptism in the New Testament* (Studies in Biblical Theology, No. 1), tr. by J.K.S. Reid. London: SCM Press, Ltd., 1950.

——— *The Christology of the New Testament,* tr. by S. C. Guthrie and C. A. M. Hall. The Westminster Press, 1959.

——— *The Early Church,* ed. by A. J. B. Higgins. London: SCM Press, Ltd., 1956.

——— *Christ and Time,* 2d ed., tr. by F. V. Filson. The Westminster Press, 1963.

Dahl, M. E., *The Resurrection of the Body* (Studies in Biblical Theology, No. 36). London: SCM Press, Ltd., 1962.

Davies, Paul E., " The Relevance of Apocalyptic for Ancient and Modern Situations," *The Study of the Bible Today and Tomorrow,* ed. by H. R. Willoughby. The University of Chicago Press, 1947.

Davies, W. D., *Christian Origins and Judaism.* London: Darton Longman and Todd, 1962; The Westminster Press, 1962.

——— *Paul and Rabbinic Judaism,* 2d ed. London: S.P.C.K., 1955.

Dewick, E. C., *Primitive Christian Eschatology.* Cambridge:

Cambridge University Press, 1912.

Dillistone, F. W., *Christianity and Symbolism*. London: William Collins Sons & Co., Ltd., 1955.

Dinkler, Erich, " Earliest Christianity," *The Idea of History in the Ancient Near East,* ed. by R. C. Dentan. Yale University Press, 1955.

Dodd, C. H., *The Apostolic Preaching and Its Developments.* London: Hodder & Stoughton, Ltd., 1936.

——— *History and the Gospel.* Charles Scribner's Sons, 1938.

——— *The Parables of the Kingdom,* rev. ed. Charles Scribner's Sons, 1961.

——— *The Bible and the Greeks.* London: Hodder & Stoughton, Ltd., 1935.

——— *New Testament Studies.* Manchester: Manchester University Press, 1953.

——— *The Interpretation of the Fourth Gospel.* Cambridge: Cambridge University Press, 1954.

Ellis, E. Earle, *Paul and His Recent Interpreters.* Wm. B. Eerdmans Publishing Company, 1961.

——— " II Corinthians 5:1-10 in Pauline Eschatology," *New Testament Studies,* Vol. VI, 1959–1960, pp. 211–224.

Filson, F. V., " Exegesis of the Second Epistle to the Corinthians," *The Interpreter's Bible,* Vol. 10. Abingdon-Cokesbury Press, 1953.

——— *St. Paul's Conception of Recompense.* Leipzig: J. C. Hinrichs'sche, 1931.

Fison, J. E., *The Christian Hope.* London: Longmans, Green & Co., Inc., 1954.

Flemington, W. F., *The New Testament Doctrine of Baptism.* London: S.P.C.K., 1948.

Frame, J. E., *A Critical and Exegetical Commentary on the Epistles of St. Paul to the Thessalonians* (International Critical Commentary) . Edinburgh: T. & T. Clark, 1912.

Glasson, T. Francis, *Greek Influence in Jewish Eschatology.* London: S.P.C.K., 1961.

——— *The Second Advent.* London: The Epworth Press, Publishers, 1945.

Goguel, Maurice, " Le caractère, à la fois actuel et futur, du salut dans le théologie paulinienne," *The Background of the New Testament and Its Eschatology,* ed. by W. D.

Davies and D. Daube. Cambridge: Cambridge University Press, 1956.

——— *The Birth of Christianity,* tr. by H. C. Snape. The Macmillan Company, 1954.

Goudge, H. L., " The Theology of St. Paul," *A New Commentary on Holy Scripture,* ed. by Charles Gore, Part III. The Macmillan Company, 1928.

Grant, F. C., *Ancient Judaism and the New Testament.* The Macmillan Company, 1959.

——— *Roman Hellenism and the New Testament.* London: Oliver & Boyd, Ltd., 1962.

Grundmann, W., " Sin in the New Testament," *Sin,* by G. Quell *et al.* (*Bible Key Words*). London: Adam and Charles Black, Ltd., 1951.

——— " Überlieferung und Eigenaussage im Eschatologischen Denken des Apostels Paulus," *New Testament Studies,* Vol. VIII, 1961.

Gutbrod, W., " Law in the New Testament," *Law,* by H. Kleinknecht and W. Gutbrod (*Bible Key Words*). London: Adam and Charles Black, 1962.

Guy, H. A., *The New Testament Doctrine of the Last Things.* London: Oxford University Press, 1948.

Hamilton, N. Q., *The Holy Spirit and Eschatology in Paul.* Edinburgh: Edinburgh University Press, 1957.

Héring, J., *Le Royaume de Dieu et sa Venue.* Paris, 1937.

Hettlinger, R. F. " II Corinthians 5:1-10," *Scottish Journal of Theology,* Vol. 10, 1957.

Higgins, A. J. B., *The Lord's Supper in the New Testament* (Studies in Biblical Theology, No. 6). Henry Regnery Company, 1952.

Hooke, S. H., *Alpha and Omega.* London: James Nisbet & Co., Ltd., 1961.

Hunter, A. M., *Interpreting Paul's Gospel.* London: SCM Press, Ltd., 1964.

——— *Paul and His Predecessors,* rev. ed. London: SCM Press, Ltd., 1961.

——— " The Hope of Glory," *Interpretation,* Vol. 8, 1954.

Jeremias, J., *" Adam," Theological Dictionary of the New Testament,* Vol. 1.

Johnson, S. E., " Paul and the Manual of Discipline," *Harvard*

Theological Review, Vol. LVIII, 1955.

Jones, G. V., *Christology and Myth in the New Testament.* London: George Allen & Unwin, Ltd., 1956.

Kallas, James, *The Significance of the Synoptic Miracles.* London: S.P.C.K., 1961.

Kennedy, H. A. A., *St. Paul's Conceptions of the Last Things.* A. C. Armstrong & Sons, 1904.

Klausner, Joseph, *From Jesus to Paul,* tr. by W.F. Stinespring. The Macmillan Company, 1943.

Knox, John, *Chapters in a Life of Paul.* Abingdon-Cokesbury Press, 1950.

——— "Exegesis of the Epistle to the Romans," *The Interpreter's Bible,* Vol. 9. Abingdon-Cokesbury Press, 1954.

Knox, W. L., *St. Paul and the Church of the Gentiles.* Cambridge: Cambridge University Press, 1939.

Laymon, Charles M., *Christ in the New Testament.* Abingdon Press, 1958.

Lee, Kenneth E., *A Study in Romans.* London: S.P.C.K., 1962.

Leivestad, Ragnar, *Christ the Conqueror.* London: S.P.C.K., 1954.

Lindars, Barnabas, *New Testament Apologetic.* The Westminster Press, 1961.

Lowe, J., "An Examination of Attempts to Detect Development in St. Paul's Theology," *Journal of Theological Studies,* Vol. XLII, 1941.

McCown, C. C., *The Promise of His Coming.* The Macmillan Company, 1921.

Macgregor, G. H. C., "Principalities and Powers," *New Testament Sidelights,* ed. by H. K. McArthur. Hartford Seminary Foundation, 1960.

Manson, T. W., "Some Reflexions on Apocalyptic," *Aux Sources de la Tradition Chrétienne* (Mélanges offerts à M. Maurice Goguel). Paris: Delachaux and Niestlé, 1950.

——— *The Teaching of Jesus,* 2d ed. Cambridge: Cambridge University Press, 1935.

Manson, W., "Eschatology in the New Testament," *Eschatology,* by W. Manson, G. W. H. Lampe, T. F. Torrance, W. A. Whitehouse (Scottish Journal of Theology Occasional Papers, No. 2). London: Oliver & Boyd, Ltd., 1952.

Marsh, John, *The Fulness of Time*. London: James Nisbet & Co., Ltd., 1952.

Minear, P. S., *Eyes of Faith*. London: Lutterworth Press, 1948.

——— " The Time of Hope in the New Testament," *Scottish Journal of Theology*, Vol. VI, 1953.

Moule, C. F. D., *The Birth of the New Testament*. London: Adam and Charles Black, Ltd., 1962.

——— " The Judgment Theme in the Sacraments," *Background of the New Testament and Its Eschatology*, ed. by W. D. Davies and D. Daube. Cambridge: Cambridge University Press, 1956.

Mowry, Lucetta, *The Dead Sea Scrolls and the Early Church*. The University of Chicago Press, 1962.

Muilenburg, James, " The Biblical View of Time," *Harvard Theological Review*, Vol. LIV, 1961.

Munck, Johannes, *Paul and the Salvation of Mankind*, tr. by F. Clarke. John Knox Press, 1959.

Niebuhr, Reinhold, *The Nature and Destiny of Man*, Vol. II, *Human Destiny*. Charles Scribner's Sons, 1943.

Oepke, Albrecht, " *baptō* " and " *gymnos*," *Theological Dictionary of the New Testament*, Vol. 1.

Petry, Ray C., *Christian Eschatology and Social Thought*. Abingdon Press, 1956.

Porter, F. C., " The Place of Apocalyptical Conceptions in the Thought of Paul," *Contemporary Thinking About Paul*, compiled by T. S. Kepler. Abingdon-Cokesbury Press, 1950.

Pratt, E. J., *Studies in Pauline Eschatology*. Toronto: William Briggs, 1917.

Purdy, A. C., " Paul the Apostle," *The Interpreter's Dictionary of the Bible*, Vol. III. Abingdon Press, 1962.

Rall, H. F., *According to Paul*. Charles Scribner's Sons, 1944.

Robinson, H. Wheeler, *The Christian Doctrine of Man*, 3d ed. Edinburgh: T. & T. Clark, 1958.

Robinson, J. A. T., *The Body* (Studies in Biblical Theology, No. 5). Henry Regnery Company, 1952.

——— *In the End, God*. London: James Clarke & Co., Ltd., 1950.

——— *Jesus and His Coming*. Abingdon Press, 1957.

Rowley, H. H., *The Relevance of Apocalyptic,* rev. ed. London: Lutterworth Press, 1963.

Rust, E. C., *Nature and Man in Biblical Thought,* London: Lutterworth Press, 1953.

Sanday, William, and Headlam, A. C., *A Critical and Exegetical Commentary on the Epistle to the Romans,* 2d ed. (International Critical Commentary). Charles Scribner's Sons, 1898.

Sandmel, Samuel, *The Genius of Paul.* Farrar, Straus & Cudahy, Inc., 1958.

Schmidt, K. L., " *basileia,*" *Theological Dictionary of the New Testament,* Vol. I.

Schoeps, H. G., *Paul,* tr. by H. Knight. The Westminster Press, 1961.

Schweitzer, Albert, *Paul and His Interpreters,* tr. by W. Montgomery. London: Adam and Charles Black, Ltd., 1912.

——— *The Mysticism of Paul the Apostle,* 2d ed., tr. by W. Montgomery. London: Adam and Charles Black, Ltd., 1953.

——— *The Quest of the Historical Jesus,* 3d ed., tr. by W. Montgomery. London: Adam and Charles Black, Ltd., 1954.

Schweizer, E., and others, " Spirit of God," *Bible Key Words,* tr. by A. E. Harvey. London: Adam and Charles Black, Ltd., 1960.

Scott, C. A. A., *Christianity According to St. Paul.* Cambridge: Cambridge University Press, 1927.

Scott, E. F., " Exegesis of the Epistle to the Philippians," *The Interpreter's Bible,* Vol. 11. Abingdon Press, 1955.

——— *The Kingdom of God in the New Testament.* The Macmillan Company, 1931.

——— *The Spirit in the New Testament.* London: Hodder & Stoughton, Ltd., 1923.

Selby, Donald J., *Toward the Understanding of St. Paul.* Prentice-Hall, Inc., 1962.

——— " Changing Ideas in New Testament Eschatology," *Harvard Theological Review,* Vol. L, 1957.

Sevenster, J. N., " Some Remarks on the *Gymnos* in II Cor. 5:3," *Studia Paulina,* ed. by J. N. Sevenster and W. C. van

Unnik. Haarlem: Bohn, 1953.

Smalley, S. S., "The Delay of the Parousia," *Journal of Biblical Literature,* Vol. LXXXIII, Pt. 1, March, 1964.

Stacey, W. D., *The Pauline View of Man.* London: Macmillan & Co., Ltd., 1956.

Stamm, R. T., "Exegesis of the Epistle to the Galatians," *The Interpreter's Bible,* Vol. 10. Abingdon-Cokesbury Press, 1953.

Stewart, J. S., "On a Neglected Emphasis in New Testament Theology," *Scottish Journal of Theology,* Vol. IV, 1951.

Tasker, R. V. G., *The Biblical Doctrine of the Wrath of God.* London: Tyndale Press, 1951.

Thompson, C. H., *Theology of the Kerygma.* Prentice-Hall, Inc., 1962.

Vermes, G., *The Dead Sea Scrolls in English.* Harmondsworth, England: Penguin Books, Ltd., 1962.

Vos, Geerhardus, "The Eschatological Aspect of the Pauline Conception of the Spirit," *Biblical and Theological Studies,* by members of the faculty of Princeton Theological Seminary. Charles Scribner's Sons, 1912.

——— "The Structure of the Pauline Eschatology," *Princeton Theological Review,* Vol. 27, 1929.

Weiss, Johannes, *The History of Primitive Christianity,* Vol. II, tr. by P. S. Kramer and S. E. Johnson. Wilson-Erickson, Inc., 1937.

Whitely, D. E. H., *The Theology of St. Paul,* Oxford: Blackwell, 1964.

Wilder, A. N., "Eschatological Imagery and Earthly Circumstance," *New Testament Studies,* Vol. 5, 1958–1959.

——— "Social Factors in Early Christian Eschatology," *Early Christian Origins,* ed. by Allen Wikgren. Quadrangle Books, Inc., 1961.

——— *Otherworldliness and the New Testament.* London: SCM Press, Ltd., 1955.

Wood, J. F., "Paul's Eschatology," *Biblical World,* Vol. 38, 1911.

INDEXES

GENERAL INDEX

INDEX OF BIBLE PASSAGES

II Corinthians